Nick Bishop has worked as a r
Henry, the Wales national sq
the author of four other boo
Graham Henry.

Alun Carter is a former Wales international who also played for
Pontypool, Newport, SO Millau and UWIC. He later worked
for the WRU for twelve years, fulfilling the role of head analyst
from 1998 to 2007. He and Nick Bishop are the authors of
Seeing Red: Twelve Tumultuous Years in Welsh Rugby, a former
winner of best rugby book at the British Sports Books Awards.

THE GOOD, THE BAD AND THE UGLY

THE RISE AND FALL OF PONTYPOOL RFC

NICK BISHOP AND ALUN CARTER

MAINSTREAM
PUBLISHING

EDINBURGH AND LONDON

To Brian Carter and Eddie Mogford

First published in Great Britain in 2013 by
Mainstream Publishing
Transworld Publishers
61–63 Uxbridge Road
London W5 5SA
A Penguin Random House company
Mainstream paperback edition published 2014

ISBN 9781780576725

A catalogue record for this book is available
from the British Library

Printed in Great Britain by
Clays Ltd, St Ives plc

1 3 5 7 9 10 8 6 4 2

ACKNOWLEDGEMENTS

The authors would like to thank the following for their contributions to the production of this book. In particular, the help and comments of Graham Price, Terry Cobner, Eddie Butler, Ray Ruddick, Bob Dawkins and Arthur Crane et al. (through the 'biography' of the club, *Pontypool's Pride*) were invaluable. Without them, the book would not exist.

The authors would also like to thank Kevin Bowring, Mike Ruddock, Corris Thomas, Jason Smith, Ray Prosser, Harry Vaux, Brandon Cripps, Bobby Windsor, John Perkins, Phil Larder, Peter Jeffreys, Karen Mogford, Gareth Kirkup, Ian Matthews, Mike Goldsworthy, Steve Jackson, Richie Thomas, Gordon Richards, Graham Henry, Graham and June Howden, Mike Gooding, Kevin Moseley, John Perkins, Neil Waite, Roger Powell, Brendan Fanning and Kevin Moseley.

We would also like to thank Bill Campbell, Graeme Blaikie, Debs Warner and all others from Mainstream for their constant help and support through to publication.

CONTENTS

CHAPTER 1

GATHERING UP THE RUBBISH

Sometime in 2003, Steve 'Junna' Jones and Ian Matthews were driving down the valley road between Pontypool and Blaenavon, chewing the fat about rugby. Ian was optimistic, enthusing about the possibilities opening up with the dawn of regional rugby in Wales. Junna maintained a sober silence. As twist followed twist in the road, and as the valley itself began to disappear into the usual vast blanket of mist, Ian's monologue gradually ground to a halt.

'What do you think, Junna?'

The car was quiet for a moment. Both tried vainly to see the road ahead.

'I think it will be the death of club rugby in Wales, and I think it will be the death of Pontypool.'

At a court hearing on 25–27 June 2012, Pontypool RFC became the first club ever to be legally defined as 'rubbish'. A lawyer for the Welsh Rugby Union (WRU) told the High Court that Pontypool was 'not good enough on the pitch' to be included in a reorganised 12-team Premiership.

Despite finishing 12th of 14 in the 2011–12 Welsh Premiership, Pontypool had failed to make the 'top 12 performers' meritocracy because of a complex WRU calculation that also included the previous six seasons. While the club was fighting its case for inclusion, it turned out that the WRU board had accepted another proposal made on behalf of the four Welsh regions for Carmarthen Quins RFC and Bridgend RFC to be added to the original ten named clubs in order that Ospreys and the Scarlets could achieve their elite player pathway standards by recruiting from within their geographical regions. Pontypool was left high and dry out in the Eastern valley.

It's not the first time – and it probably won't be the last – that Pontypool has been accused of being the 'rubbish' of the game in Wales. In November 1973, London Welsh broke off fixtures with Pooler, complaining of excessive violence in the home game between the two clubs at Old Deer Park. Welsh finished the game with only 12 men on the pitch. Needless to say, Pooler won.

We were rubbish, and I loved it – never more so than on that momentous Easter Tuesday in 1973. The crowd at Pontypool Park was packed in, bigger than I'd ever seen it. People rose like a human cathedral on the far-side bank, opposite the main terraces. You could get 15,000 people or maybe more on that bank for the really big games. Reputedly there were 20,000 in occupation for the 1989 tour match against New Zealand. There would be so many they would be hanging off the trees.

I remember playing rugby with the other youngsters – all of us only seven or eight years old – underneath the scoreboard in the large in-goal area behind the posts. Occasionally I'd look around and see those Welsh heroes of mine in the red shirts – Geoff Evans, Jeff Young, John Taylor, Tony Gray and, of course, JPR. Strange feeling in the pit of my stomach not to be rooting for them for once . . . But I was a Pontypool boy and it was a day for the red, black and white. Pooler stampeded to victory, 22–3. The human cathedral came to life at the end of the game, flooding the pitch as Pontypool RFC was crowned Welsh Merit Table champions for the first time in its history. 'We are the champions' dissolved into the more guttural cry of 'Poola, Poola' that swirled around the ground. It still swirls around my memory to this day.

Six months later and the rubbish was thrown out. After Pooler's dominance had been confirmed with another 28–9 win, a London Welsh official announced: 'It is not the kind of game to which we are accustomed here at Old Deer Park.'

We were rubbish, and I loved it. No one ever arrived at Pontypool Park by straightforward means or ever came as an established star. Some of the rubbish had been blowing about the Welsh club rugby scene for several years, its value unrecognised. Bobby Windsor and 'Charlie' Faulkner had both played for Cross Keys and other lesser lights before they found a home at Pontypool Park, with the broad coaching arm of Ray Prosser around their shoulders. Neither had 'made it' on the first-class scene when they came.

When Eddie Butler first graduated from the junior playing ranks at age 19 in 1976, his ambition was to play for his home-town club of Newport.

'I remember going along to the pre-season sessions at Rodney Parade. The first questions they asked me were, "Have you played for any of the Wales age-group sides?" and "What representative experience do you have?"

'The answer to those questions was "No" and "None", at which point I was gestured to the far side of the field to be, as I soon found out, with all the other also-rans.

'They just didn't want to know unless you already had a "name" or reputation. So I thought I'd find somewhere where my talents might be appreciated.

'A couple of weeks later I presented myself for training at Pontypool Park, a callow 19 year old. No one knew who I was, but Ray Prosser was the first to greet me with a firm, warm handshake. Standing by his side was someone I already recognised from the TV. It was all I could do to keep my mind on what "Pross" was saying.

'After ten minutes or so, he stopped talking and said, "Graham will show you around the ground and clubhouse."

'For the next half-hour, Pricey showed me the facilities and patiently answered all my queries about the club. Graham Price. Here was a genuine star of the domestic game, an established Wales international, who would become a first choice for the British Lions only one year later, behaving as if *I* was the rugby celebrity!

'Of course, if you didn't have the desire to hang around and plough through the misery that Pross put you through afterwards, you were gone just as quickly as you arrived – maybe quicker. But that first impression, that sense of democracy, of how everyone started on the same level whether you were an unknown or a capped international, never left me. Pontypool was a place where they rescued the value in the rubbish and saw the jewel in the dross.' (Eddie Butler)

My early life, up until the age of 14, was fragmented. So much time spent away, following my dad as he shuttled between teaching jobs in locations as far apart as Scotland, Germany and Zambia! It's time I can hardly remember: first in Wilhelmshaven, a German deep-water naval base where Hitler constructed his warships during the Second World War. The *Admiral Graf Spee* was built and launched there. When I was seven years old we moved to Silverdale, a Staffordshire mining town.

The only common link between my early lives was the regular journeys back to Pontypool. Going back to family was great, but my dad and I were secretly rubbing our hands at the prospect of Saturday afternoon at Pontypool Park. The sense of building expectation on the walk along the Monmouthshire and Brecon canal to the Pontymoile Basin, then off toward the south end of Pontypool Park and through the ornate 'Sally' gates – so called because they were a gift from the eighteenth-century Duchess of Marlborough, affectionately known as Sally, to the Hanbury family; the sudden grandeur of Hanburys' Park, with its giant oaks, beeches and elms.

The weather would dictate our position. My favourite place was on the terracing above the 22-metre line at the 'lower' end of the ground (Pontypool Park slopes steadily downhill into the corner nearest the leisure centre). Many of the faithful would arrive an hour before kick-off to assure their positions and then the banter would start. On a wet day it would be the big stand on the west side of the ground. On an autumn day, with the bandstand on the Blaenavon side and the flame-like colours of the trees licking the hillside, there could be no finer place to play rugby – or get beaten up.

Whilst we were away from Pontypool in Staffordshire, we followed the progress of the club's international players on TV. Unfortunately in those days terrestrial TV allowed just one choice of game on the main channel. We were some 30 miles from the Welsh border and the English BBC did not broadcast the Welsh games themselves.

In 1976, Wales travelled to Ireland seeking the Triple Crown. England were playing Scotland in a Calcutta Cup match on the same day which was the main televised game. On that cold Saturday in February, we jumped into our Austin Allegro and ventured to the nearest highest point looking for a strong enough signal to watch 'our boys' play.

Keele University stands overlooking the Potteries below. We parked in the grounds and Dad grabbed the portable TV, to which he had already made some crafty wiring adjustments. He connected the TV wires to the car battery and carefully put the bonnet down and laid the TV on top of it. Then he fiddled with the channels and bent and twisted the old aerial until a clear picture from the transmitters in North Wales was found.

We huddled up in the front seat of the car with the engine running, a thermos flask of hot sweet tea and some chewy teacake sweets. BBC Radio Wales was going in the back seat and the telly was on the bonnet. The dulcet tones of Lyn Davies tasted sweeter than the tea! We watched Wales beat Ireland sitting on top of a hill in England. The Pooler boys did us proud, and at that moment I believe I had a small glimpse of my future, a future that could tie all the rubbish of the travelling and rootlessness of my childhood together.

CHAPTER 2

EDDIE MOGFORD, MAX HORTON AND WEST MON

It is a cold, bright Tuesday morning. I am sitting in the front room at Merchant's Hill, Pontnewynydd, with Valerie and Karen, the wife and daughter of Eddie Mogford. Eddie is lying in the coffin in the hallway. I sit quietly with the other coffin-bearers, unsure whether to drink coffee or take the tumbler of whisky on offer. Eventually, like everyone else, I take the tumbler. Looking across at Karen, I smile faintly, remembering my visits to Eddie's treatment room. Eddie would always be looking to set up his daughter, the only child, upon whom he so clearly doted, on a date 'to get her out of the house'. Karen needed no help in this respect, but nonetheless the memorable physical and verbal pummellings Eddie dished out in the name of 'physiotherapy' or 'massage' always began with: 'She's a lovely girl.'

For a young athlete in need of repair, negotiating that ten-minute minefield with a measure of diplomacy was only one of many tests to be passed in the following couple of hours. As Eddie worked both your mind and body into shapes you never thought possible, you would find yourself broken and rebuilt a hundred times or more.

On the morning of Worcester's Premiership game with Newcastle Falcons in February 2010, I'd visited Eddie at the County Hospital in Panteg. He was in a bad way, rambling incoherently. Every now and again our eyes would meet and his face would contort briefly: 'Carter, you f***ing prick.' Nurses stopped in their tracks and the whole ward looked over as one; Karen had to leave to go back to work. I sat still and took Eddie's verbal battering. If I so much as twitched a muscle, he would turn around: 'Don't leave me now, Carter, you Black-and-Amber b*****d.' It was the last time I was to see Eddie before he passed away in December 2011.

The preacher finishes a short blessing and the murmur of family prayers fades into the background. I half-expect Eddie to rise up and give me one last tongue-lashing before he leaves for the Gwent Crematorium: '. . . And another thing, Spring!' I gratefully pick up my corner of the coffin and hoist it aloft. Two of the other shoulders that bear Eddie out of 'Welsford', his home, for the last time, belong to Graham Price and Terry Cobner. Nothing is said between them. Pricey and 'Cobs' will exchange pleasantries for the first time in about 15 years later that afternoon, sharing a pint and a table in the Little Crown, Eddie's local. I keep my eyes to the front as we go out into the blinding morning sunlight. The coffin feels as light as balsa wood. Black and white, love and hate, and nothing by halves; it is the Pontypool way.

No one epitomised that way better than Eddie Mogford, particularly during the time of the resurrection in Pontypool RFC's fortunes in the early 1970s. I was only 14 years old when I first met Eddie. That was when I had my first serious rugby injury. My dad told me there was a man in Merchant's Hill, Pontnewynydd, who could help. As we approached the extension on the side of a large detached house, I could hear this loud chuckling coming from the other side of the door. It opened to reveal this large, jovial man with a beaming grin. I thought he was Father Christmas, then he swore violently at my dad. Brian Carter and Eddie had been at George Street School together. Dad seemed to think the volley of profanities was funny. I was introduced to Eddie Mogford and asked to take a seat.

The room was dark, illuminated only by the bright red glow of four lamps burning gently into the bare flesh, some taut and some saggy, of Eddie's patients. Three people lay on tables that ran, end on end, along the entire length of the room. On the windowsill a radio purred away quietly in the background as Eddie rubbed the shoulder of a man sitting on a small wooden stool. I felt my eyes start to water from the powerful smell of liniment in the room.

Famous faces that I didn't know stared down at me from walls covered in framed pictures – a Welsh boxer, a runner with the three feathers clearly visible on his vest and many, many others. But there was one wall that held my attention, the wall dedicated to my heroes from the Pontypool rugby team. Peter Lewis, David Bishop, Eddie Butler, Charlie Faulkner, Bobby Windsor, Graham Price, Terry Cobner: they were all there.

Before my imagination could carry me away on a tide of pleasurable mental replays of 'heroic moments' at Pontypool Park, I was jolted suddenly awake. Eddie was cursing and turning the air blue with one of his jokes. The eyes of his victim grew wider and wider as Eddie remorselessly took him to pieces while everyone else laughed, thankful that they weren't the butt of his humour for the time being. Eddie Mogford was at the centre of his wicked theatre, chuckling away. I started to relax and enjoy it. I remember thinking, 'I like this . . . I'll be back for more.' As if sensing my new-found relaxation, Eddie swivelled around, he looked straight through me – and then he started talking . . .

*

Eddie had first developed his interest in physiotherapy as a young medic in the army in Malaya during the Second World War. In 1966, he took over from his father Bill as the resident physio and masseur for Pontypool RFC, just three short years before Ray Prosser's arrival as coach. He finally retired in 1993, having given the club 27 years of loyal service, and was promptly made a life member of the club.

Eddie was, I believe, the kind of person you need at every successful club or sporting organisation, from the highest to the lowest. He was well-nigh invisible in terms of his public profile outside Pontypool, but his 'unseen guidance' – whether barked out from the touchline, or whispered, kneeling by an injured player's ear, or rasped out via a humiliating put-down in the treatment room – was key to reinforcing the messages Ray Prosser was trying to embed in the culture of his new model Pontypool. Terry Cobner remembers Eddie as 'a complete one-off, the most politically incorrect man I've ever met in my life and a great friend. He complemented what Pross was trying to do perfectly because he didn't respect excuses, even when they were valid. "Get up!" he'd say, "I'm not wasting my time on you!" (though in far more direct language) after he came on the field for an injured player. With the advance of sports science and medicine, we've gone in completely the opposite direction, but I don't believe it's necessarily a good thing. We don't promote mental toughness because we believe too much in susceptibility to injury. Sometimes you just have to buckle up and play on through the pain.'

It wasn't just what he was saying, but the way he said it. Believe me, some of Eddie's jokes could strip paint from the walls. He had an uncanny knack of being able to formulate and then give voice to those questions that we would all love to ask but so rarely do. His innate ability to make people laugh, then relax physically with the quality of his massage created a small, unguarded chink in the patient's armour through which the stiletto of the question, or the cruel joke, could enter. There was no defence – and the wound was deep because there was always an audience to listen to it.

Eddie touched the lives of many people through his work as a physiotherapist. As long as you were not being targeted, you could sit back and relax as he tore into his various patients, one by one. When your turn came, as it inevitably would, thoughts of any injury were secondary as Eddie got into his flow. In front of a full room and a captive audience, no profession was exempt: the poor Catholic priest who had to answer for the many failings of his Church; the postman who could only deliver bills and bad news; the solicitor who had to defend extortionate charges; the policeman (me) who could not keep people safe at night: 'You must be the worst copper ever to wield a truncheon in the Gwent constabulary . . . the criminals must have a field day when you are on duty, Spring!'

But Eddie's patients always came back for more; they loved him. Eddie once confided in Graham Price that one of his clients insisted on continuing his treatment sessions for many months after his ailment had been cured. There was no longer anything wrong with him; he just came back for the culture and the conversation. The treatment room was one of the crucibles in which the Pontypool spirit was forged and sustained.

After the death of his parents, Eddie and his wife Val moved into his childhood home. The house was dishevelled and in need of considerable renovation, and Eddie would shake his head sadly. I can still recall an army of Eddie's patients and ex-patients marching down the main road to help with the many labouring tasks that needed to be done, much to Eddie's surprise. It was their way of repaying him for his priceless help in getting to the bottom of their 'issues'. They rebuilt his house for him.

Bob Dawkins, an ex-captain and coach of Pontypool in two different eras, remembers both the calculated and not-so-calculated carnage caused by Eddie Mogford: 'I had my first rub-down from Eddie Mogford. At the time his dad was involved with Pontypool Youth. He was a delightful man – but not at all like Eddie, with his wicked, dark sense of humour. Bill Mogford was a completely upfront "I do exactly what I say on the tin" type of man; completely genuine and dependable.

'I was about seven years old and there used to be regular "disagreements" between the boys in Fowler Street and the kids from Cwm Ffrwd Oer. We would all go down to the railway line and pelt each other with stones, slings, sticks and whatever else happened to be lying around at the time. It was a pitched battle, like some kind of miniature biblical warfare. If things were going badly, the cry would ring out, "Get the big boys!" – and Eddie was the biggest of the big boys, about 12 or 13 years old. He always arrived with the force of the military police.

'Later I used to go to Eddie for the treatment, but I also knew people who'd go just to hear his jokes, or even take delight in being on the butt-end of them! Eddie's treatment room became a centre of rugby culture and conversation in the area, a hub of joyful irreverence, of abundant and very clever mickey-taking.

'There was one game, Eddie was the trainer on the touchline and one of the Pontypool players went down injured, clutching his hand. Eddie ran on and took a look. "Right, you've dislocated your thumb . . . Look away now," he said. He was quite definite and authoritative about it. Then I heard a sharp double click . . . just "click-click" cutting through the white noise on the pitch.

'Later, the player went to the infirmary to get it checked out. They did the X-ray and said to him, "You've broken your thumb in two places!"

'In a way it was typical of Eddie's sense of humour. He could take the mick out of you, sometimes quite cruelly, and you wouldn't even feel the bones breaking, you'd be laughing so hard . . . And I never met anyone who didn't think the world of Eddie Mogford. You knew Eddie always had your best interests at heart, but his humour would break you down in the subtlest of ways. Put you down, pick you back up and rebuild you again.' (Bob Dawkins)

Not that Eddie was in any sense a medical fraud, you understand. The same episode was repeated almost verbatim in 1991, 23 years later. A young Cwmbran hopeful named Gareth Kirkup had turned up for training at Pontypool. Kirkup is now the forwards coach for the Cwmbran side in Swalec League 4 East: 'I joined Pontypool RFC in the summer of 1991 from Cwmbran. Pontypool was as usual riding high in the Premiership, and I kept my head down while doing my apprenticeship with the Athletic [2nd XV] squad.

'As a young forward it was a great environment in which to learn my trade. Everywhere I looked there was someone who had earned his stripes at the highest level, whether it was Pricey or Junna Jones or Staff Jones – or indeed our captain, Mostyn "Upside-down Head" Davies.

'Things were going well for me until one Thursday night training session. We'd done the fitness, and John Perkins had picked his starting XV for the Saturday. Then as per usual he picked another XV to oppose them in a 30-minute full-blooded contact game to round off the session.

'Making this second XV was no mean feat in itself, as 60 players or so would regularly turn up to training and it was a very competitive environment; nobody wanted to be among those ordered off for an early shower, with everyone else looking on.

'As the ref, "Perky" began by exhorting the second XV to

have a real go at the first-teamers, so we both went out and knocked seven bells out of each other. There was no quarter given or taken. About halfway through I tried to stop a driving maul and predictably ended up in a heap on the floor with stud marks tattooed along my back and a dislocated finger hanging off the end of my hand! A long forefinger curled towards me like a snake. It belonged to Perky. "That will teach you," he muttered darkly.

'I looked at my hand. My index finger was at 90 degrees to all the other fingers! I shoved it towards Perky and he pulled back sharply: "Keep that thing away from me. Go and see 'the Jaw' [Ivor Taylor]." I took myself and my finger over to the far side of the pitch, as instructed, and showed Ivor, who turned away in horror. Pross, who was standing nearby, just swore at me.

'Despite some misgivings, Ivor consented to take me over to Eddie's place in Merchant's Hill; as usual he was to be found in the Little Crown, blowing the top off his first pint of the evening as I entered feeling sorry for myself with my mud-soaked kit and ballooning finger. Everyone in the pub stopped and turned to watch as I stopped right in front of him and held out my finger without saying a word. It was humiliating. "What the f**k have you done now, you dopey dick? Come here and look over my shoulder."

'After a bit of manipulation, a couple of pulls, a yelp from me and one final push, the finger popped back into place. An indescribable sense of relief came over me. "Cheers, Ed. Thank you so much."

'"OK, now piss off so I can enjoy my pint," he replied, with a cheeky glint in his eye. Whether he was taking the mick out of my clothes, my hairstyle or my belly, or simply introducing me as "the ugliest man in Cwmbran" as I stepped into the packed audience in the treatment room, there was always that glint in his eye. It became almost a privilege to be injured, just to take my place in Eddie's congregation, with Radio Wales belting out the hymns and Eddie belting out the abuse. It became a religious experience for me, like a pagan rite.' (Gareth Kirkup)

Eddie was not immune to counter-attack from those he had slighted – far from it. Eddie loved his garden and at 'Welsford' he was able to immerse himself in his beloved vegetable plot. He would spend many hours tending to his veg, whilst every now and then glancing up nervously to check if his old mate Johnny 'Short Fuse' Morris was spying on him with his binoculars from Leigh Road, on the other side of the valley. Eddie also loved his Sunday lunchtime pint of Albright with his mates 'Harpo' and 'Tiger' at the Little Crown.

Occasionally, he would have one too many and in order to keep out of Val's way until he sobered up he would spend his time pottering around in the garden. On one occasion he actually fell into a trench that he had recently prepared for his runner beans and fell soundly asleep. The word spread around town like wildfire, fanned by the man with the binoculars on the other side of the valley!

Eddie's nicotine intake always went through the roof on match days at Pontypool Park as he watched intently from the sideline, treatment bag at the ready. His fast feet would always get him to an injured Pooler player quickly.

Away from his daytime work – Eddie worked as an executive officer at the Royal Ordnance factory in Glascoed for 33 years – he ran his clinics on a Sunday morning and on weekday evenings in his spare time. Over 20 years, the small change that was left in the little saucer on Eddie's mantelpiece was an unrepresentative token of the huge hidden value he brought to Pontypool's cause on the rugby field, especially after Ray Prosser took over the coaching reins at the club. Those pennies and shillings rarely took inflation into account.

As Graham Price put it in his eulogy at Gwent Crematorium on 6 December 2011: 'Eddie was a very important cog in the Pontypool Rugby Club machine. You would invariably find Eddie busy behind the scenes, ensuring that the injured players were receiving the expert treatment that was required to get them back to full fitness. It is impossible to quantify how many important games Pontypool won because of Eddie's contribution in making sure that the best team and the most influential players were fit enough to take the field. However, I have no doubt that they were many.'

Eddie Mogford was the glue within the Pontypool environment, the person who ensured that the Pontypool mentality on the field was constantly being supported and refreshed off it, in those little moments when a player got too big for his boots or suffered a crisis of confidence, or couldn't separate his rugby from his private life, or felt like chucking it all in.

The small change in Eddie's dish distilled only a public perception, or more accurately a public ignorance of the 'man behind the scenes', and it was a small price indeed to pay for the 'treatment' you received in that room. Having knocked you down, he would pick you back up slowly, asking how you were and getting to the bottom of the psychological issues glimpsed beyond the physical ones. As his fingers worked their way deeper into your muscles, the voice softened and the questions became more pointed. You would leave stronger than you had arrived.

I remember vividly the various greetings that welcomed me – 'You coppers are all c***s!', then 'Ah, the Black-and-Amber b*****d's back again!' – all 'terms of endearment', as Prosser used to say. Eddie was at the core of the Pontypool rugby meritocracy – every player received the same treatment, every person received the same treatment. There were no preferences, no favourites and there was no hierarchy. Eddie's barbed sense of humour saw to that.

Eddie Mogford was one important part of a strong support network that was ready and waiting to be given direction by Ray Prosser in 1969. As Bob Dawkins says: 'Eddie was part of the nucleus of Pontypool in the glory days, along with Ray and one or two of the committeemen, like the secretary Bob Jeremiah. Bob Jeremiah – salt of the earth. When he was secretary of the club, Bob would do everything on the cheap, but he wouldn't stint at how far he'd go to arrange the social visits and club tours. He always made a special effort for those. I always looked forward to the end-of-season tours to the West Country. We would visit Bridgwater on the Friday, Weston-super-Mare on the Saturday and then it was on to the Winter Gardens in the evening. It was superb.

'It was characters like Bob and Eddie who made it such a privilege to play for Pontypool. They gave it substance because they connected you back to the community you grew out of; they would never let you get away from that. They had a way of showing you the continuity even if they weren't talking about it.'

Bob Jeremiah's sense of loyalty to the club went far beyond the 25 years he spent as club secretary. On 5 November 1966, a promising young Wales Youth prop called Roger Addison had been selected to play for Pontypool against Rugby in a match at William Webb Ellis Road, the birthplace of rugby. He was 21 years old. His sister Barbara Owen recalled that he had a 'funny feeling' about the game but was reluctant to let anyone down at the eleventh hour.

A quarter of an hour into the match a scrum collapsed and Roger Addison's 'funny feeling' became a life-threatening reality. His neck was broken, with the complicating factor that the gum he had been chewing since the start of the match had become trapped in his throat. The home doctor, John O'Hanlon, was forced to perform an emergency tracheotomy out in the middle of the field.

The prognosis for rugby quadriplegia was anywhere between three weeks and six months, but Roger Addison went on to live for another forty-four years, with the majority of that time spent at the Rookwood Hospital in Cardiff.

Every week for the 39 years Addison spent at Rookwood, Bob Jeremiah would make the 60-mile round trip from Pontypool to Cardiff by bus to visit him. When his own health issues put a stop to the visits by bus in 2009, Bob Jeremiah picked up his pen and started writing letters to Roger Addison instead. As Bob recalls: 'He couldn't move from the neck down and could only whisper, so we had to lip-read, but he always asked about Pontypool and the players . . . He had a wonderful sense of humour . . . he once told me he could run faster than a particular Pontypool winger! And he joked a few years ago about how he qualified for a bus pass.' (Bob Jeremiah)

The Pontypool club chaplain, Revd Alf Williams, would also go to see Roger regularly. Max Horton, my former sportsmaster at West Monmouth Grammar School, would visit Roger every other week and on one occasion I accompanied him. Whenever possible, Roger would come out to the front door in the wheelchair that he navigated with his head. He loved to get out of his room and see the sun, to play host to his visitors. I think that little act of moving out beyond the front door at Rookwood allowed him to feel he was still an active part of life. The big miracle – that he survived his condition for so long and with such patience – was fed and supported by a host of other more modest 'Eastern valley' miracles, including Bob's visits late into his 70s and his letters when he couldn't make the bus journeys any more. These were the understated miracles, performed by real people and born out of a living sense of community; so softly whispered they were nearly inaudible; so quiet they had to be lip-read.

'Whether it was Eddie's parlour or Bob's tours, you always

had the feeling that, as a player, you were representing them and all the people who came into the parlour or went on those tours. Pontypool RFC was a binding force in the social fabric because it was the focal point, and Bob and Eddie – and others like them – had unique ways of showing you the connectedness. You were never bigger than the club, or else there'd be someone like Eddie to answer to . . .' (Bob Dawkins)

Another silent guardian of the club spirit was Berwyn Lewis. Berwyn used to run the line regularly for Pontypool and he took a young and apprehensive Graham Price under his wing when he first joined the club. Pricey remembers him as 'a man of Pontypool . . . He used to come and scout us boys out when we played for Welsh Schools in the age groups – me and Dicky Barrell and Haydn Stockham. As far as Berwyn was concerned, any boy who went to West Monmouth Grammar School should have been thinking of playing for Pontypool RFC and he made sure we all knew it!'

Graham Price continues: 'He kind of took me under his wing and looked after me when I was in my late teens. He'd take me to the Comrades Club and the Clarence Hotel and calmly point out all the old guys with pot bellies draining their pints: "He played for Wales Youth . . . He was a Wales Schools player," as his gaze circled around the room. He'd then be quiet and let me digest it all in the fusty, smoke-darkened atmosphere. "He wasn't willing to do that little bit extra, didn't like the training . . . let himself go to pot."

'He'd say it all very quietly and without judgement, but I got the message. If ever I needed an incentive to train hard and get myself super-fit, the sad sight and smell of "what might have been" hanging around those clubs and pubs and hotels was a constant reminder. It never left me.

'Whenever I looked up at the Grotto, waiting at the top of that impossibly narrow, winding path, whenever I felt a branch snap forward and sting my face, whenever I couldn't get a foothold on the loose slate and shale and thought, "F**k that, I've had enough," there was the ghost of Berwyn sitting on my shoulder. The smell of the stale beer and cigarette smoke in my nostrils came back to me and I remembered the sad faces of "what might have been". That kept me going throughout my career.' (Graham Price)

West Monmouth Grammar School, or West Mon, as it was affectionately known, was a hotbed of young Welsh rugby talent and a key source of supply for Pontypool RFC. Ken Jones, possibly the quickest man ever to play rugby for Wales – he was a member of the silver medal-winning Great Britain 100m relay team in the 1948 Olympics in London – Terry Cobner, Graham Price and Iestyn Thomas all represented both Pontypool and Wales after attending West Mon, and three of those went on to become British Lions.

Long before those later generations, John Phillips 'Jack' Jones, the first Welsh 'superstar', had been unearthed through the potent combination of a West Mon/Pontypool rugby upbringing. Born on 2 March 1886, he attended West Mon, where he demonstrated a remarkable all-round facility at sports. He captained the school's soccer team in 1902–03 and won no fewer than eight sporting events on the same school sports day, including five races ranging from 100 yards to one mile, both jumping events and 'throwing the cricket ball'! He played his first-ever game for Pontypool three months shy of his 17th birthday and became a vital part of the club's push for first-class status, which duly arrived in the 1907–08 season, with Jones as the club captain.

Despite his status as a three-quarter of rare brilliance, Jack Jones stuck to Pontypool principles that were still as valid under Ray Prosser 60 or 70 years later: 'Never pass the ball if you can find a better way to get it up the field.' During the 1911–12 season, Jack and his fellow centre, W.J. Thomas, tried every trick they knew to break down a stubborn Llanelli defensive wall, but towards the end of the match it remained proud and unbreached. Jack said to Thomas, 'Next time you get the ball from a scrum, keep hold of it, whatever happens. Whatever you see or hear, ignore it!'

From the very next scrum, Thomas made a break with Jones alongside him crying out for the ball at the top of his lungs: 'Give it here, you fool! Pass it! Pass it, man!' The Llanelli defence was duly distracted.

W.J. Thomas did his part, keeping the ball and crossing for a try before anyone, except Jack Jones, was able to work out quite what had happened.

Jack was part of the Pooler side that claimed its first Welsh club championship in the 1913–14 season, although in the meantime he had established himself in the Wales national team and been selected for the British Isles squad to tour South Africa in 1910, where he was acclaimed by the South Africans as 'the Prince of Centres'.

Like Eddie Mogford, Jack Jones was a member of the medical profession; like Eddie, when he was finally laid to rest on 23 March 1951 at All Saints church in Llantarnam, all his coffin-bearers – William Vallis, Tom Probert, George Veater and Joe Williams – were Pontypool players. The lifeblood of rugby is, and has always been, in its ability to uphold the continuity between past and present.

The senior sportsmasters – for which read 'rugby nuts' – in charge at West Mon had an important role in developing the future of Gwent rugby. Ken Jones was mentored by Gilbert Garnett in the late 1930s before flowering for Pontypool, Wales and the British Lions (and the GB sprint relay team) a decade later. Garnett was a formidable individual who could dish out beatings to 'sinners' among the schoolboy population equal to any administered on the pitch at Pontypool Park. In the '60s, the torch was passed to Max Horton, a notable Pontypool captain from 1949 to 1951 whose leadership coincided with the beginning of an era of 'champagne rugby' at the club – Pontypool lost only seven of their thirty-nine matches in the 1950–51 season – and the well-starred formation of the Pontypool Youth side, which was to prove another important plank in the platform for Pontypool's success twenty years on. One year later, in 1952, Ray Prosser played his first game for the club in the second row, having graduated from Pontypool United. It turned out to be an important conjunction of personalities for the club's future.

There was a Spartan edge to West Mon that bordered on the brutal. The school's motto, 'Serve and obey', was cheerfully – or not so cheerfully – expanded by pupils to 'Serve and obey . . . There is no other way'! West Mon never closed, not even during the 'Big Freeze' in the winter of 1962–63: pupils had to attend classes in their overcoats, fortified by the issue of throat lozenges and mints.

There was a tendency to push students to the limit, where they either sank or swam, metaphorically speaking. In 1947, in one unfortunate accident, a boy with his shorts caught on the grating at the bottom of the school swimming pool really did drown. The accident was in part attributed to the heating system, which created an indoor fog, and a chlorination process that turned the water opaque. It was as hot and unpleasant as the Florida everglades. In the ubiquitous pea-souper, Max Horton could enter the swimming-pool area and shout, 'I know you are in there, now come out at once!' and never notice the two sniggering pranksters hiding beneath the diving board no more than a couple of feet away. For some time after the accident, the swimming pool was left unheated and boys were forced to swim naked in the ice-cold water piped directly into the pool from a local stream above West Mon.

Cross-country runners sent out through the back of the school and around the Upper Race frequently found themselves ploughing through snowdrifts waist-high in the bitterly cold winters of the '60s. The rugby field by the Quarry was built on a steep slope whereby players would enjoy one downhill half and try to survive the other against the gradient as best they could – an experience repeated at Pontypool Park in the 1970s and '80s.

Max Horton looked for all the world like a dyed-in-the-wool rugby man. Any pupil who had the temerity to mention soccer would invite a response as deep and booming as any First World War howitzer: 'The ball is OVAL, boy, OVAL.' Only the school's rugby representatives were permitted to wear the exclusive navy-blue tie with its embroidered golden lions. They were the elite.

Horton also oversaw a wide-ranging sports programme, however, that included cross-country running, track-and-field, swimming, gymnastics and cricket in the summer. In many ways he had an alternative view and was a man ahead of his time. He believed in concepts such as 'shared ownership' of the team between coach and players as a matter of intuition rather than theory. He wanted all his charges to be athletes first and foremost before they became 'rugby players' or positional specialists.

Terry Cobner says that his first experience of seeing rugby from a coach's perspective – 'as a teenager with hair' – came from having to assume responsibility at school.

'I played from the age of 13 at West Mon and we had a game every Saturday. I was like a young professional. Max used to be the head rugby master, but he preferred the players in the team to organise things on and off the field. So there were the best boys in the valley, pooled together and working things out for themselves. It was a powerful cocktail. We organised the tours, the dances, the buses, the fixtures, everything – and Max tagged along.

'There was a tremendous tradition of support within the community, and it was one that was acknowledged and advanced by the boys themselves at West Mon. We were West Mon and we were conscious of the people who had attended the school before us and progressed to higher honours.' (Terry Cobner)

I used to watch Graham Price in his Capri, and Terry Cobner driving past in his Granada as I walked from Griffithstown to West Monmouth School, and I felt that same connection. I recall thinking at some level, 'Oh, they went to West Mon too and now they've become Welsh internationals.' My stride used to quicken involuntarily because I felt I could tread the same path as them. That's how things always used to work in towns like Pontypool. One man would come from Abersychan, another would come from Griffithstown. Pontypool represented the population centres of Cwmbran, Blaenavon and Abergavenny – well over 100,000 souls – but it did not need to be an artificially constructed region to do that.

I ended up at Pontypool because it represented the region at club level and from there you could see across the horizon to the national team – much as you can see the seven counties from the top of the Grotto on a clear day. The anatomy of selection was quite lucid and natural. You started at one of the nerve centres of Welsh rugby and once you were in the lifeblood of Welsh rugby (your club), it would move you closer to the beating heart (the national team) organically – if you were lucky enough and good enough.

Most of Terry Cobner's experience of rugby as a teenager came from playing the game at school: 'Coming from Blaenavon, I didn't go down to watch Newport or Pontypool or even to watch Wales play. My earliest recollection is of watching my father play on the Rifle Green at Forgeside with Colin Evans, who had one Welsh cap, before going north to play league for Keighley. They walked from the Rifle Green down to St Peter's church to take a bath outside after the match. They stripped down stark naked and got into those tin baths in the biting wind under the gaze of the Holy Trinity!'

Terry Cobner goes on to recall: 'I didn't watch a first-class game of rugby until I was 13 years old, and it was Blaenavon versus Pontypool in 1959, a championship year for Pooler; Blaenavon lost narrowly. It was 16–13 and we gave them one of their toughest tests of the season. We used to play touch rugby on the Bank up there as the game was going on, or we'd go up to the Saw Mill at Big Pit to collect a big brown bag of sawdust to mark out a pitch for ourselves at Rifle Green. So my experience wasn't the norm in those days.'

Horton also encouraged his prized rugby students to try their hand at other sports. He knew rugby was strong in the Eastern valley and encouraged pupils to expand the range of their sporting experiences as much as possible. It was Maxie who first introduced soccer (despite his contempt for the game!), hang-gliding off the Blorenge and the Duke of Edinburgh award scheme to West Mon. Graham Price was part of the Welsh Schools shot and discus team when he was at West Mon: 'I was Welsh Schools champion at both and I was an all-round sportsman at school. *Victor Ludorum*, they used to call it, but they never gave me a wreath! For me, rugby and athletics went on parallel courses for a long time and I was happy doing both. I even tried my hand at the pole vault just for a laugh.

'At West Mon it was: "Be a rugby player or get lost." They'd send you off on a cross-country run if you didn't want to play – out of sight, out of mind. I was a big lad and I had some skills, so school was like playtime to me.

'I went to lessons in between playing rugby and kicking a

tennis ball around in the school yard at break times, or running around playing tag. I played regularly, I got better and everything moved forward without interruption, even though my schoolwork suffered, of course.

'Max Horton, the sportsmaster, was highly instrumental in my development. He had been a captain of Pontypool in the 1950s, so he had already been to a place I wanted to go. I think he had a Welsh trial at fly-half. I felt I could learn from him and so I listened.

'Rugby lessons, athletics lessons, PE lessons, gymnastics lessons. It was all properly organised playtime and I credit that for developing a very wide range of skills in me on the rugby field.

'At 14 or 15 years old, I didn't have a position I could call my own. I think it was something Max Horton deliberately avoided, a young man specialising too early in his rugby life. I played back row for my age group, but I was willing to play anywhere for the year above me. Wherever they wanted me, I'd fill in. I loved running with the ball in my hands. When I trialled for the Pontypool Under-15 Schools team, I played everywhere – flanker, number 8, second row, then finally I finished playing centre! Max, who also ran the Under-15s in his spare time, insisted on playing me at centre.

'So, at one stage I was playing centre for West Mon on Wednesday afternoons and the next weekend I'd be propping for Pontypool Schools! Max was thinking, "We want him in the side somewhere for his skills and athleticism" – I think it was an example of modern professional thinking about rugby. If you want a bloke in the team, create a spot for him to play.

'I played all year at centre for Max Horton; the next year, I played at prop and that was when I started to train and play "full time" with Pontypool Youth. I knew I wouldn't be staying at school beyond my O levels.

'It was Max Horton who first asked me whether I wanted to play for Pontypool Athletic when I was in Year 6. There were a few of us from West Mon who would go up to the Athletic to play – Dicky Barrell and Maldwyn Davies and myself. After that I used to go to Pontypool regularly and take my kit bag with me . . . It got to the point where if they were short, they'd ask me to play – although at the time I was only 17, so I'd have to graciously decline. You couldn't get away with being 17 in the front row in those days, even if you could get away with it in the backs!' (Graham Price)

In his insistence on shared ownership of the team and players learning the requirements of 'foreign' positions, Max Horton was, without knowing it or elaborating it in theory, already developing a model for the professional rugby union player 40 years later. He was developing a model that Ray Prosser could and would use at Pontypool: good footballers who could scrum, run, handle and adapt. Forwards who could run quicker for longer than their opposite numbers and contribute as effectively in the final quarter as they did in the first, who could get involved fully with ball in hand and still dominate in their set-piece tasks, like Pricey; forwards who could think independently and organise on the field within the structure of the general game plan, like Terry Cobner. It was some education.

CHAPTER 3

A NEW ERA OF PROSS-IBILITY

Thomas Raymond Prosser came to rugby relatively late in his athletic career. He didn't join Pontypool and play first-class rugby until he was 25 years old, having dipped his toe in the water during a brief stint at Pontypool United. It is not generally known that prior to that Ray had played soccer – and played it well – as goalkeeper for Pontnewynydd Blues! He hadn't had much interest in rugby in his early 20s, the developmental years that are normally considered vital for a young player. Max Horton – at least the enlightened side of him – would have approved.

A 'good butty' of Ray's, Jimmy Munday, persuaded him to come up to Pontypool United and have a run-out. Jimmy was a tall fellow with a dubious reputation for hairdressing despite owning a barber's shop. The red-and-white 'barber's pole' advertising his services outside the shop was considered by the locals a grim reminder of the blood and bandages involved in the service. Barbers in the Middle Ages would also regularly perform tooth extractions and blood-letting and customers approached Jimmy Munday's with the same medieval feeling of apprehension. It was only Jimmy's exceptional sense of humour that enabled him to maintain a regular clientele.

Prosser played his first game for the United against Old Luctonians in Herefordshire. Each player had to sing a song or recite a poem after the game, and he took to the atmosphere and culture like a duck to water. He and Jimmy Munday packed down in the second row together, which would have earned Ray another nod from Max Horton. The physical nature of rugby, and the camaraderie after it over a pint or two, appealed to Pross and he decided to give up the goalkeeping for good. Before a game Jimmy Munday would say, 'Raymond, I think it is an occasion for Stead and Simpson today.' Pross would chuckle quietly, looking forward to the mayhem ahead as he tied his bootlaces and screwed in his studs.

His athletic ability soon attracted notice and he joined the big club on the opposite side of the Eastern valley at the beginning of the 1951–52 season. Ray was travelling from Cwmbran and was paid expenses – two shillings for the cost of his return journey – by one Mr Cormack, the Pontypool team secretary. Having an alert and questioning mind, Pross soon found out that stars like Malcolm Price and Benny Jones were being paid £5 a week, and what made it worse was the fact that they both lived in Pontypool! Pross made a mental note and the next time he bumped into Mr Cormack he queried the discrepancy. He was told bluntly, 'They have shown they can play rugby.'

'I was told I'd never make it.'

It could almost have been the Pontypool clarion call. It was the same for Eddie Butler, both at his first wide-eyed trial for Newport and when he left rugby completely at the age of 28 to become an assistant producer with the BBC.

'I was told that *I would never make it* as a presenter or commentator. I joined the BBC as an assistant producer and they said, "Oh, we don't think you've got the voice for it." You have to have a bit of faith and just stick with it. Be stubborn,

don't get typecast and keep on going – the Pontypool bywords.'
(Eddie Butler)

One of the anomalies of Ray Prosser's playing career is that, while he went from strength to strength propping for both Wales and the British Lions for five good years after winning his first cap against Scotland in January 1956, he continued to play second row for Pontypool throughout the same period. He was even selected in that position for the combined Pontypool/Cross Keys side that confronted the touring Springboks on 2 November 1960 in the twilight of his playing days.

At 5 ft 11 in. and just over 15 stone, Pross was seen as a middle jumper in the lineout and an athletic support player outside the set-piece. The *Western Mail*'s eminent reporter John Billot described him as 'the cleverest and quickest thrower from a lineout in Wales, with his instantaneous single-action timed jump, twist in the air and delivery'. It was only in Welsh trial matches of the mid-1950s that he began his conversion to prop.

Apart from illustrating the selflessness, bordering on self-effacement, that allowed him to accept selection in a different position to that which he was accustomed to playing at the highest level of the game, Pross was becoming the living embodiment of the mantra that Max Horton would later preach at West Mon. He was versatile, he refused to be typecast in one role and he had a strong background in another sport – in Ray's case, the game with a round, not an oval, ball.

Moreover, like many who were to graduate through the Pontypool school of excellence, he was a player with a point to prove, whatever position he was playing. He had that hunger for success that could only come from being told he might not be good enough. When he became coach, there would be no Mr Cormack: Pross would never create inequality by paying players to play.

Under Ray Prosser's captaincy in 1957–58, Pooler recorded twenty-seven wins and eight draws from their forty-four matches played. In the following season, they went one better, losing only four matches out of forty played, and winning the Welsh Club Championship for the fourth time in their history. One of the best games in those two seasons was their 14–9 home victory over Llanelli, described by J.B.G. Thomas in the *Western Mail* as 'a thriller, full of incident and played at a cracking pace throughout. Although there was precious little dividing the teams, Pontypool were the fitter and Ray Prosser, who was tireless and majestic throughout, an inspiration to his forwards, gave a magnificent display in the second row.'

J.B.G. added as a (second) prophetic afterthought, 'At outside-half Benny Jones was far more decisive in his play than was Carwyn James.' It was the first, but not the only, time that the two greatest coaching minds in the Welsh game during the '70s would collide.

*

It is December 2012, coming up to Christmas, and all the decorations are already out in Pontypool market. The streamers are up, the lights are winking on and off, and there's the constant, surprised buzz of old friends reunited for ten minutes or half an hour. Everywhere in the market small congregations come together and fall apart, as often as not talking about rugby and the hallowed days of the club.

I bump into June Howden. June is the wife of former Pontypool committeeman and the local postman Graham. The Howdens run a bric-a-brac stall at the top of the market. June is a big supporter of the club and worked behind the bar at the club HQ, Elm House. It has since closed down.

'Eddie [Butler] was here just the other day, signing his book. It was so lovely to see him again,' she says. I'm about to embrace the nostalgia when I notice Graham scowling. He nods towards a teddy bear with a black-and-amber scarf, looking lost and lonely on the floor beneath the market tables.

'I use it to buff my shoes!' he explains, before giving it a slight admonitory 'shoeing'. There's a pause and he adds, 'Black-and-Amber b*****ds!' with a knowing grin on his face. We both laugh.

He points to a cafe down the aisle. 'There's someone down there who will be pleased to see you.' From where I am standing, I can already make out the broad smiles on those familiar faces.

I'm one of many who make the pilgrimage to this cosy, ramshackle cafe to refresh themselves at the source and to meet the man who shaped my rugby career and was my real 'rugby father' – Pross.

Thomas Raymond Prosser greets me: 'Hello, Spring. Good to see you.'

'Hi, Pross, you are looking well,' I reply.

'It is all a veneer. I'm falling apart inside. I've got to shoot off soon and see the doctor. I'm stiff in just about every joint bar the right one!'

*

The first thing you need to know about Pross is that he's a hypochondriac, and my first mistake is therefore to comment on his state of health. Graham Price has spent many years trying to invent ways of avoiding a conversation that begins with 'How are you, Pross?', for to do so is to write off the next couple of hours of your life listening to a catalogue of Prosser ailments, real and imagined.

As a player, my main memory of him in the '80s was his endless moaning about one affliction or another. It never stopped. He always used to make sure that the club doctor, Hefin Jones, sat next to him during a game – just in case any symptoms of a potentially life-threatening condition arose in the course of it. If nothing arose, Pross would instead list all the aches and pains which had arisen in the course of the last week and how they were keeping him awake at night with the worry. Poor old Hefin would be required to give a running commentary while the game was in progress on the consequences of all Raymond's symptoms and how a fatal result could be avoided.

Occasionally Prosser hypochondria would collide with Prosser superstition. One season we went on a winning run when Ray happened to be wearing a pair of khaki shorts and a Hawaiian shirt. So he had to keep wearing the shorts and the shirt the longer we remained unbeaten, just in case – and that year the run extended deep into January. It was a treat to look over at Pross shivering to death in the stand in his colourful beach wear, his mind no doubt swooning over all the viruses and bugs lying in wait, ready to prey on him.

Both the superstition and the hypochondria stem from the British Lions tour of 1959, which was really the apex of Ray Prosser's playing career. At least it would have been the proof absolute that Pross had indeed made it were it not for the injuries that dogged his tour, and the fear of flying, and the frequent bouts of homesickness. The flying and the injuries were the worst. Talking to Terry Campbell of the *Western Mail* back in February 1987, Pross said: 'When Wales played Ireland I would take the boat over the Irish Sea, but I couldn't do that in New Zealand. Other players would often take a sleeping tablet, but I'd have two and then wake up after ten minutes. I'd be listening to the engines and looking out at the wings and worrying what was going to happen.

'On tour we'd fly on two planes. If I swapped planes with one of the other players, I'd keep thinking, "Perhaps I've swapped to the plane that's going to crash." And I'd be swapping from one plane to the other and back again like a madman. It used to leave me as weak as a lamb, so I wouldn't even be able to carry my baggage off the plane. I'd let my mind dwell on it for a day or two and I'd tie myself in knots.'

When you mention the injuries to Ray, he still grimaces at the memory: 'In New Zealand I broke my nose so badly I could see it in front of my right eye, I got the flu and I had blood and fluid leaking out of my ear, all in 24 hours. I felt my life was draining away through that ear, I was in and out of hospital so often with it.' (Ray Prosser)

Despite emerging by the end of that tour as one of the very best forwards the Lions possessed and playing in the only Test of the four that the Lions won – by 9–6 in the fourth Test – Pross felt a bit like a square peg in a round hole. Only the redoubtable Scottish prop Hughie McLeod and another man of Gwent, Haydn Morgan, came from the same working-class background as Ray. Only a minority of the forwards, such as Bill Mulcahy and Roderick Evans, agreed with Ray that the Lions should be dishing out at least some of the punishment that they were taking. The longer the tour went on, the more painfully aware he became of the fundamental difference in attitudes between New Zealand and British forward play, highlighted by the selection of Ronnie Dawson at hooker ahead of Bryn Meredith, another West Mon product and one of the best in his position to have ever played the game.

Pross didn't feel it was right. Selection was wrong, onfield reactions were wrong. When the Cambridge, Harlequins and England lock David Marques was kicked in the head by Maori prop Albie Pryor in only the third game of the New Zealand leg of the tour, he calmly got back to his feet, shook his assailant's hand warmly and satisfied himself with calling Pryor an unpleasant name. Pross liked Marques as a man and they got on well – barring the odd complaint that Marques 'will keep on using words like "corrugated iron" and "marmalade"' – but he suspected that the Harlequins and England approach to forward play just did not pass muster in New Zealand.

There was no corrective action taken, either by the referee during the Auckland match or by the Auckland union when Pryor was again selected to play for NZ Maori against the Lions later in the tour. When Bill Mulcahy was kicked out of a ruck a couple of minutes into the match against Wanganui, he looked up to see the referee standing over him disapprovingly. 'Serves you bloody well right,' he intoned. 'You should get off the ball.' A word was coined for the repeated attacks of violence that the Lions endured on tour: 'Pryorisms'. As the respected Kiwi scribe Terry McLean put it: 'They [the Lions] affected to be appalled at the fanaticism with which New Zealand played its rugby and it became a cliché on their side of the argument that they themselves "never" went looking for trouble.'

The Lions were their own worst enemies. This was not a place for bowler hats and gentlemen – and there were too many gentlemen in the Lions pack. In turn, this allowed the minority of Lions forwards who were prepared to mix it to be targeted by the All Blacks. There was nothing akin to the '99' call of the 1974 Lions tour to South Africa, where it was a case of 'one in, all in'; when Prosser and his fellow Welshman Roderick Evans resolved to pay back Albie Pryor for his misdeeds in the Maori game, they were penalised four times in as many minutes of play.

The forwards like Pross who fronted up in time-honoured Old Testament fashion got booted mercilessly: 'We were done up front and we were done by "the Boot". I had my head booted so far up my arse I didn't know whether I was being kicked in the face or the behind. When I got back home, I made a silent pact with myself that I'd never allow any pack of forwards I was involved with to be stood over like that. We would stick together and we would be the aggressors, the one who did unto others before they did it unto us.'

In fact, the Lions were undone by two 'boots' and the second belonged to Don Clarke, who in the first Test of the series at Carisbrook Park kicked six penalty goals to beat the Lions' four tries. The Lions went on to outscore the All Blacks in tries over the course of the series by nine to seven, but they still lost the series itself by three matches to one. Clarke kicked 36 points out of the 57 scored by the All Blacks and there were no fewer than 40 penalties awarded in the first Test alone. It left an indelible mark on Prosser, as did the heaviest defeat of the entire tour, an 8–26 trouncing administered (again at Carisbrook Park) by Otago. The Lions pack that was trampled by the South Islanders was led by none other than the forgiving gentleman himself, David Marques.

The defeat by Otago was the tour event that really engaged Prosser's coaching intelligence. As Terry McLean observed, 'The Otago forwards were superb. They had vitality, they hunted as a pack, they were completely tireless. "Red" Conway covered acres of countryside at incredible speed and at one stage when he covered 20 yards at his highest speed to enter a ruck the bones of every man jarred in sympathy.' One year later, Conway would have an injured finger amputated so that he could join the 1960 All Black tour of South Africa. It was an act of mental toughness Ray Prosser would understand and use as an example of the level of commitment required in order to play for his Pontypool teams of the 1970s and '80s.

Otago had a rich history of innovation in the game. The 1905 'Original' All Blacks had been coached by the province's very own Jimmy Duncan, who first devised the wing-forward position that has translated to the number 7 'fetcher' and link man in the modern professional game. He was also responsible for introducing the 'five-eighths' attacking system in the 1905 team's backline, which had the effect of making the scrum-half the fulcrum of the team.

In the Otago Boys 1st XV back home, Duncan had a willing disciple in the shape of 'young' Vic Cavanagh, whose father had designed a system for his undersized university student charges whereby small forwards could compete against much larger opponents at the breakdown by entering it low and hard-bound and relentlessly attacking the space beyond the ball. When Young Vic's career as a player ended prematurely, he followed his father into coaching and further refined the system at the Southern club before eventually embarking on a highly successful coaching career with Otago. Over three seasons between 1947 and 1949 his teams outscored their opponents by 374 points to 80, despite losing eleven All Blacks to the South African tour in 1949.

As with other visionary coaches – such as Carwyn James and Ray Prosser himself in Wales – the home union was thoroughly intimidated by the prospect of appointing such an innovator as Young Vic and chose the 'safe' but disastrous option for the tour of South Africa in 1949. At the end of the whitewash tour, it was universally acknowledged that the New Zealand Council had made an appalling blunder in not giving Cavanagh the appointment.

He had his revenge indirectly, however, through one of his coaching protégés in the Waikato, Dick Everest, who was also an All Black selector in the 1959 Lions series. The start of the match between Waikato and the touring 1956 Springboks represents perfectly the sweeping intensity of the Cavanagh concept of 'rucking', as Ray Prosser experienced it on the Lions tour of 1959: the concept of low, collective driving forward play he would take back to Pontypool and develop in his own coaching regime ten years later. The Waikato forwards hit contact so forcefully that it looked 'as if they were leaning into a strong wind', as one contemporary commentator put it. Warwick Roger in his book *Old Heroes* quotes Fred Labuschagne, a leading South African journalist of the time, who observed the beginning of the game as follows:

> Waikato kicked off. A high swirling ball which Jan Pickard, as was his wont, awaited with monumental calm. With the ball arrived eight hoop-shirted terrors and the giant Western Province forward practically disappeared into the Mooloo mud under impact. Ian Clarke dribbled on. Buchler couldn't stop the rush. Neither could Nel. Van Vollenhoven left his position on the wing to try and help, and the astute Ponty Reid switched direction as the ball came to him from the ruck. He gave the Waikato winger Malcolm McDonald an armchair ride to the Bok line.
>
> In just sixty seconds of hurricane rugby the Waikato side had practically wiped out the aura of Springbok invincibility. That dramatic first minute sealed the fate of the test series.

When he took over as coach at Pontypool Park in 1969, Ray Prosser wanted those 'two boots' – an Albie Pryor and a Don Clarke – to be a part of his team and its outlook. They would be the ones administering the kickings. He had a clear model in mind for the team as a whole – and the pack of forwards in particular that he wanted to develop. They would become the first 'South Island'-style team in the northern hemisphere, with certain local allowances – such as the frequent replacement of the ruck by the maul, with the ball staying up and in hand.

Ex-Welsh international referee and current IRB law-making consultant Corris Thomas took charge of Pontypool matches on no fewer than 35 occasions and he was quick to see a definite pattern: 'The Pontypool players were all of the same type, like eggs in a box. The core element was not physical size or even strength, but hardness. They were all physically and mentally hard men. You could feel it palpably out on the pitch, you could see opponents becoming discouraged because they saw no sign of weakness, no signs of self-doubt. What you have to understand is that the Pontypool eight – outside Bobby Windsor in the '70s and Kevin Moseley in the '80s – were nearly always the smaller pack. More often than not the opposition were bigger than they were, but the Pontypool forwards were bigger men collectively, as a unit, and they were bigger on the inside.

'Pontypool were a brutal team, there was no two ways about it. That was part of their philosophy: they wanted to intimidate the opposition. They were entirely democratic about it, of course; they'd boot their own players on the ground almost as much as they'd boot their opponents. When they drove over the ball, it didn't matter to them what colour shirt was near it. That jersey – along with the player inside it – would get churned out of the back of the ruck like a field being ploughed up.' (Corris Thomas)

In his experiences of the late '70s and early '80s, Mike Ruddock – at the time a loose forward for Tredegar and Swansea – noticed the disparity in size:

'Pontypool did not have a big pack of forwards – certainly not as big as Swansea, when I moved down to St Helens. We were bigger than them in every position in the pack, except maybe hooker. I was the baby of the Swansea forwards, but even I was bigger than John Perkins! But they all had great body positions in contact and they were tough as old boots, the lot of them.'

These new 'eggs in a box' were also a product of an old Pontypool tradition both inside and outside rugby. The accounts of the Pooler 'Terrible Eight' of the early 1920s are remarkably similar to those of the forward pack of the 1970s, as Arthur Crane et al. describe in *Pontypool's Pride*:

They were on the smallish side, but it was their wonderful vigour and everlasting vitality in the loose which made them renowned, and it required an unusually brave man to go down at their feet when they were in full cry for they were exponents of the foot rush, an essential feature of the game in those days.

One of the eight, Tom Woods, was only 5 ft 9½ in. and 14 stone, but he could play in any position in the pack, and even turned out at centre as a substitute for the superhuman 'Jack' Jones when he was injured – much like Terry Cobner 50 years later.

Even further back in time, a generation of iron-workers at the turn of the century were for a short time called the 'Pontypool Ironsides' when they took to a rugby field. As J.B.G. Thomas noted, 'the men of the Osborne Forge, if dressed in club jerseys, would challenge any terrible eight. What matter the name as long as the Pooler blood and spirit flows through the veins of the scrummagers and decade follows decade?'

*

The second thing you need to know about Pross is that he was one of the two coaching innovators in Welsh rugby in the '70s, although that capacity to innovate was carefully disguised by his natural instinct for self-effacement and a wicked sense of mischief. I am convinced that many of Ray's innovations were ignored because they happened in the forwards rather than in the backline and because he refused to undertake the union's coaching certification process.

The forward pattern he brought with him from the South Island of New Zealand had a natural emphasis on the scrum-half as the main tactical controller of the game. Like Sid Going for the All Blacks in the ten years from 1967 to 1977, the number 9 tended to be the main kicker and organiser in the team. This brought Ray Prosser's playing philosophy into direct conflict with the near-mystical status of the number 10 in Wales, the traditional position from which the creative orchestra was conducted. The conflict was sharpened by Carwyn James's success with the 1971 British and Irish Lions in New Zealand *against* Going and the style afterwards championed by Pross at Pontypool. Of course, Carwyn's magician at fly-half on that tour was Barry John, and I believe John's journalistic crusade against Pontypool in his career after rugby – he memorably called the club 'a cancer on Welsh rugby' – was strongly influenced by his experience in New Zealand in 1971.

The value placed on a 'mercurial' number 10 by the West Walian myth-makers also worked against the selection of a scrum-half as good as David Bishop for the majority of his career. 'The Bish' was the best number 9 in Wales by a country mile for most of his seven-year stint at Pontypool (1981–88) but he tended to run games single-handed and that told against him – particularly in 1988, when the Welsh selectors were looking to replace Terry Holmes and opted for a typically quicksilver West Walian distributor in the shape of Robert Jones instead of Bishop, the Gwent one-man army.

As Terry Cobner recalls: 'Pontypool played off 9. Most teams would play off 10 or 12, but Pontypool played off 9. Everything, the box-kicking game and the sniping runs to get the loose forwards into the game and the constant use of the short side, came off the scrum-half.' (Terry Cobner)

Graham Price reinforces the view that 'the most important player for Pross by far was the scrum-half. That went against the grain in Wales, where the outside-half was always looked upon as the player who made most of the decisions. But at Pontypool, as in New Zealand, it was the 9 who managed the game. The 10 was regarded as a "first five-eighth" and part of the ball-using duo at 10 and 12 who would link play up to the three-quarters. There was a joke going around at the time, "If

Pross can find a number 8 to do the kicking, he won't be giving the ball to the scrum-half!" And at Pontypool, the 9 always used to train with the forwards, not the backs.

'So while there were two outstanding club coaches at the time – Carwyn James down at Llanelli and Ray at Pooler – their views on rugby were diametrically opposed. It was like the geographical position of Llanelli and Pontypool. One was east, the other was west, and the two met only to clash philosophically on the rugby field. Carwyn James would say, "Let's get the ball moving through the hands, let's show them that the pass will always beat the man." Pross would reply, "Why are we passing the f***ing thing? Let's boot it 50 yards down the bloody field with one well-aimed kick!"' (Graham Price)

Although Pooler took a lot of undeserved flak indirectly because of comparisons with the way the 1971 Lions played the game, it was in fact a period of extraordinary good fortune for Welsh rugby to possess two great rugby minds who thought in completely different ways about the game. I believe it ensured that the national team never – or only occasionally – lost its balance between creativity in the backline and necessity up front.

The remarkable irony of the situation is that both Ray and Carwyn remained stubbornly outside the system throughout their periods of influence. Where Carwyn James had demanded a control over the selection process if he was elected Welsh coach, Pross never took up the union's standing invitation to coach the national team forwards. The offer was conditional on him undertaking the WRU's coaching certificates and that was something he resolutely refused to do. He remained a 'rebel without a cause' right up until the end and reacted strongly when those he'd nurtured chose to progress within the establishment, even into the upper echelons of the Welsh Rugby Union.

In tune with a coaching life led outside the well-defined boundaries of WRU coaching qualifications, Ray Prosser had a slightly piratical edge to him. He was always on the lookout for 'booty'. He didn't care much what it was, as long as it was cheap, or preferably free. On one occasion, he discovered a well-known Ebbw Vale winger was a builder by trade and so he was set the task of rebuilding Ray's front garden wall. The poor man sweated and strained; he was there for a couple of weeks, as Ray kept on finding new little jobs for him.

Ray also took a liking to the police shirt issue when I was working shifts as a copper in Cwmbran. I received six new blue shirts per year as part of the annual clothing agreement. At the end of the three years, there was a shirt surplus. I had hardly used any of them; they had just accumulated in my wardrobe. Prosser knew almost instinctively that there was a bargain to be had: 'Spring, does that police force give you anything worthwhile?' When I mentioned the shirts, his eyes lit up and the deal was done. Apparently, he used them on his garden and in the allotment. Every time I saw him I'd be greeted with: 'Got any more of those nice police shirts, then, Spring?' Even after I'd finished playing and was no longer in the police force, he would hanker after more of those shirts.

In coaching terms, I've no doubt that Ray Prosser knew the revolutionary nature of what he was attempting to do, particularly in view of Pontypool's historical success achieved through a brilliant backline in the late '50s, but he passed it all off with a characteristically devilish splash of humour.

Bob Dawkins remembers: 'One of my best friends, Dai Wigley, used to be the chief engineer down at Panteg Steelworks. At the time, Ray was driving one of the big bulldozers on the scrap-metal site there. Anyway, there was a chap, one of the labourers at Panteg, who absolutely worshipped Ray – he used to come to work in his Pontypool colours. He always used to tip his hat and call Ray "Mr Prosser"; he made a bee-line for him on a Monday morning to discuss Saturday's game.

"'Mr Prosser, I can't understand how we're winning game after game after game," he'd say. Ray would reply with his poker face firmly in place, "Well, it's all down to you supporters."

"'Is it? Really?" said the labourer, his eyes widening and his chest puffing out with pride.

"'Yes. Whenever I sit on the bench and I hear the supporters shout 'RUN THE BALL!' I shout 'KICK IT!' . . . And when they shout 'Kick it', I tell 'em to move it. Works like a charm, never fails. My success is totally down to you people in the crowd!"

'Ray would then start up the excavator – still with a straight face – and leave the poor man standing there, dazed and confused.'

Here is the key to the Prosser sense of humour. It was usually self-deprecating, and frequently mischievous – in tune with a man who did not want to be in the limelight himself. If praise was to come, it would have to come for his team. It was a sly grin rather than a jovial belly laugh.

As Bob Dawkins remembers: 'Pross always made a big thing of being dull, or challenged upstairs – but not a bit of it to anyone who knows him! He was, on the contrary, a great raconteur who understood the psychology behind storytelling.' (Bob Dawkins)

When the famous front row of Charlie Faulkner, Bobby Windsor and Graham Price were reunited in 2005 to be inducted into the Welsh Rugby Hall of Fame, all three invited Ray Prosser along.

Pricey was prepared for the inevitable response: 'It was a proper formal dinner, with all the bells and whistles, just the sort of do Ray hates. He loves hospital – you can't stop him going to the Nevill Hall to get his latest ailment checked out.

He'll even take his own medical dictionary with him and tell the doctor what he thinks might be wrong with him.

'But can you get him to accept an award or make a speech in public? Not a chance. So when the dinner was first mooted I knew he would try to make an excuse and get out of it. I was prepared for all eventualities. He said he hadn't got a dinner jacket: "I haven't got a DJ, Pricey. I can't come." I replied, "No worries, Pross. I've borrowed my son's for the night just for you."' (Graham Price)

For Corris Thomas, Ray Prosser was the one coach who never badgered him after the match; he was the only one who stayed firmly in his own space both during and after games. He never sought explanations from referees after games had finished and he never tried to influence them before they began. That was a part of both his honesty and his desire to stay in the background: 'Ray Prosser and I were on grinning terms. We never had any in-depth conversations after the game, and he wasn't the sort to chase refs or cross-question them about their decisions – unlike some other coaches of my acquaintance! I guessed he smiled at me because they usually won when I was refereeing – as they did with every other ref!'

*

The third thing you need to know about Pross is that it requires iron discipline and absolute transparency to come and work for him; there are no half-measures. In return, he will be absolutely transparent with you. It is his way or the highway. Your role in the team is black and white, too, nothing in between, and it is spelled out to you with total clarity.

There was never any doubt about what was expected of you, in terms of either your commitment or your function within the playing structure. Tactically, there was a clear plan in place for every part of the field and that enabled the players to relax because they knew exactly what they had to do in every situation. From lineouts in our own third of the field, for example, it would always be 'two ball' and a box-kick off 9 with the blind-side wing chasing it down. In the middle of the field, it was off-the-top ball from the middle and two scripted phases. In your opponent's 22, there would be a peel around the tail of the lineout, usually by Pricey, to take out their midfield defenders. It was a crystal-clear structure to work from.

Pross would be equally clear in spelling out exactly what he expected of any player either joining or leaving the club. For any player joining, there would be no extra financial incentives, no 'gravy'. To anyone thinking of leaving the club, he would say, 'Anyone want to leave Pontypool? The door's always open . . . but don't forget – you'll never come back. Go, by all means – but you'll never come back.'

However, I sometimes wonder whether Ray Prosser's attitude was related to his hypochondria. Ray had zero tolerance towards 'that which was not Pontypool', just as he could not abide the mere thought of a virus lurking somewhere in his own body. He created a siege mentality: an 'us versus them' outlook that could also make enemies.

Gordon Richards and Richie Thomas are two West Mon old boys who are now both honorary life members of Panteg cricket club. Gordon worked with Pross and knew him from Panteg Steelworks: 'One evening after a Pontypool–Cardiff game at the Park we were in the president's lounge talking to two members of the Cardiff committee, Alun Priday and C.D. Williams. We knew Alun and C.D. well from our encounters between Panteg CC and St Fagans.

'Pross came storming up to us as if someone had breached the fortress walls. "Who let you two in 'ere and how do you know them so well?" he demanded, pointing at our drinking buddies. It irked him that two mere "cricket players" were hobnobbing with two stalwarts of Cardiff rugby.

'Pross didn't always realise that such relationships, and bridge-building between clubs, could be a good thing. A few seasons later Alun Priday called me to say that Cardiff was thinking of cancelling fixtures with Pontypool. Alun had overheard one of John Perkins' motivational speeches while running the touchline for Cardiff and his report to the Cardiff committee hadn't gone down too well. Luckily I was able to inform Pross just in time for him to make a conciliatory phone call and mend the fences. Ray probably respected Cardiff more than any other opponent. But this wasn't the case with every club we played, who saw the dark side of Pontypool on the pitch.'

The black-and-white commitment he both demanded and gave created a tremendous depth of emotion within the club. I recall going through a tough time personally on one of Pooler's trips to Canada in the 1980s and my chosen way of expressing that dissatisfaction was to let off fire alarms in our hotel. I even set one off inadvertently when I hooked up my model aeroplane to the water spray system on the ceiling – I wasn't trying to do it deliberately. The climax occurred at a residential hotel we were staying at in Toronto. Most of the upper floors were occupied by old retired folk and when the sprinklers went off they were forced to troop, half-soaked, all the way downstairs, through the hotel lobby and past all the boys in the bar. Looking and feeling rather sheepish, I joined them a few minutes later. The Perk took one look at me and said, 'Any more of this, Spring, and we'll have to send you to Newbridge.' At that moment all the confused circumstances of my life came to a head and I burst out in loud, uncontrollable sobs. 'Noooo, please don't send me to Newbridge, Perk . . . I don't want to go to Newbridge.' I thought Perky really meant it and when I 'came to' I saw that it was a joke. But, like most Pontypool jokes, it had a point. I understood that Pontypool RFC was the only pin holding all the confusion together. It was humbling.

After his experience as a player with Mr Cormack, Pross ensured that there would be no wage scale at Pontypool. If you lived in and travelled from Cwmbran, and you paid 10 pence on the bus to get to Pontypool, and it cost you 10 pence to get back home again, that is what you would be paid to play. Pride in the jersey and the people you were representing came first. There was no room for 'tall poppies' with Pross. As Peter Jackson recounts in his excellent book *Bobby Windsor: The Iron Duke*, when Bobby mentioned the fiver he had got previously from Cross Keys as a semi-professional sweetener and asked what he might expect in return for his services at Pooler, he was met by an unequivocal response: 'F**k all.'

That applied to everyone. It was a completely level playing field with Ray Prosser and that was typical of the man for as long as I've known him.

As Terry Cobner recalls: 'Everyone was told in front of everybody else what they were doing right, what they were doing wrong and it was full on. There was no taking a player around a corner and telling him in private, there was no place to hide, it was utter transparency. It didn't matter if you were a British Lion or played for the Athletic, the treatment was exactly the same.'

Pontypool RFC was an amalgam of people from all walks of life: the majority were blue-collar workers – colliers, carpenters, steel workers, electricians, policemen – with a sprinkling of doctors, students and businessmen, and the odd crook – or should I say 'loveable rogue'. Pross would love to take the piss out of the more white-collar types: 'We've got more bloody medical men, lawyers, students and teachers than *University Challenge*. We're keeling over with eggheads!' he'd say, but ultimately it was the same rule for all. Ray Prosser's way of showing he cared about you, like Eddie Mogford and Junna

Jones, was to subject you to a tirade of verbal abuse, usually based on how you looked physically or what you did for a job. Prosser's cruel-but-apposite nicknaming was part of that. The sharp wit cut through all social distinctions and variations in character and reduced everyone to the same level.

In fact, Pross got so used to remembering everyone by their nicknames and his mental caricature of them that he sometimes forgot their real names. The club archivist Ray Ruddick tells a story about the 'doyen' of sporting commentators Bill McLaren once turning up to commentate on a Pontypool game. McLaren was always very assiduous in his research before matches and he approached Pross with a couple of pages of closely annotated foolscap in hand. He wanted to know the Pontypool squad for the match. This was not Ray's thing at all and signs of panic appeared: 'Ivor, where are you?' he screamed. When 'the Jaw' was not forthcoming, Pross desperately rummaged through his memory for the names of the backs: 'Well, we've got "the Doc" at full-back and "Sheets" on the right wing. "Bill Sykes" is playing outside-half . . .' Pross ground to a halt. He could only remember the nicknames, never the real names – and certainly not if they were playing in the backs!

Prosser would also go to some extraordinary lengths to help the people he knew to be worth helping. Bob Dawkins recalls an occasion when 'while he was still a player, Ray drove all the way from Pontypool to Bristol to pick me up and drive me to the game. Remember, there was no Severn Bridge in the early '60s, so he had to drive all the way up to Gloucester and come back down again to Bristol. That was a good three-hour haul. Then after the match had finished he drove me all the way back again in the middle of the night. I was astonished that he'd do that for me. It opened up a window for me onto his character.

'Although he'd never coached before, it was no surprise when things began to move forward quickly after he took charge. It inspired me, and when our ships passed in the night in 1969 it became a matter of regret to me that I never played with him as my coach. I missed him by only a few months in 1969, but I missed him nonetheless. If he'd come at the time I was still there, I've no doubt I would have stayed.' (Bob Dawkins)

The flip side of the coin was that once Pross had written a player off in his head, he would hardly ever waste any time on him at training. When he wasn't seeing the world in red, black and white, Ray saw the world in monochrome – everything was either black or white. He had a clear, well-ordered way of doing things. For Ray, there was a protocol in every situation, the right way and the wrong way of doing things.

Graham Price comments: 'His great strength was his simplicity and his bluntness. His language used to be so blunt and colourful that the process of knowing where you stood with him was usually painful. People would take offence at his jokes, which were often very personal, but he never meant them that way, it was just his method of getting everyone singing from the same hymn sheet.

'You have to be able to say the things people don't want to hear. Sometimes straight talking isn't very palatable, especially in public, but that was the Pontypool way. The more Prosser liked you and rated you and the more he thought he could get out of you as a player, the harder he would ride you.

'So he used to chivvy guys like Staff Jones and Charlie Faulkner mercilessly. He'd be on their backs all the time. If Ray didn't say anything to you, it was because he didn't care and didn't see any potential. We all knew that was the worst thing that could happen to you at a Pooler training session. You wanted Pross bawling in your ear, with the rain falling on your head and mud seeping up your legs; then you knew you were on your way. Just like you'd want the cruellest jokes turned

at you by Junna Jones or Eddie Mogford in his massage parlour.'
(Graham Price)

Mike Goldsworthy, Prosser's regular number 10, took his
son to Pontypool recently, travelling to the Eastern valley from
his home town of Penarth on the South Wales coastline. 'Aby',
as Mike was known some 20 years earlier, placed great
importance on his 17-year-old son meeting 'the Pross'. Many
other ex-players now make the same pilgrimage.

As an outside-half, Aby had great attacking flair and the
ability to beat a defender with a sidestep and a good turn of
pace. But what Pross took delight in was his ability to kick the
ball a long way. Mike had a great spiral punt and could keep
the Pooler pack rolling forwards, especially when his target
area was the far right-hand corner with Pontypool playing
'downhill' towards the leisure centre. That corner became a
graveyard for many a visiting team.

Before one Saturday afternoon match, Mike was settling
down underneath his usual peg in the dressing-room at the
back of the main stand. He was sitting underneath his number
10 jersey and was going through his usual pre-match routine
when Ivor 'the Jaw' Taylor appeared at the door and beckoned
him over.

'Aby, "the Doc" has dropped out and we want to ask you a
big favour for today's game: could you play at 15?' 'The Doc'
was Peter Lewis, Pooler's prolific goal-kicking full-back, who
was another crucial part of the 1st XV jigsaw.

The Jaw was suitably deferential: would Mike Goldsworthy
mind playing full-back for this game only? Mike agreed without
hesitation; Ivor was gushing with his thank-yous. Aby moved
his stuff and little Dai Thomas from the Garn came in nervously
a few moments later to sit underneath the number 10 peg
instead. It was only 30 minutes before kick-off.

Mike recounts the rest of the tale with some incredulity. 'Do you know, even though I was playing out of position, at short notice and without any training sessions behind me at full-back that week, Pross still debriefed me after the match as if I'd been playing there for years? "I thought you did well there, Mike," he said. There was a pause, then he threw out his arms. "But why the f**k did you drop that ball in the first half?" Ray had a mind like a steel trap and could remember every moment of every game. "Hold onto the ball as if it's your baby, even if you are a f***ing volunteer!"'

Eddie Butler has his own outstanding memory of the searing Prosser tongue in action. Eddie played for Pontypool, but his further education occurred at Cambridge University. He recalls bringing a Cambridge University team of which he was part down to Pontypool for an early season game by special arrangement. It was a clash of two worlds, chalk and cheese.

'I remember bringing a Cambridge University team back to play Pontypool when I was up at Cambridge as a student in October 1977; I'd arranged it through my links with the club. I thought it would be a great experience for the boys to lock horns with guys like Pricey, Bobby, Charlie and Jeff Squire and broaden their rugby experience. At least, that was the theory.

'I was walking out onto the pitch before the game when I saw Pross already there, talking in animated fashion to Perky and Charlie, who were both nodding vigorously. I could only hear snatches of the Pross vernacular.

'"They're just a bunch of f***ing children. They've come to learn. Whatever you f***ing do, don't touch 'em. No booting and no punching, eh?"

'The Perk and Charlie nodded enthusiastically, their heads going up and down like they were on invisible pulleys.

'Come the game, and everything went to the script until the last five minutes or so. Pooler were winning comfortably by 33–16. Our flanker, John Evans, had been causing the Pooler forwards some heartache by falling on the wrong side of rucks consistently and killing the ball. Finally, Charlie couldn't resist it and unzipped his head good and proper. The claret flowed freely; it was everywhere. I looked over to see Pross jumping up and down on the touchline.

'As the players walked off at the end of the game, Pross went straight for Charlie and grabbed hold of him: "What did I f***ing tell you? No booting and no punching." It went on and on. I could see Charlie getting more and more distraught. He had his head in his hands and his body was rocking from side to side. I could hear him doing his penance in that unmistakably nasal, metallic whine of his: "Aw . . . sorry, Pross. I couldn't help it. No. Aw . . . sorry." The more Charlie apologised, the more animated Pross became!

'It was typical Pontypool. Tried to behave, ended up giving the best and only lessons of which they were capable.' (Eddie Butler)

CHAPTER 4

CLIMBING THE GROTTO
TO THE PROMISED LAND

'There's a pot of gold up in that Grotto, for any of you who care to go looking for it . . .' That's how it would all start, with a grin and a wink from Pross, followed by an hour of pure torture.

Before that, there would be a good deal of apprehension and not a lot of talk in the changing rooms. I say 'changing *rooms*' because one was never enough. At least 40 and sometimes as many as 70 players would turn up for training sessions and both home and away sheds would have to be used regularly. You would be rubbing shoulders with men who wanted your spot, so there would be the same level of concentration you normally associate with matches. You did not attend a Pooler training session in order to get fit; if you did, you were already placing yourself at a massive disadvantage in the desperate scramble for places, not only in the 1st XV but also in the Athletic side.

Pross and Ivor Taylor would change separately in the referee's room underneath the main stand at Pontypool Park. Ivor was Ray's right-hand man and a Blaenavon man; he was Peter Taylor to Pross's Brian Clough, Ernie Wise to his Eric

Morecambe: 'The reason they call me the coach is that I've got a lot more mouth than Ivor. But sometimes he has been my legs and he is almost always three parts of my brains.' In my opinion, Ivor was also Pross's main pipeline to sanity. He had joined Pontypool as a player in 1971, having played for seven seasons down at Rodney Parade, and went on to play another twelve seasons for Pooler. During Pontypool–Newport matches, the Jaw was therefore nowhere to be seen. He usually went off to watch the 2nd XV instead. If anyone could survive contradiction with his sense of humour intact, it was Ivor.

I used to arrive early for the seven o'clock session. Sometime in the hour leading up to training the Jaw would appear at the changing-room door and give some poor individual the summons to the ref's room. Everyone else would breathe a sigh of relief, or wince in empathy, as the player shuffled off to get his 'feedback' face to face with Pross. Ivor would be there, too, playing the good cop as best he could.

Pontypool Park was the arena, and I mean it in the gladiatorial sense. Training was regimented and nobody would say a word as Pross entered the ring; we knew how the session would begin – running two by two in an orderly fashion around the iron fencing separating the pitch from the park proper. Pross would jog along just inside the long line of 'butties'. Four laps with a sprint for home on the last lap and that would normally conclude the warm-up.

In the warmer months, Ivor would disappear a couple of laps from the finish and you'd find yourself looking across at your running partner, exchanging a knowing glance, understanding what lay just ahead. Something would drop to the bottom of my stomach like a lead weight.

Pross would make his comment about the pot of gold and then add, 'No slacking, now. Me and that long-jawed c**t will be watching you all the way.' There would be a mad dash into heavy undergrowth on the corner of the pitch opposite the leisure centre before everyone settled down into single file. Ray would then walk off to find his post on top of the second steep ascent on the Grotto run.

*

The path upward is all loose stones and shale, with a gulley in the middle of it, grooved by the rain that tumbles down the hill in the wet months. On either side of the path, branches await their opportunity to whiplash the unwary. The excitement of the dash to get to the corner first and jostle my way into the first five or six up the incline is still inside me. My foothold keeps slipping and I feel my lungs collapse, as I have to go back over the same ground.

A couple of hundred yards into the ascent, the gradient begins to even out and a generous grass verge appears on either side; the path becomes broad and open. I can get into my running and I start to pass some of those ahead of me on the climb. Chris Huish looks at me startled, as if I'm mad, but I sense a rhythm building; it's a familiar feeling from my days as an 800-metre runner and I let my lungs fill with air like a pair of bellows. I know this is the time to push on, while I feel the ease in my body.

Without warning, a wall appears in front of me and the horizon disappears. It feels like a door has been suddenly slammed shut in my face. There is no more running to be done and I find myself instead looking for footholds, for inches clawed back from an unforgiving host. I'm thinking, 'Little steps, little steps, keep your rhythm.' Occasionally, I trip and have to put my hand down on the ground for support. My breath comes in rasps. Jesus, this is harder than the beginning. I force myself to remember: there *is* an end, it is called the Grotto and it is some 100 feet above me. That keeps me going.

The impact of the Grotto run is black or white. I saw many men driven to destruction by it. The mere act of coming back for more somehow gave you a sense of invincibility.

As Eddie Butler recalls, 'In August 1976, Pontypool not only became a new sphere of experience, it swallowed me whole. My mother broke the news: "This strange man has been on the phone, dear, a Ray Prosser. He wants you to go to training. You will take care, won't you? It all sounds very rough."

'At the first training session, I found out that cricket was no longer played on the park. Not much rugby either. The pitch served merely as base camp for warm-up before the assault on the hills began. Time has dulled the pain of the Grotto: memories revolve happily around the figure of Bobby Windsor, never the greatest on the slopes, seeking each week the key to the mystery of the uphill climb. Sprint, stride or walk: the middle man of the famous three tried all speeds but somehow always needed to be scraped from the soil two-thirds of the way up.

'That damned Grotto serves as a murderous example of Pontypool at its very best, of how the most gifted of players must sometimes go through the worst humiliations so that both the club and they may prosper. The indestructibility of Pontypool owes much to the moaning, cursing, spitting and swallowing of gnats to be witnessed late on a summer's evening high above the town.' (Eddie Butler)

When I arrive at the top, 'the long-jawed c**t' looks me up and down forensically. In some grim way, he looks satisfied as I weave slowly along the ridge. There is a slight nod of acknowledgement.

The sensation upon reaching the Grotto during our training

runs is one peculiar to Pontypool. Your body is screaming for recovery time, your lungs are working overtime to get oxygen back into your bloodstream, you feel as if you're at the limit, but at the same time it's as if you've emerged into a new world. You're looking out over seven counties; over Torfaen, over the Park, over the town of Pontypool itself, out even over England on a clear sunny day. Your breath is taken either by the mixture of exhaustion and relief in your body, or by the spectacular pleasure of your surroundings – or, more likely, by both.

Look up to your left and only a short distance away there is the stark grandeur of the Folly Tower, built or rebuilt – depending upon the extent of your immersion in the local lore – by the Hanbury family in the eighteenth century. Mythology insists that it exists on the site of an old Roman outpost; what is certain is that it has been demolished and rebuilt at least three times in the last three centuries. On the last and most notable occasion, on 9 July 1940, it was taken down stone by stone at the order of the Ministry of Defence. The Folly was considered to be a navigational landmark used by Nazi aircrews on their bomb runs to the nearby Royal Ordnance factory at Glascoed. It was not rebuilt until 1992.

For centuries the Folly was a land-bound lighthouse that gave notice to travellers and Celtic pilgrims alike that they were in sight of home:

Here where the hill holds heaven in her hands,
High above Monmouthshire the grey tower stands . . .
(Myfanwy Haycock, 1937, a local poet and artist)

Latterly, it became a panoramic rallying point for holidaymakers. Reputedly as many as 20,000 people gathered here to celebrate the Silver Jubilee of King George V in 1935, building a bonfire nearby to light up the night skies, usurping for once the traditional red glow of the ironworks. The Folly was a centre of social interaction. As the owner of Ann's Pantry noted in the *Pontypool Free Press* of 1948, 'loaded with boiled ham, fresh rolls and butter, ice cream, oranges, sweets, tea and mineral waters I used to go with my helpers to cater for the many holiday makers up there at Whitsuntide'.

Look down to your right and a very different monument is visible, one particular to the late twentieth century. As Harry Vaux (a talent scout and committee member of the Prosser era) once told me during a conversation in Pontypool market: 'Who else would have 'em running to the top of the Grotto but Pross? Pot of gold's up there, he'd say. And when you got to the top you'd see that view. Seven counties and the great monument to '70s design squalor, the tower block in Cwmbran, next to Ty Tudor in Southville and its sunken garden.

'What a horror! It is the biggest skyscraper in Wales. Two hundred feet tall and built around two huge chimneys that bled away gases from the heating for the nearby shopping centre – a "landmark" building indeed.'

Nothing represents the dark industrial heart of the Eastern valley better than that tower at the centre of Cwmbran, an enormous waste-disposal unit disguised not-so-carefully as a contemporary living space.

This stark conjunction of the time-honoured and grand with the mundane and the squalid is there even in the Grotto itself. In the 1970s, the exterior was that of any old neglected farm outbuilding – the roof had partially caved in and the walls were crumbling, harshly treated by the weather and vandals alike over the years. It wasn't until over 20 years later, in 1996, that the restoration work was completed. In the eight years or so that I ran like a madman to the top, and for many years before that, the Shell Grotto firmly withheld its secret from all passers-by.

Inside, as your eyes adjust slowly to the semi-darkness, a new world dawns, a world composed of the materials belonging to the local landscape. It is like a living socioeconomic history book. The roof and walls are decorated from top to toe with shells, mostly cockles and periwinkles, with some exotic oysters and conches, stitched around natural stalactites. They were brought in on the boats that transported the local industrial products, coal and iron, abroad. The floor, which at first glance looks like another shell mosaic, in fact contains the bones and teeth of animals hunted within the park grounds.

Wherever you look, in the landscape as in the outlook of the rugby team, there is that typical jolting dichotomy of the Pontypool character. There is the historical stature of the Folly, Hanbury Park and the Grotto set against the design scab of the Cwmbran tower and its toxic flues, or the overgrown remnants of abandoned sluice-gates and the old ironworks' tunnels pock-marking the valley; the utilitarian exterior of the Shell Grotto set against its secret beauty; even within that beauty, the semicircle of animal teeth and bones yawning beneath the footfall of the unwitting visitor, ready to snap and devour; the glory of the view set against the pain of the run.

The breathtaking setting of Pontypool Park existed as a kind of contradiction – part hilarious, part serious – to the kind of rugby played on the field.

It was like one of Eddie Mogford's colourful jokes.

As Eddie Butler says: 'What always struck me about Pontypool Park is how beautiful it is. It is the most picturesque setting, and I always loved that sense of contrast with the rugby that was played here, its brutal hardness. The two together, for me, spelled "home".'

Corris Thomas experienced the same contrast as a referee, especially during Wednesday evening matches at the Park.

'Wednesday night at Pontypool Park was a unique experience. If you hadn't had that experience, you hadn't really lived, particularly if you were a referee!

'Walking onto the pitch was like entering the Roman Coliseum. As you walked out, the giant uncovered bank rose in front of you like a great mountain crag, but a mountain alive with people. It always took my breath away, however often I experienced it. It must've been able to accommodate 10,000 people or more on a really busy evening. Pontypool Park is a two-sided ground, so you wouldn't see many spectators behind either set of posts – it would be just the main stand on one side and the Bank on the other: 9,990 rabid Pooler fans and ten cowering visitors, wondering why they'd come . . .

'There would be that quiet sense of purpose in the Pooler changing room. You could see all the players mentally preparing themselves. You'd never hear much, if any, banter; it was almost silent, ominously silent, as I checked the players' studs – like a big wave before it breaks on the shoreline. Then you'd walk out and the chants of "Pooler, Pooler!" would hit you and you'd see that, once again, the mountain had indeed come to Pontypool Park.

'I don't think many of the "away" teams wanted to be there on those Wednesday nights. They were frightened of the ordeal to come; some of them would be ashen-faced. A lot of players didn't like playing in midweek anyway because they'd have been working all day and then had to get up to Pontypool from Cardiff or Newport or wherever – all to get a good booting and a battering.

'It was as unforgiving a place to be as it was spectacular, and I always felt it was worse on those Wednesday nights than it was on Saturday afternoons. There was a palpable difference in the atmosphere.' (Corris Thomas)

I have to discover my own 'pot of gold' in Ivor's slight nod of approval as I begin the descent. This is my favourite part of the race, flying downhill full pelt without a care in the world. Not everyone enjoys 'descending' as I do, or shares my willingness to surrender to the risks involved. This is where I'll be looking to hold off the challenges of Mark Picton or 'Hat-trick Patrick' Hayes – or get ahead of them. Getting ahead allows you to control the pace before you reach the next 'no overtaking' area. There is danger in those bushes and scrub at the bottom of the valley and I may need to slam on the brakes to avoid careering right into some prickly undergrowth. Looking up to see Prosser silhouetted on the next peak, screaming at the more timid souls, cancels all my doubts and I let my body go completely.

Then it's the final ascent, a real strength-sapper. Sinking ankle deep into flat, thick slabs of turf with every step, feeling my strength ebb away. I have to drag my legs out of the long grass even though I'm winding down faster than a clockwork toy. It's hard to describe the feeling of elation when that second peak is conquered, Pross is left behind and there only remains one last gallop down to the committeeman and his stopwatch standing by the side of the pitch! I think I lived for that moment at each and every training session.

The 'F' in Fitness was a huge letter, probably the most important letter in Pooler's alphabet under Ray Prosser – bigger than the 'S' in Scrum or the 'M' in Maul. Again, it was a necessity he'd understood on that painful 1959 Lions tour to New Zealand.

Even then, New Zealand sides were semi-professional in outlook, as Terry McLean relates in *Kings of Rugby*:

The NZRFU's active encouragement of summer training schools and specialised methods of physical training from 1956 onward . . . placed an importance which was certainly semi-professional in extent upon physical fitness in New Zealand rugby. Provincial teams were encouraged to engage in working-up fixtures [for the Lions tour]. Combined provincial teams were brought together for practice matches. The New Zealand Maori team made a two-match tour and its players lived and trained and played together for two weeks before they met the Lions. As in 1956, a dozen or so national trials were staged up and down the country, even as the Lions were going into action in their matches in Australia.

The directive of the International Board that international teams should not be quartered in hotels for training earlier than 48 hours before the start of a Test match was openly ignored.

Playing for Pontypool was a professional business, without the money, and I believe we were the first club in the UK to take a professional attitude towards fitness.

Terry Cobner says: 'Fitness was huge for Pontypool. If there was one word that could encapsulate the Prosser philosophy, it would have to be "fitness"; if it was a phrase, it would have to be "fit for purpose". We aimed to be fitter and harder than everyone else and as a result we stuck to our game objectives for longer than anyone else. We had the attitude that even if someone scored more points than us, they would never beat us. We would be there waiting for them the next time. If you're not fit, you're buggered, because when the legs go the mind follows. It's inevitable. Everything stems from your physical conditioning. Pross would say, "I don't mind you coming off, as long as your head's under your arm!" Eddie Mogford would just come on with his magic sponge and smack you around the chops until you got up.

'I don't know how many other clubs would have had the guts to implement the programme Ray did. I don't think the players would have accepted it, and moreover I'm not sure that Ray's methods would have translated to the national team: there would have been too many players coming in from too many different environments. I doubt they would have been willing to subject themselves to the harshness of an environment to which we had become accustomed – and even grew to like after a while.' (Terry Cobner)

Ray Prosser would say, 'Use your fitness as a weapon against your opponents because that's what it is.' Most games were won and lost in the final quarter, and that was our time. Pross made a point of reminding us to square our shoulders and stand tall at all those fourth-quarter lineouts, when there would be four or five opposition forwards with their hands on their knees and blowing hard. It was a huge psychological, as well as a physical, advantage for us whenever we saw that tell. We were there, looking down on them as they struggled. We knew we had them where we wanted them, that we could sustain our patterns of play more accurately and for longer.

Eddie Butler remembers: 'Pontypool looked at it as a compliment to be seen as short-haired, humourless, one-pint-and-we're-off types, and we didn't discourage people from forming that image of us. For us, it was business – as near to professionalism as you could get without actually being professional. We didn't have much time to smile because we took our rugby very seriously and were proud of that fact.

'Two weeks before the end of the season we would still have thirty willing bodies turning up for training and doing an awful lot of hard work. Fitness, especially among the forwards, had a huge emphasis at Pontypool. When you had eight very fit, big men roaming around the pitch at high speed, you could do a great deal of damage.

'We trained all the way through the summer; there was no "time off". We just kept up the pace and ran straight on through until September arrived; it was business as usual at Pontypool. We looked at ourselves as professionals long before they ever thought of professionalism in rugby.' (Eddie Butler)

Graham Price found that his athletic background naturally complemented Ray Prosser's demands in the area of physical conditioning: 'My athletic background helped me understand what was necessary on the training front. I never took that for granted. I did six hours' training a week, every week, and because of my background I knew that fitness would benefit my performance on the field. I just carried it all straight into my rugby and I never found it a chore – or even a means to an end. It was what I did, it was what I was used to and it was what I enjoyed doing.

'There were no fitness advisors or nutritionists around in those days, so I used to sit around after a match or a training session trying to earwig and pick up little training tips from the guys ten or twelve years older than me – but it turned out I could have been the one giving them the tips!

'"The hardest part is making that first step outside your front door" – that's what I remember from those earwigging sessions. Someone saying, "Oh, I was going to go for a run last night, but it was a bit cold and dark and then I smelled the wife's cooking . . ." Then he added, "The hardest part is always that first step outside your front door." That stuck with me; it became my mission statement.'

The single largest element in 'fitness' is in its strengthening of the invisible muscle called 'mental toughness'. Confidence in your physical conditioning easily translates to confidence as a rugby player on the field. During the 2011 World Cup, both Wales and New Zealand attributed the upsurge in their fortunes to a secret recipe for a fitness level that gave them an edge over their rivals.

Objectively it wasn't true, of course – certainly not in the professional era. The value of Wales's well-publicised pilgrimages to Poland for their cryotherapy sessions in temperatures of minus 120 degrees centigrade were not mainly about physical conditioning in itself; they were about using 'fitness' as a peg on which to hang self-belief. Cryotherapy fools your body into flooding the bloodstream with endorphins by convincing you that you are dying. So when the Welsh players entered the 'evil sauna', as Sam Warburton put it, the enhanced training endurance was strictly secondary to the toughening of the mentality associated with that situation. If some part of your body thinks you are going to die, it is fair to say that it will commit to the challenge in front of it more fully and give you the 1 per cent or 2 per cent extra you're after.

The Grotto run developed that ability to control physical pain, agony even, and turn it to your advantage. At times you really did feel you were going to die; it was that hard. Training at Pontypool Park consistently forced you to your absolute limit because of its competitive nature. If something inside you wasn't ready to make that commitment on one particular Thursday evening, you knew that there would be someone else who did have it and who was ready to fill that breach. If Perk wasn't up to it, he knew Pross would not have a moment's hesitation in replacing him with Haydn Moreton in the 1st XV pack; it was the same for Graham Price with Mike Crowley, or Staff Jones with Paul Jenkins.

There were no excuses at Pontypool, and that went for the walking wounded too. The worst possible outcome would be to find out that Junna was also sidelined with one of his many injuries. No player wanted to be part of 'cripple training'. If you couldn't take part in the main session, then you were usually handed over to Junna instead and that meant you were a duck in a Chinese restaurant. Cripple training would be even more gruelling than the main session with Pross, Perk or Bobby Windsor. This alternative session finished some 20 minutes after the main body of training and it was far, far tougher. Basically, you'd have to complete most of the same tasks as the able-bodied except at a walk, hobble or jog. It encouraged your body and mind to 'play through pain'.

It didn't end with the Grotto run either, though the run was one part of it. After a few warm-down laps, in the dry months it would be time for Prosser's unique version of 'touch rugby'. With the Pooler sense of humour in full swing, 'touch' actually translated to 'full contact' – or 'murder ball', as it was called by the players. Many a rookie was caught out by Ray's announcement that there would now be a session of touch rugby and relaxed just a little too much. I found myself bounced five or six metres backwards by a Chris Huish charge on my debut. I wondered what had hit me.

'Murder-ball' developed into a game of rugby league in the 90's under the coaching of Goff Davies and John Perkins. Pooler could never have too many candidates in the tight five and word would get around like wildfire in the changing rooms before training about a new player who'd come in that evening. For Nigel Meek, a Blaina boy who had previously played for Ebbw Vale, it meant his own personal Passchendaele opposite the incumbent Wales hooker Garin Jenkins.

'I'd played against Garin before, but even with the benefit of that experience I had no idea of what awaited me in the "touch" session . . . ,' recalls Nigel. 'The first time I got the ball I got Garin too. Knees. Elbows, head, he was all over me – then he shouted, "Touched!". Of course it all went off after that, and even "Sheets" copped a few as he tried to separate us!'

Nigel Meek went back to Blaina that evening a chastened man after his trial by fire, but he came back again for the next season and that marked him out as a Pooler player. He was accepted after that, and went on to win three Wales caps in the early 1990's.

In mid-season, the game of touch would be replaced by a 30-minute match between the 1st XV and the Athletic, and that was far more violent. The fight to wear the red, black and white starting jersey produced regular training battles that were as intense and bloody as any game. The Athletic had quality players and some very tough men. In the 1980s, I used to watch Hayden Wilmott take on the heavyweights of the first team, who tried to bully the Athletic players. I was playing one night as 'Haydo' gave the Perk a bloody nose. It showed the first team were not going to walk all over us, and on the occasions when the Athletic gained the upper hand Pross would have no hesitation in switching Athletic players into the 1st XV, however celebrated or capped the incumbent might be.

The other major aspect that enabled Pontypool to move far ahead of their competition in terms of physical conditioning was the building of the leisure centre in 1974 underneath the bottom corner of the rugby pitch. The centre was only a 50-metre walk from the changing rooms and had a variety of facilities, including a 25-metre swimming pool and a multi-purpose gym/weights room. It was ideal for the generation of players and the professional approach to physical conditioning that Ray Prosser was nurturing.

Bob Dawkins recalls how the attitudes of Steve 'Junna'

Jones were revolutionised by the appearance of the leisure centre: 'Laurie Daniel [a Pontypool old boy] came down to coach the United side and one night it was far too wet to train out in the open – our pitch was a mud-heap at the best of times – so we all went down to Twmpath school instead.

'We were there in the weights room, and I think it was the first time Junna had seen anything like it. I was wearing my blazer and grey flannel trousers and spectacles, having come down straight from Fairwater school. At that time I'd been doing weights for many years and I casually bent down to pick up one of the barbells. There must have been about 35 kg on the bar and I did a couple of curls with it.

'I could see Junna gimleting me from the corner of the room; he was itching to have a go. But when he went to pick it up . . . nothing happened! The bar remained obstinately glued to the floor. Junna stood up and eyed me suspiciously. He jabbed out a threatening forefinger: "I know who you are now."

'Quivering in my flannels and pushing back the glasses on my nose, I replied, "Whatever can you mean?"

'He said: "Clark Kent."

'But Steve was genuinely bewildered, and I could tell he was already hooked. "How can you do that and I can't?" he continued.

'"You're probably a lot stronger than me," I replied, "but it's a matter of technique not strength."

'Junna nodded and I could tell his brain was working overtime. After a brief pause, he just said, "Can you teach me?"

'So I started taking Junna down to Pontypool leisure centre, which had just opened, with a glossy new weights suite, and began to show him the ropes. Within a couple of weeks he was there five or six days a week, working out every night.

'Within six months Junna could leave me for dead on the weights. He was so competitive, and he wouldn't rest until he could make the most out of himself and be better than the other fellow. He quickly became the strongest man in the gym.' (Bob Dawkins)

I first met Junna down at the leisure centre, doing weights with Dai Leighfield and Neil Waite, two other Pontypool players. At the time I was an athlete turning slowly into a rugby player and although I had a strong background in aerobic activities I needed to build myself up physically, especially when Pross started selecting me in the second row. Dai and Junna showed me how things were done and helped me develop overall muscle tone and increase the power in my legs and arms. They did the same with others and the culture of gym work began to spread from one generation of players to the next. In time the culture in the weights room produced some real 'weights monsters'. Mike 'the Bear' Crowley, for instance, was capable of bench-pressing 180–200 kilos, which I've not seen bettered during my time as team manager for the Worcester Warriors over the past two years.

The transformation of Pontypool didn't happen overnight. Ray Prosser took over as coach in 1969 after what the club historian Arthur Crane calls 'the Wilderness Years' of the mid to late 1960s, a period in which Pontypool were not only unsuccessful but also the butt of everyone's humour on the Welsh club scene. Pontypool's decline, in fact, coincided with Ray's retirement as a player in 1961 and only revived with his appointment as coach in 1969–70. The force of his personality was that important to the club's fortunes as a whole.

It was a grim time for Bob Dawkins, who had returned from college in the south-west to play rugby in his home town.

'I first played for Pontypool in 1960 before going to St Luke's College in Exeter. In 1966 I returned home because I was able to get a four-bedroom council house in Cwmbran. In the south-west I was struggling in a tiny one-bedroom flat in Bristol.

'In 1966 Pontypool was probably at one of the lowest ebbs in its history. We were feeble up front – ironically so, in view of what happened afterwards under Ray Prosser.

'Clive Rowlands came to Pontypool and I felt the fortunes of the club were tied too closely to his own personal welfare for its own good. He had captained the club quite successfully in the 1962–63 season when the "Big Freeze" that winter put an end to all club rugby for two months in January and February [1963], and he went straight into the Wales team as captain in 1963.

'However it was a disaster as far as Pontypool was concerned. He was frequently out injured for long periods and never trained with the team. He'd left his teaching job in Cwmbran before the beginning of the 1965–66 season for a job with BP. He lived in Upper Cwmtwrch in Swansea and that is pretty much where he stayed. You never saw him except on match days. As a player, he only wanted to kick the ball – playing for Wales in 1963, he was largely responsible for the 111 lineouts on the paddy field against Scotland. The IRB changed the laws about kicking directly into touch after that.' (Bob Dawkins)

In the 1964–65 Home International Championship, Rowlands won his 13th consecutive cap on the day of his 13th consecutive captaincy, leading Wales to the Triple Crown against Ireland on 13 March 1965, the first Triple Crown Wales had won in 13 years. It was indeed unlucky for some, particularly those involved at the Pontypool club. A couple of months later, a fire started in the wooden main stand overnight and it burned to the ground. The cause of the fire was never discovered, but it was an event in tune with the times.

Bob Dawkins says that 'the nadir, perhaps Pontypool's all-time nadir, was the 1966–67 season and a playing record that yielded only 14 wins from 51 matches. It was a couple of wins less than the club's record two years later. That was Clive's last season as captain.

'When I played in the centre for Pontypool, I never saw the ball! Well, I did see it, but only being punted up in the air by Rowlands. It was soul-destroying, and it forced me out of the club to Pontypool United. The United side was playing a much more expansive game at the time. It would regularly move the ball and score from underneath its own posts and I enjoyed my rugby there.'

Without wishing to pin all of Pontypool's failure in the mid to late 1960s on poor old Clive Rowlands, it is clear that his move to Swansea and his absence from both the local community and the rugby club had a damaging effect on his ability to lead it and improve its fortunes. His situation was an echo of the Welsh Rugby Union's attitude 40 years later, with success at national level being taken in exchange for a certain indifference towards the grass-roots level of the game. Both were, in my opinion, Faustian pacts; in the mid-'60s, the heart of Pontypool as a club was withering, if not burning to the ground – much like the club game in the valleys as a whole after regionalisation was introduced in 2003.

'Ray Prosser and I started at Pontypool at almost the same time, around 1969. I was just a little before him. The atmosphere at the club before Ray got there was terrible. My first game, they wanted to fine me for not having my boots in a bucket! We were bottom of the Merit Table at the time and they wanted to fine me for not having boots in a bucket. Unbelievable.' (Terry Cobner)

Terry took over the captaincy of the club for the 1969–70 season from Laurie Daniel, having attended college in Staffordshire and resisted overtures from the Newport club down the road: 'I had played for Welsh secondary schools and then attended Madeley College in Staffordshire. In the summer before I attended Madeley, I used to hang around on the twmp by Forgeside; we used to call it the 'Ponderosa', in honour of the *Bonanza* programme we were watching on the telly at the time. I remember one day my father came running over in a high state of excitement: "Son, son," he said, "you've got a try-out for Newport!" I looked back at him blankly. When he'd got his breath back, he thrust a paper in front of my face. "It's all here in the *Argus*!" he repeated. I said calmly, "Dad, I don't want to try out for Newport."

'"Son, you've got to go, it's in the paper!" he replied. I was buggered.

'So off I went to Newport, dragging my feet, to have my trial. I didn't know anybody there. I was just trying to keep my head down and change underneath this peg when I hear a big, booming voice behind me. "Oi, you can't have that peg, it's my peg." I turned around and there was the big, shaggy figure of Glyn Davidge, Welsh international, in front of me, stinking of booze, having just come in from the pub. I moved my clothes. You could plot a pattern of where every ruck and maul had been that day simply by following the smell of beer – the smell of where Davidge had been. The smell seemed to hang around on the pitch forever.

'Newport thought I had some promise and invited me to play for their United side. I played one game and then bolted off to college with a sense of relief. I played for Staffordshire while I was there and began to attract good reviews from

Gwyn Bayliss, a Welsh full-back from Brynmawr who filed rugby reports for the *Wolverhampton Express and Star*. He wrote a letter to Pontypool and they contacted me. "How would you like to play for Pontypool?" they said.

'"Well, I'd like to come home," I replied.

'"We can organise a job for you in teaching," they said, and I promptly agreed.

'I couldn't wait to come home. I missed the Eastern valley and the character of the people in it and their sense of humour, so I jumped at the chance. I came back to teach first at Abersychan school and then at Llantarnam, and play my rugby for Pontypool.' (Terry Cobner)

There were no quick fixes. It took the best part of a couple of seasons for Pross's dictum – *train in an orderly fashion, play in an orderly fashion* – to be understood and accepted. A lot of old wood had to be chopped away before the new growths could take. As Terry Cobner recalls: 'So, the following year, Ray was appointed coach; I had already been appointed captain and our relationship blossomed. I bought into his philosophy and Ray began to instil a discipline that had previously been lacking. The first year was very difficult because there were still elements within the camp that weren't prepared to accept that discipline, but they were gradually weeded out or left of their own accord.'

As a callow 18 year old fresh from school, Graham Price saw the cultural change at the club: 'Pross went on the 1959 Lions tour of New Zealand and he came back a different man. He saw how the Kiwis viewed the game, he saw their training methods and he brought it back with him to Pontypool. But he struggled to get his ideas across in his first season coaching the club. There were too many "old hands" there for his liking. In particular, we lacked the fitness values his style of play was going to demand. When you're tired, you go back to doing what you automatically do and that was the case in Ray's first season.'

Recruitment of a new generation of players who could be moulded by Ray in his own image became key and his recruitment drive was to receive invaluable scouting assistance from the likes of Harry Vaux and Gwilym Williams. As Ray Prosser used to say, 'To coach a first-class club, I think it's more important to be a poacher than it is to be a coacher! It's being able to see a player you fancy playing for another club and to inveigle him to come over to you.'

Up until Ray Prosser took over, the tradition used to be that all the good valley forwards would go down to Newport and play there. So Ray's first aim was to make Pontypool an attractive alternative to travelling down the valley to the big city. Pontypool always had the reputation for having a good backline in the '60s, with men like Laurie Daniel and Adrian Hearn. The Newport backs would travel up the valley to play and that trend accelerated in 1971, with men like Ivor Taylor, David Cornwall, Martin Parry, Gordon Collins and Phil Waters all joining the club in the same season. They called it the Newport 'brain drain'.

With Prosser in charge, we also began to attract some good young forwards to the club. Graham Price came up from West Mon in 1971, along with Bill Evans in the second row. Ron Floyd, our main lineout forward for most of the decade, formed a productive partnership with Bill for the next few years. Cobner, Mike Harrington and Brian Gregory were already in place in the back row.

Bob Dawkins comments: 'The recruitment traffic gradually became all one way, up the valley. Ray was determined to make Pontypool the biggest club in the area and it had a marvellously positive impact when that started to become a reality. Good players in clubs like Talywain, Cross Keys and

Cwmbran all aspired to play for Pontypool. When Pontypool were strong, so too were those other satellite clubs, so the effect was mutually beneficial. It lifted everyone in the Eastern valley. In those days, clubs like Talywain were quite capable of crossing the border to beat the likes of Gloucester United in England.' (Bob Dawkins)

The Pooler pack took another huge step forward when Ray Prosser acquired Charlie Faulkner from Cross Keys the following season (1972–73), then Bobby Windsor the year after. The incumbent hooker Alan Talbot played an influential role in persuading Bobby to join up with Pross at Pontypool. The key, however, was the ability to hang on to home-grown talent in the Eastern valley. Bobby Windsor and Charlie Faulkner were the exception rather than the rule, as all the other forwards came from the catchment area between Cwmbran and Blaenavon. What they all had in common was the desire to improve and make Pontypool a genuine challenger to the big city clubs in and around the M4 – Cardiff, Swansea, Newport and Llanelli. They didn't come for the money, because there wasn't any beyond expenses, 'bar money' and Pontypool's generous investment in tours to locations such as Canada and San Francisco, which were always fully funded by the club.

Part of Ray Prosser's genius was his ability to detect potential in men who – if they were far from 'rubbish' – had been drifting around the Welsh club scene for a number of years without making an indelible mark on it. They had certainly not been able to find a permanent home for themselves. In Charlie's case especially, it looked like his rugby career was coming to an end.

Bob Dawkins says: 'Bobby and Charlie were both what they now call journeymen when they arrived at Pontypool. They'd been around the block. I remember playing against them when they played for Newport Saracens. It was the environment at Pontypool, and the people they were playing with, that made the difference in their careers.'

Graham Price takes up the theme: 'Bobby Windsor had been floating around the valley clubs. He started at Cross Keys and went down to Cardiff for a while, but they wanted to convert him into a prop. Bobby was undoubtedly strong enough to have played prop and that is what he did later in his career, even starting a Welsh Cup final against Swansea at loose-head with an entirely steel-grey head of hair. But at that time he was caught between two stools and a lot of clubs didn't know what to make of him.

'Charlie had already joined us the previous year from Cross Keys. He has always managed to keep his true age a secret, but I can now reveal that he was 29 years old when he joined Pontypool in 1970 – I will leave it to you to work out how old he was when we were winning those Grand Slams together in 1976 and 1978 . . .

'In those days you didn't have much rugby life left after 30, and you'd be packing it in at 32, but that's when Charlie's career took off. When he first got selected for Wales in 1975, Charlie was 34 years old. His career was like an unexpected fairy tale dug out of the coalmines and steelworks.' (Graham Price)

Having acquired a lot of the 'boot' he needed up front, Ray Prosser turned his attention to the other boot, adding a reliable goal-kicker in the shape of first David Morgan and then Robin Williams, who had left the club to make the journey down to Newport only to follow the magnetic pattern of the other Newport backs and re-join Pontypool for the 1973–74 season. Robin went on to set a club world record of 517 points in one season the following year.

Ray Prosser displayed a degree of ruthlessness in his quest

to establish Pontypool as the premier club in the area and all other clubs as 'feeder' clubs to its needs.

Bob Dawkins remembers: 'One of the first things to happen was Ray organising a meeting between Pontypool and the United, with a view to amalgamating the two clubs. I think he was only after United's best players, as it turned out!

'I looked him in the eye and said, "Ray, you just want to cream off our best assets, don't you?"

'Pross looked straight back at me and smiled: "Well, that's about the long and the short of it, Dawks."

'It might have worked if there had been an agreement to run United as the Pontypool second string instead of the Athletic team, but that wasn't forthcoming. It did, however, show Pross's extraordinary drive to explore all the avenues available to improve Pontypool's fortunes as quickly as possible.'

Pontypool's success in that breakthrough 1972–73 season not only encouraged local players – and those based as far afield as Newport – to join the ranks, it also began to project their players onto the international stage, which in turn snowballed the recruitment drive. The first of the Pooler players to achieve international recognition was the captain, Terry Cobner. The club climbed ten places in the unofficial Welsh Merit Table to finish in a respectable 8th position in 1971–72, their highest position since 1962.

As Arthur Crane put it in the official club history, in 1972 Cobner was already 'reinforcing his reputation as one of the finest wing forwards in Wales. He was already considered to be in line for senior Welsh representative honours to add to his selection for the Welsh Under-25 teams against Fiji in 1970. The road to "Pross-perity" was just around the corner!'

'Cob' duly earned his first full cap against Scotland at the start of 1974, at the age of 28, and, as it turned out, he opened the floodgates for others such as Graham Price and Charlie Faulkner to follow.

The relationship that developed between Terry Cobner and Ray Prosser was crucial to Pontypool's success. As Harry Vaux says: 'Terry Cobner approached Ray about coaching the club in 1969 and, as you know, they were like blood brothers, although they haven't talked to each other for years now.'

Pross and Cobs spent so much time on the phone together you could have mistaken them for a couple of young sweethearts. Ray would even call Terry to help him with the daily crossword: 'What's six down, then, Dick?'

The club archivist, Ray Ruddick, believes that, although Ray Prosser has a lovely daughter, Beverly, Terry Cobner was really the son that he never had. Cob himself adds: 'We used to talk all the time. We'd either be on the phone, or Ray would leave the tip at Panteg where he used to work and appear at the school. That old ash-truck would pull up out of the blue and I'd have to get Stuart Harrison [another teacher at the school] to take the lesson for me! We'd meet every Sunday morning, discussing who we needed, who we wanted to get rid of, then we'd get on to his beloved garden and allotment and the theory of planting potatoes. We'd have a good drink together and it was a very close relationship.' (Terry Cobner)

Terry Cobner was Ray Prosser's captain for ten years in a row. Pross typically did not trust academic or intellectual types, but he realised that he needed intellect on the field to get his ideas put into action successfully, to take the message and translate it for the rest of the team. The likes of Cobner and Eddie Butler in the next generation at Pooler were therefore invaluable in the leadership of the team. Both Terry and Eddie were excellent communicators and both went on to demonstrate their ability to apply their intellects to rugby after their playing careers finished. Eddie is a successful journalist and Terry became the WRU's first Director of Rugby and a major driving force behind the regionalisation of the game in Wales in 2002–03.

Ironically, it was that same rugby intellect, mixed in with a fair bit of obstinacy on both sides, that eventually created a great divide between Pross and Terry; as Harry Vaux puts it, 'Pross just can't get it out of his mind now . . . that Cobs left Pontypool to go into the Welsh set-up and was responsible in part for the regionalisation of rugby in Wales. Pross thinks he was the one responsible for the coming of the regions and blames him for the decline of Pontypool. So they don't talk any more. But I don't think Ray was quite right about that, mind.'

Armed with the feeling for 'shared ownership' of sporting teams that had been cultivated at West Mon, Terry Cobner was more than happy to take responsibility for what happened on the pitch and he was used to acting independently of the coaches once that opening whistle had been blown. As his experience of the captaincy increased and his authority within the game in Wales grew, Cobner began to exert a huge invisible influence on games. In David Tossell's book *Nobody Beats Us – The Inside Story of 1970s Wales Rugby Team*, the Bridgend and Wales centre Steve Fenwick recounts the story of being caught on the wrong side of a ruck against Pontypool in a club game the weekend before a big international; of seeing Terry Cobner coming straight for him, not to administer punishment but to protect him physically as the boots came whistling in; of the terse warning not to f***ing get caught there again followed by the broader picture – 'See you next Saturday.'

Cobner even exerted this influence over referees. Corris Thomas recalls refereeing a cup game in Maesteg between

Pontypool and second-tier Maesteg Celtic in December 1976: 'It was the second minute of injury time and I'd already looked at my watch a couple of times. A huge upset was on the cards because Maesteg Celtic had a two-point lead. The crowd was going wild, delirious. They were already creeping over the touchlines, swaying to and fro as more and more people pressed forward to get a glimpse of the action. I had to keep telling the linesmen to move the crowd back off the field. I suppose you can't blame them, they were anticipating what would have been without doubt the greatest moment in their club's history.

'Pontypool were attacking, and it was very late in the game. I looked at my watch and there was only about a minute and a half left and I was conscious of the need not to award a technical penalty that could potentially decide the game. I always made it a rule to stick to clear and obvious offences, infringements that I couldn't ignore, in those circumstances.

'There was a breakdown and a Celtic player threw himself recklessly over the top of the ruck and killed the ball. I looked at the crowd seething back and forth on the sidelines. Out of the corner of my eye I noticed Terry Cobner, looking straight back at me as if to say, "If you don't blow the whistle, he's going to have it." It was just a look, and Terry didn't do anything, but I had to make the call. Cobs gave me the look and I thought, "Well, yes . . . you're quite right there, Ter . . ." and up went my arm. Robin Williams was the best goal-kicker in Welsh rugby and he stepped up to kick the penalty and Pontypool escaped by the skin of their teeth with a one-point victory, 13–12.

'But both Cobs and Bobby [Windsor] had that kind of presence and influence on the field; it reached the stage where they were almost like shop stewards on the pitch. They made a strong impression on everyone around them – opponents, referees and supporters. They were every bit as key to Wales's success in the '70s as Gareth and JPR, in my opinion.' (Corris Thomas)

It was no surprise, given the force of his personality and his background in Welsh club rugby, that Cobs became such an important forward leader in the British and Irish Lions pack of 1977 in New Zealand.

John Dawes was fundamentally a backs coach and I know from conversations with those involved that Terry's centrality to the coaching on the trip grew as that of John Dawes diminished. The occasion at training in Timaru when John couldn't find the players when he turned up to lead the session (they were all hiding behind the advertising hoardings) was somehow symbolic. Dawes was also sensitive to criticism and had disagreements with some of the pressmen covering the tour, including Mervyn Davies, with whom he'd shared some of his greatest triumphs with both Wales and London Welsh.

Graham Price recalls: 'We had gone through half of the tour without a forward sitting in on the selection panel or organising the technical aspects of the forward play that needed to be coached. The RFU's Don Rutherford even sent Dawes a paper on what the Lions needed to do up front but it was ignored!

'That was when Terry took a step forward to give the forward play some structure, after we'd been stuffed in the 1st Test and before the 2nd Test in Christchurch. For the rest of the tour, Terry took on the major coaching role. Cobs was a school teacher by profession, so it came quite naturally to him, and he'd been given a lot of leeway by Pross in that respect. For the last three Tests, it was Pontypool, Pontypool and more Pontypool, as Cobs used all the methods he'd learned off Ray Prosser to convert the Lions pack from the punchbags of the 1st Test in Wellington to probably the best set of forwards ever to tour New Zealand.' (Graham Price)

Terry Cobner explains further: 'When we went out to tour New Zealand, there was no system of lineout signals in place and no overall policy at the lineout. Would we block at the lineout? How would we support our jumpers? Would we move across the lineout and try to occupy the gap or stay in our own space? What were our positions at kick receptions? Would we try to ruck or maul the ball in the loose? None of these decisions had been made before we left the UK and so we departed with a blank sheet of paper, as far as planning was concerned.

'To begin with, there wasn't that consistency of policy in any area of the game and that came back to bite us in the 1st Test against the All Blacks. We also had some key people missing. Traditionally if the forwards could hold their own in New Zealand, the British backs would be good enough to do the rest, but in 1977 the situation had been completely reversed. If you talk to some of the backs on that trip, they will tell you that the support they received was disappointing. Brynmor Williams told me that the only person on the coaching panel who talked to him was me, and I'm not a backs coach!

'My coaching role began after the 1st Test. We were on the way up to Timaru and I found myself in the WC with John Dawes. He said to me, "Where are we going to go from here, Cob?" and I replied, "Give me the forwards." He looked unconvinced for a moment, so I said it again. "Give me the forwards, you must have thought about it already." He zipped up his fly and said, "All right," and I took over from then on. Our next game was against a District side and we won handily and then we beat Canterbury on the next Saturday. They had kicked the s**t out of the last Lions tourists in 1971 and we said to ourselves, "There's no way that's going to happen us," and it didn't. All of a sudden the mood of the tour party was elevated with that win and I felt I had earned my coaching spurs; I had the respect of the senior players. We won the 2nd Test and the show, as they say, was back on the road.

'I was at that time of my playing career – I was 31 years old – when I was ready to take on the extra responsibility. It came as second nature to me – I'd had the schooling at Pontypool and I knew about forward play and I was able to right the ship with the help of that club background, particularly in the area of selection. The biggest decisions were made in the front five: selecting Peter Wheeler ahead of Bobby Windsor, switching Fran Cotton to loose-head and bringing in two new second rows in the shape of Gordon Brown and Bill Beaumont. I also chose Derek Quinnell at number 6. When you make six changes to a Lions pack, you know that if things don't work out, your cock's on the block.' (Terry Cobner)

If this was a symbolic passing of the torch from London Welsh to Pontypool, it was one that occurred in distinctly unhappy circumstances. The strength of Welsh rugby in the '70s had always been in the creative friction between the philosophies of the two clubs, even after London Welsh severed all playing ties between them in the winter of 1973. The heat generated by that friction became a blazing fire on international days with Wales, with Gerald and JPR and John Dawes providing a deft counterpoint to the brutal-but-intelligent 'boot' of the Pooler front row and Terry Cobner. In 1977, the balance had been lost. There had always been as many 'cavaliers' from London Welsh and Llanelli as there were 'roundheads' from Pooler. That all changed in 1977 and the Lions' back play was the worse for it. Where there had been no fewer than seven London Welshmen on the historic tour of New Zealand six years earlier, none toured in 1977.

There were four Pontypool forwards on the trip and three of those played in the Test matches.

From the Christchurch Test onwards, Cobs led the forwards on to one of the most complete dominations of an All Black forward unit ever witnessed, particularly in the set scrums and driving mauls, those two articles of Pontypool faith. In one sense, it was a case of 'Prosser's revenge' for 1959, to the extent that the All Blacks were forced to accept lineouts instead of scrums whenever they had the option. The final indignity was the enforced use of three-man scrums by the Kiwis in the 4th Test, for which they were roundly booed by their own fans. The Lions forwards didn't just control the last three Test matches, they stripped the All Blacks of their rugby manhood.

The morphing of player into coach as the tour developed did not occur without some obstacles along the way, as Terry Cobner recalls: 'The most difficult decision on the 1977 tour was picking Peter Wheeler over Bobby for the 2nd Test, a match we had to win. Bobby was my best friend and we always roomed together on tour.

'Was it the right decision? Did I wish I would never have had to make it? The answer to both those questions would be a resounding "Yes". But if you're on a ship that is sinking fast, as the 1977 Lions were, there is no room for sentimentality in selection. You can't pick your best friends first.

'Bob had injured his leg before he went on the tour and he couldn't run freely, so Peter was yards ahead of him in training. Peter was also a better thrower into the lineout, so the only area in which Bobby was clearly better was at scrum-time. With Fran Cotton and Graham Price miles ahead of anything in New Zealand at the time, we could forego the scrummaging power for the extra speed around the field and Peter's accuracy at the lineout.' (Terry Cobner)

A sizeable amount of what would now be called 'intellectual property' was transferred in the process, from Terry Cobner to the likes of Peter Wheeler, who took the Pontypool techniques of forward play back to his club, Leicester, and to Wheeler, Fran Cotton and Bill Beaumont, who made them the basis of England's Grand Slam in 1980. As Terry observes in today's game, 'I certainly see the Pontypool imprint in Leicester. It's there even now. Richard Cockerill, their current Director of Rugby, would be a Pontypool hooker. No doubt about it. He'd suit us and accept our standards and our behaviour. He'd fit right in.'

The sense of ownership and confidence in his leadership abilities Terry had first developed at West Mon had spread a long, long way out of the Eastern valley. When he was eventually invalided out of the 1977 tour with a knee ligament injury in the game against North Auckland, the opposing All Black coaches and selectors were left in no doubt that they had seen the back of one of the best back-row forwards to visit the 'Shaky Isles'. One of those selectors, J.J. Stewart, said: 'Quick wits and experience count for a lot. Cobner was the best tackler among the Lions' loose forwards. He was only a little guy but boy, he was strong. I think he was a helluva good footballer.'

Cobner's ascent, after his career as a player ended, into the world of first coaching and then selection and directorship on a national level, was first signalled by the prominence of his role in New Zealand and confirmed when he was invited back into the Wales camp to coach the forwards before the Autumn game against New Zealand in November 1978. However, his move towards the rarefied realms of rugby politics and policy-making (he became the WRU's first Director of Rugby in 1996) placed him increasingly at odds with the interests of the club he loved so much. Terry Cobner always had a much more wide-ranging view of what might be best for Welsh rugby than a Ray Prosser or a John Perkins and, given the stubbornness of both parties, a split was inevitable.

CHAPTER 5

GETTING DOWN AND DIRTY

The impact of Pontypool RFC upon Welsh club rugby, and club rugby in the British Isles as a whole, was magnified by the 1977 Lions tour of New Zealand. The three members of the Pontypool front row in particular were transformed from mere human beings into creatures of myth after their appearance as a unit for the British and Irish Lions against Bay of Plenty. They were renamed the 'Viet Gwent'; Max Boyce wrote one of his most famous songs about them. They were even transformed into 'Groggs', possibly the most famous of John Hughes's well-loved clay figurine creations.

The Pontypool scrum had acquired such a totemic significance that all kinds of unlikely counter-measures were considered in response – even ones that had never worked in the first place, like the All Blacks' three-man scrum. Grand Slam-winning coach Mike Ruddock experienced the reality behind the myth first-hand while playing with Tredegar: 'I started playing against Pontypool for Tredegar in 1977–78. The British Lions had just returned from a tour of New Zealand in the summer of 1977 and everyone knew about the impact Pontypool, via men like Terry Cobner, had had on the coaching of the Lions forwards. It was massive. Cobner ended up coaching the Lions forwards on that trip, and Bobby Windsor and Graham Price were also Test match forwards – to be joined by Charlie Faulkner as a late replacement. Charlie was always last to the party.

'They had humiliated the All Black forwards and dominated the scrums so completely that New Zealand had even resorted to three-man scrums by the end of the series. At Tredegar we got really excited and thought this was a great idea to get away from their main point of strength as quickly as possible, and I was given the job of being the chief decision-maker at the base behind the front row. I could pass left, pass right or take it on myself.

'We played Pontypool at Pontypool Park in September, and I remember the intake of breath from the crowd in the stand when we only packed down a front three in our first scrum. The Pontypool boys squatted down for the scrum and when they saw what we were doing they all started laughing out loud. When the ball came back, I had no chance to pick it up and make any decisions. Our front row toppled backwards over the top of me to be followed by the entire Pooler pack. I was trampled to bits – they were still laughing – and came out of the other side of the scrum like I'd been through a threshing machine! I could see bits of what was my jersey on the ground all around me like confetti . . . I just lay there like a sardine, and now I could hear the crowd laughing themselves stupid.

'We'd pinned all our hopes on that three-man scrum, so I ended the match looking like a bit of roadkill. An American football coach once said about his offensive line, "These guys are mean, and I mean *mean*. They won't just run you over, they'll reverse back over the top of you again just to make sure you're dead." That was the Pontypool pack, all right. They took no prisoners.

'Pontypool pursued me my whole career. I remember driving up the M4 with some mates to watch the England–Wales game at Twickenham in 1980 – the infamous game in which Paul Ringer was sent off and Wales lost 9–8 despite scoring the only two tries. We'd had a few to drink by then and one of my mates was nudging me, "Hey, Mike, there's a car right behind us and it's been there for a few miles now. There's a bloke waving his arms out of the window." The car speeded up and drew alongside us and the window started to wind down. Then the head of the Tredegar RFC secretary Mike Edwards appeared at 70 mph. I thought his hair was going to blow off. I tried to slide down in the back seat. Mike Edwards was shouting and gesturing: "Mike, you're playing against Pontypool on Monday night!" What a mood-breaker that was.' (Mike Ruddock)

For Pontypool, the scrum was the point of contact at which they set the mood for the game ahead and established a psychological advantage.

As Corris Thomas explains: 'If you couldn't live with them in the scrums, they would squeeze the utmost out of that advantage. The scrum didn't end with the ball coming out to the scrum-half . . . Oh no! Pontypool would keep on driving until the opposition collapsed, then they would trample all over them. For a referee, you needed to have eyes in the back of your head because it was a real flashpoint situation. And remember, there were three times as many scrums in those days and they all went on for far longer than they do now.' (Corris Thomas)

At the centre of the Pooler scrum was Bobby Windsor. He was the first of the three members of the so-called Viet Gwent to be capped by his country. As a physical specimen, he was way ahead of his time. Bobby was not a striker for the ball in the scrums; he wasn't one of those flexible types like Brian Moore or Peter Wheeler. He was the first of the really big physical hookers, of the men who could have comfortably played first-class rugby as a prop – as indeed Bob did for Pontypool in the twilight of his career to accommodate Junna Jones.

Bob was always listed in the programme as 14 st 10 lb and we used to have a good laugh about it in the changing sheds because we all knew his best fighting weight was between 16 and 17 stone, and he'd rarely be less than that. In South Africa with the British Lions in 1974, given the high-protein diet out there, he weighed even more. It was no coincidence that on the rare occasions that the front row struggled, for either Wales or Pontypool, it was invariably because the opposition had a hooker as strong and as heavy as Bobby, like Argentina or France when they had Alain Paco playing for them. Paco left such a strong impression on Bob that he even named his boxer dog after him.

Bob Dawkins remembers: 'Ray Prosser said to me, "Bobby is more influential in the pack for us than Terry Cobner. It all revolves around Bobby." Bobby was the policeman of the rolling maul that we developed in the '70s and '80s. He was also the biggest man in our tight forwards. He was probably two stone heavier than Charlie and three stone heavier than Pricey, whatever it said in the match programme. Bobby was a monster. When he played for the British Lions in 1974, Bobby was playing at somewhere between 17 and 18 stone. Pricey was only 14 stone dripping wet!

'No one could scrum against Bobby; he would just enjoy popping them through the roof of the scrums . . . One of the abiding memories I have of the '70s is of opposing front rows being lifted up into the air wholesale. Bobby was at the centre of all of that. He was the first of the breed of big hookers in the UK, men who could do all the footballing elements required by the position but had this enormous physical presence.

'And Bobby was, of course, a great footballer, having played fly-half for Newport Schools at Under-15 level. He knew when to give a pass and he was even a competent kicker!' (Bob Dawkins)

Bobby Windsor's right-hand man, Graham Price, was a quite unique player in my experience. He played on the tight-head side, which demanded more strength and technique because of the weight coming through on that side of the scrum. Yet Pricey was 14 stone even – and barely that – when he won his first Welsh cap against France in Paris in 1975. In the early stage of his career, he regularly used to give away anywhere between two and three stone in weight to his opponent.

Terry Cobner recalls: 'When Pricey first started in the 1st XV, he was only 18 years old; we pitched him in really young. That was very unusual for a prop. He would come off the field hardly able to put one foot in front of the other. His head would be hanging on his chest in the changing room after a game because he couldn't physically hold it up. He was stuffed.

'But Pricey always had this huge resolve, an incredible single-mindedness and sense of purpose. He worked like a dog in training and ran like a stag during games. He was an excellent runner and handler, and he was technically very good in the scrum. It was all about the hit, for Pricey. He always scrummed 'heads' not 'shoulders'. He'd aim to hit the top of the loose-head's head with his right shoulder and if he did that part successfully, it didn't matter how big or strong the loose-head was – even if he was Gerard Cholley! He'd have his shoulder on his neck and he'd have his "elbow to heaven", as we said in Pontypool. He'd be using his right arm to lock up the loose-head in that uncomfortable position.

'Once the prop was wrapped underneath Pricey, the idea would be to take him down as low as possible without pushing him beyond his limit so that he collapsed completely – keep him low and uncomfortable, but keep him up. If an opposing tight-head ever tried to take the scrum down on their ball, all hell would break loose! He would get a right good booting so that he didn't do it again, so that we could use the advantage we always anticipated we'd have in the scrums.' (Terry Cobner)

I remember playing behind Pricey for the first time as one of Ray Prosser's exercises in positional versatility. He used to ask Eddie Butler and myself to play in the second row to toughen us up and get us used to a new set of requirements, and I was only 6 ft 2 in. and under 14 stone at the time.

When Graham packed down in a scrum, the sensation for the second row pushing behind him was quite extraordinary. He would be on the move constantly: one moment he'd be taking the scrum down low, the next he'd be sliding in on the hooker or suddenly driving his opponent upwards and out of the top of the scrum. He did a huge amount of work in every scrum to find just the right position, the one in which he felt most comfortable and his opponent felt most awkward. Few of those opponents could keep up with Pricey's combination of movement, strength and work-rate at the set-piece for the whole game. Towards the end of it they would be so exhausted that Graham could just wrap them underneath his right shoulder and take the scrum gently to ground. They would be so tired they couldn't hold it up any more. That was the cause of most of the collapsed scrums. Graham took a lot of flak for those collapses, but it was nearly always the fault of his opposite number. As Gordon Brown told him after one of the Lions' games in 1977: 'Pricey, I'll pack behind you anytime.'

Size was not an issue for Pricey: 'I played for the 1980 Lions in South Africa. We were up against a Barbarians select outfit, the kind of team they used to test men who were on the fringe of the full Springbok squad. All week the locals were telling me about the man I'd be facing in the scrums, "Flippie" van der Merwe: "Wait and see what happens to you on Wednesday at Potch." He was Danie Craven's blue-eyed boy and they were lining him up to play in the Test series. I was told he was 6 ft

4 in., 23 stone and as strong as a rhino. At that time, my fighting weight was about sixteen stone, so I was giving away about seven stone in total.

'Anyway, we played the game at Potchefstroom, the site of an old British concentration camp in the Boer War, and the atmosphere was as raw as you'd expect. They had no great love for the British in those parts and the game was played on a dry, bone-hard field under a very hot sun. It was nothing like Pontypool on a wet Wednesday night, that's for sure!

'I looked across at the man-mountain opposite me at the first scrum and he was every bit as big as they'd said. The first engagement was phenomenal; I'd never felt such weight coming through the scrum, even against France! I knew there would be no point in simply standing in front of Van der Merwe all day, so I looked up at that hot sun and decided, "Let's see how hard you can work."

'That was the Pontypool way at the scrums. When Ray Prosser first started coaching at Pooler, he insisted on an eight-man effort at the scrums for the full 83 or 84 minutes of the game. Bobby was a giant hooker who never struck for the ball, so it would be eight very fit and committed scrummagers against seven when their hooker raised his foot to strike. On top of that, we were usually up against opposition who would have maybe one or two men who didn't really want to scrummage all day and we could always smell that weakness. That would make the contest eight versus five and a half. Given our conditioning and our attitude to the scrum, it was an unfair contest.

'So I decided to make Flippie work hard for his living under the hot sun. After a few experiments, I soon discovered that his height was his weakness. He didn't like it when I went low – and I preferred to scrum with my nose about three inches off the deck anyway. As the match wore on, with his body mass, under that sun, he began to wear down like the Duracell bunny! His second rows started screaming at him because he wasn't making any impact on our scrum . . . I remember one scrum in the second half where he let out a long wheeze that sounded like a death-rattle; it was as if all the air and the life went out of him.

'Before the game I was supposed to be cannon-fodder for Danie Craven's protégé. Afterwards I was the *sterkman* [strongman, in Afrikaans].' (Graham Price)

I think this is why both Ray Prosser and Graham used to place such a premium on live scrummaging and only ever used a machine when it was absolutely unavoidable.

As Graham says: 'We were both disciples of live scrummaging. It was a problem for the Lions in New Zealand in 1977 until Cobs took over the coaching of the forwards after the first Test because all the work we'd been doing was on a machine.

'You can get a certain amount out of work on the scrum machine, but ultimately it doesn't test you when you hit it. It doesn't argue back. You're not getting worked into awkward positions or in the constant process of adjustment you're in with live opponents. You don't learn to react to changes of angle or pressure, which is exactly what you have to do in matches.

'Nowadays if a wheel comes on, the whole scrum tends to disintegrate. In those days you learned to stay together and found a way to get back square collectively. Even if you started to go backwards, you could stay together as a unit. If you could manage that, the opposition would run out of steam and the ball would still be there at the number 8's feet.' (Graham Price)

Pricey went through the tough apprenticeship that was typical of life for a young prop making his way in the game in Wales.

'In the scrums at school you could get away with murder just by a stern look at your opposite number! When I first started playing for Pontypool, I found myself up against experienced opponents who had all tried out for the club at one time or another. They would be playing for Talywain and Garndiffaith now, men such as Jeff "Stikes" Davies and "Slogger" Baldwin, and they viewed the games against Pontypool like their very own cup finals. They wanted to show the club what they were missing and I bore the brunt of it!

'I'd end up looking back between my legs at our second row for most of those games and as I'd come off Pross would come up to me and say, "What was going on there? You were getting a right bollocking." I'd reply, "Well, he was doing this and that and it's against the rules." Pross would burst out with that cackle of his and reply, "That's how it is, son, it's the law of the jungle!"' (Graham Price)

The educational process didn't stop there: 'Charlie, Bobby and I [and in a later generation, Staff, Junna and myself] were always looking for ways to improve, simply because other teams were finding ways to counter our dominance at scrum-time. There were some bloody good front rows in Wales around that time. Newport had Colin Smart, "Spike" Watkins and Rhys Morgan; for Bridgend, it would be Ikey Stephens, Geoff Davies and Meredydd James; at the Talbot Athletic ground, Aberavon could put out Clive Williams, Billy James and John Richardson, a cold killer with baby-blue eyes. "I looked at John Richardson and there was death in his eyes!" as the Llanelli winger J.J. Williams once told me. Down at Cardiff Jeff Whitefoot, Alan Phillips and Ian Eidman would be waiting for you. It went on and on and after a while there never was an easy game. From a Wales vantage point, I never wanted to miss a game because an Eidman or a Morgan would be ready to take my place!

'We came up with answers on the field and improvised solutions. For example, we went through a period at Pontypool when opponents realised that, although they couldn't push us backwards, they could wheel us around. First South Wales Police started doing it and then Meredydd James at Bridgend took it up. As the ball was put in, Meredydd, who was a canny operator, would crab sideways and pull Charlie onto him, while Ian Stephens would try to come up and around my right shoulder. So we developed a move off the back called the "Charlie", where we encouraged the wheel and let it develop. Then we would roll off our number 8 at the back with a driving maul, leaving all those Bridgend forwards out of play on the far side of the ball!

'I remember when John Dixon went down to Cardiff. John was a typically awkward tight-head from the valleys who used to play for Abertillery. He had a style all of his own, where he would bore in towards the centre of the scrum and get his head into our hooker's face. That in turn would enable his hooker to strike for the ball while ours was paralysed! John could get into this position where he was almost sideways-on and somehow he could maintain it. So when he played for Cardiff we had Charlie bind onto his shorts and pull him even further around until he was at right angles to the touchline. Then we sank and drove when he couldn't push back.

'I think one of the key games for us as a scrummaging pack was the game against Neath in March 1973. Like us, they were going for the Merit Table title that year and it was the game that really showed us what we could do, as they had both Walter Williams and Glyn Shaw in their ranks. In particular it showed me how far I could go in the game. I was playing against a current Welsh international prop in Glyn Shaw and there were a couple of scrums where we must have shoved them 20 or 30 yards up the field and they just couldn't stop us. Glyn was a great prop with the ball in his hands, but I don't think he enjoyed it one little bit. That gave us great faith in the "bible" that Pross had always preached about the value of scrummaging.'

(Graham Price)

The great strength of the scrum at Pontypool was in the depth of the front-row pool that we had available to us by the start of the 1980s. Top quality props and hookers would be playing for both the 1st XV and the Athletic, which was in turn due to the competitiveness of the environment created by Ray Prosser.

In addition, we were able to bring in other decent operators such as Brandon Cripps under the rules of the club loan system that applied at the time. Brandon played his rugby for Newbridge, one of our most deadly enemies in the Eastern valley, but if Pricey was for some reason unavailable Pross would not hesitate to ask for Brandon's release and he would invariably do a solid job.

As Brandon recalls: 'Whenever I had played for either Newbridge or Abertillery against Pontypool, Pooler always seemed to recognise one of their own playing in the opposition ranks. They were a hard bunch and they'd often target me, but as soon as I showed I was quite happy to give a few digs back everyone was happy. They didn't expect you to moan when you took it and they never moaned themselves if they got it back in return.

'On the advice of Steve Jones, Ray Prosser would ask me to come down to the Park and play in games when Pricey was injured because he knew I could lock out a scrum whatever the pressure. When his first choices [who could usually do a bit of everything] were out, Ray would always go for the next best pure scrummager available after that, not the best all-round prop. Those were his rules of selection. Ray had asked me to play for Pontypool on a full-time basis, but at the time I would have had to switch to the loose-head and it would have been a big ask for me. Pricey was already playing tight-head down there and no one was going to uproot him. So I stayed at

Newbridge.

'Prosser always called me "big man". He once said to me, "Be careful hitting the ruck carrying all that weight, big man, you could kill some c**t."

'I had some memorable games with Pontypool. The Eastern valley clubs all felt the same way about Newport, of course, so it was always a pleasure to get stuck into the likes of Colin Smart or John Rawlins. Whether I was wearing red, white and black or black and sky-blue, it didn't matter.

'Colin Smart would be awkward for the first 20 minutes or so, but after I dropped him on my right leg he'd be quiet as a baby. In the other game I played for Pooler against the Black-and-Amber, I remember Ray Prosser running onto the pitch afterwards and heading straight towards me. My first thought was, "What have I done now?" but then I noticed Ray had a big grin on his face. "That Rawlins . . ." he said, "you buckled him up good and proper, like a chicken with duck's feet!"

'When we played against Cardiff, I was looking to Pross for some technical guidance. They had a good front row in Jeff Whitefoot, Alan Phillips and Ian Eidman. Instead Pross told me: "I just want one thing from you, big man. At the first lineout, you tip up Bob Norster. Perk will do the rest." I did as I was told and Norster never spoke to me for two years after that.

'The best loose-head I played against was probably the Gloucester boy Malcolm Preedy; he would keep going for the full 80 minutes.

'But my best memory was a game we played against Munster; we came back to win after going behind early on. I punched Donal Lenihan and it was a cracker. He was spark out. Chris Huish watched the whole incident and I could see him chuckling. "The wind off that one would have been enough to put him down, Brandon," he said. "If you'd hit him any harder, they'd have marched you straight down to the clink." Needless to say, Pross didn't see it that way. "You only f***ing clipped him," he said. "Why didn't you hit him harder?'" (Brandon Cripps)

There were times when there were as many as five Pooler front-rowers all in contention for a Wales squad place. Junna Jones and Mike Crowley both came close to playing for the national team while still representing the Pontypool Athletic 2nd XV, and Junna sat behind Alan Phillips for the 1980 New Zealand tour match and the whole of the 1981 Five Nations tournament without managing to step onto the field.

Junna came closest to winning his Welsh cap in Scotland in 1981 at Murrayfield when Alan Phillips went down injured with 20 minutes left in the game. The sight of Steve Jones warming up on the sidelines seemed to have an unfortunate galvanising impact on the Cardiff hooker, who limped along to the very end of the match and denied Junna that elusive cap. Knowing Steve, he probably thought Alan did it deliberately to thwart him!

I believe that Junna might also have started the game against the visiting All Blacks in 1980 had he not got himself sent off in an October club tussle with Gloucester at Kingsholm. Unfortunately for Steve he was on the far side of the field when he received his marching orders. I remember his head bowing ever lower as he had to endure the 'long walk' around the edge of the pitch with the verbal stonings of 'the Shed' pouring abuse down on his head. It was almost biblical in its intensity. I think at that moment Steve somehow knew he would never bear the three feathers on his chest.

The case of Mike Crowley was another heart-rending story of Pontypool's characteristic ability to inflict as much pain upon itself as it did upon others. The ex-Waterloo prop Steve Peters describes a typical encounter with the 'big bad baldy Bear': 'I used to dread coming down to Pontypool on Wednesday nights with Waterloo. We had a fixture with them, but boys would always find themselves having unexpected niggles before the game and pull out! You know, that sudden need to attend an unknown uncle's funeral or the bad attacks of dandruff.

'I remember once coming down as the starting loose-head to Pontypool Park and steeling myself for the confrontation with Graham Price, who was one of the top props at the time, if not the best tight-head in the British Isles.

'For about 50 minutes, the match was everything I expected it to be. It was like being thrown into a washing machine or a tumble dryer at every scrum. I was bent down, my nose a couple of inches off the turf, felt I was going to black out, then the scrum would pile-drive upwards as the power came on. My head was spinning as the chants bounced back from the huge bank on the far side onto the field.

'Early in the second half Pricey went down and stayed down. I had a look of concern on my face, but inwardly I was jumping up and down like a little kid at a tea party. I was thinking, "Christ, my life just got easier . . ."

'It was at this moment that I remember hearing a call ringing out along the touchline from the Pontypool bench: "Get 'the Bear' ready!" All of a sudden anxiety started to flood back into me. Who the f**k was the Bear?

'Then I saw this giant stripping down, shaven-headed and with a thick beard like a pirate, and I swear he looked twice the size of Pricey! When he came on for that first scrum, my worst fears were confirmed: he was probably the biggest and strongest man I ever faced. Pricey was a British Lion, but the Bear was something else. I couldn't believe he didn't go on to win a hatful of caps for Wales.' (Steve Peters)

The Bear could prop on either side of the scrum. He was a powerhouse and would have relished the gymnasium culture of the modern game because he had credentials as a bench-presser and a squat-lifter impressive even for the professional era. Mike worked for South Wales Electricity Board as a painter and decorator; however, he had an unfortunate experience, much like Junna's, when it came to selection for the national team.

Mike was playing for Pontypool Athletic against Caerleon on 23 March 1985. Everyone knew that Wales were set to pick him for the forthcoming international against France after Ian Eidman had pulled out of the game with an injury. So all the Bear had to do was get through the game without injuring himself and he was set fair to win his first Welsh cap. He was the kind of player who, had he been given the chance, would have made it stick and remained part of the national set-up.

Late in the Caerleon match there was an incident and Mike was called over by the referee. All the Pontypool players became very animated and surrounded the referee, who had spotted some over-vigorous rucking. Bobby Windsor clasped his hands together and was on the point of sinking to his knees: 'Please,' he said, 'don't send him off . . . Send me off instead, I was just as guilty.' Bobby was desperate for Mike to play and earn his first Welsh cap. It was water off a duck's back to the ref and that was that. Mike was off and got suspended; an equally big man – Stuart Evans of Neath – was chosen instead of him and played outstandingly well in Paris. That was the end of Mike Crowley's international career, without him ever having stepped on the field for his country.

Graham Price noticed a subtle but significant change in the scrum, particularly at the beginning of the 1980s and especially in the attitude of referees to the set-piece: 'When I first started in 1970, there were only two things you'd get penalised for, either the hooker striking too early or the scrum-half not putting the ball in straight. The refs didn't want to know after that, they left you to sort out your own problems. There was never any attempt to micro-manage the scrum, as there is now – the binds and pulling down on the arm, or taking it low, or boring in or popping up. Everything went in those days and the game – and Pontypool, in particular – were all the better for it.

'I began to sense a change in the atmosphere during the game between Pontypool and the visiting Australians in 1981. We had already dismantled them at the first scrum and were in the process of doing so again when their front row just fell back over the top of their second row, who had lost their footing. The scrum duly collapsed and the whistle went. "Penalty to us," I thought. I looked up to see Roger Quittenton's arm pointing towards the Wallabies and he muttered something about not holding the scrum up. We all understood that one of our biggest weapons had just been neutralised by a refereeing interpretation on the day and that knocked the stuffing out of us completely. We lost 37–6.

'I believe that the importance of the referee changed with the coming of Clive Norling. Clive was a natural showman and something of a "celebrity ref". He looked at himself as a player would; he wanted to have more influence on the game. This could have both positive and negative consequences on the play.

'So one day we were playing Bridgend, and Meredydd James and Ian Stephens did their stuff and they put the wheel on us. Everything as per normal, then. Suddenly play was interrupted by an urgent blast on the whistle: "Peep, peep . . . Peee-eeeep." Norling had blown the whistle and penalised Bridgend for wheeling the scrum. I looked across at Meredydd, he looked at me. We were both non-plussed.

'Norling, and probably by implication the Welsh Referees' Association, had rummaged through the rules and come up with a new interpretation of the law that you must always push straight.

'But the result was that the referee threw himself forward

into the action and subtly took away the responsibility of the front-row players to sort issues for themselves. It's the same now, but far, far worse. Refs have no idea what's going on in the scrum but like to pretend they do, and they won't allow players to resolve problems on the field themselves. Everything is resolved by the whistle instead.' (Graham Price)

What Graham is describing in embryo is the issue of 'political correctness' in modern rugby – and the situation we have now in the relationship between referees and law-making to the scrum in the professional era. Most refs do not have the same sense of theatre as Clive Norling, but there is the same emphasis on the micro-management of the scrum. The referee has started to carry a heavier law book onto the field with him, and it is a big negative in practice, however politically correct it may be in theory.

The bureaucracy of law-making has also grown, which means more people are involved in every change to the scrum laws. This in turn guarantees that they hardly change at all. There are too many voices involved in the process, agreement comes via compromise and the result is that 'Crouch-Touch-Pause-Engage' can become 'Crouch-Touch-Set', with no verifiable improvement whatsoever.

Meanwhile referees and their touchline assistants are required to monitor a host of micro-details as the scrum engages:

Does the loose-head get his bind?
Does the loose-head put his hand on the ground?
Is the loose-head 'hingeing' (bending at the hips)?
Does the tight-head bind on his opposite number's arm?
Is either prop pushing in at an angle?
Is either side trying to pull the scrum around by giving ground on one side and promoting on the other?
Are the front rows popping up after contact?

This is just a limited selection of the issues that the referee and his assistants are collectively attempting to 'manage', with the result that you're lucky if a ratio of one in four scrum completions is achieved. More often than not, the referee will bail out by picking from one of the myriad potential offences and give a penalty or free-kick.

The most fundamental truth of scrum dynamics is that, for the vast majority of the time, *no one knows who is responsible* for the set-piece failing to function, not even the players themselves! Corris Thomas remembers arranging to take Peter Rogers, the ex-Wales Test prop, through a couple of hours' footage of penalised scrums to try and identify the true culprits. Even Peter threw up his arms and gave up after half an hour!

By cluttering the scrum scenario with a 'folly' of laws and interpretations of laws, the referees and law-makers have progressively eroded the players' responsibility to resolve their own problems. It is a huge mistake and sensible ex-referees and policymakers such as Corris Thomas know it. It is why Corris introduced the concept of *materiality* back into refereeing theory. (In other words, you only penalise the clear and obvious offences that actually affect the outcome of a situation on the field, nothing more.)

Ironically, at the same time the law-makers and law-shapers have not insisted on the application of the three most basic laws of the scrum, namely:

1. The ball must be put in straight, along the middle line of the tunnel.
2. The hooker must be in a position to hook the ball.
3. The scrum must be stationary before the ball is fed into the set-piece.

If these three laws had been honoured – but most particularly (1) and (3) – there would not have been the need for the other peripheral interpretations. I believe that this is one of the more important departures from the virtue of the Pontypool era. Pontypool wanted to scrummage; for the most part we wanted to keep the scrum up and keep the opposition working and to use it as a platform for attack. If there was a problem, we understood it was up to us to resolve it, technically and physically. We did not expect to be either spoon-fed or scapegoated by the ref.

The principle of 'letting the players play' and not over-managing the game – giving players the space and time to resolve the great majority of the issues they create for themselves – also applied to the issue of violence on the field in the 1970s and '80s. Referees in those days were prepared to adopt best business practice and 'delegate' authority to the players.

Graham Price continues: 'It was a brutal game in the '70s. If the referee didn't see something, then it didn't happen. Because they were all on the circuit, the refs knew the guys who were looking for trouble and they knew the ones who weren't interested in it. They would monitor the reactions of those groups during the game and tailor their refereeing to it.

'Whereas nowadays refs will yellow- or even red-card anyone they see committing foul play, back then the refs would see retaliation for what it was. If a player who was known to belong to the non-violent faction got enraged and threw a punch or a kick, the ref would usually ignore it and look for the root cause. The most violent or psychotic blokes also tended to be those endowed with the most sheer animal cunning, so they knew the situations in which they were unlikely to get caught!

'Mickey Burton told me a story once about how he got belted in a game against Pontypool and took a wild swing at the man he thought was the culprit. There was a prompt response on the whistle from Ken Rowlands, who called Burton across in his most severe school-teacher manner.

'He stood there for about two minutes, wagging his forefinger in Mickey's face in front of the bank. I thought he was going to poke his eye out. Mickey told me afterwards that Ken had said, "Well, I know there must have been a reason why you took a swing, Mike, and I have a fair idea who did it, but I have to make an example of you in front of these b*****ds." The finger wagged even harder. ". . . So I'm going to stand here giving you a telling-off and give them a penalty." As Rowlands sent Burton away like a naughty schoolboy into the corner, he muttered under his breath, "You've earned yourself one punch in retaliation. Make it count!"' (Graham Price)

Pontypool were the masters of playing to the outer limit of the law in this respect. Ray Prosser had learned from his experience in 1959 that you had to make the game as physical as you could in as many situations as possible, and intimidation was a big factor in our approach. In the week before every game, he would exhort us to 'get a picture in your mind's eye' of our opponent, to visualise ways in which we could hurt him or outplay him. Ray didn't mean 'deliberately go out on the pitch to hurt him physically', he meant 'find ways to damage his self-confidence and break down his will to play the game he wants'. 'Do whatever it f***ing takes.'

It all started even before the game. There would be the eye-balling in the tunnel as the players prepared to go out onto the field, then the test at the first lineout or scrum by fist or boot. 'How are you today, butt?' John Perkins would say as he stood opposite his opponent in the tunnel. 'I'm looking forward to doing battle with you.' Many players, even some of considerable ability, failed the psychological test before the opening whistle or at the first lineout and as a result failed to make the impression on the game they wanted.

Like most things Pontypool, it was also a double-edged sword, and on one memorable occasion I recall the hulking Aberavon lock Adrian Owen chasing Perk around the park mercilessly all afternoon, trying to provoke him into throwing the punch that would end his chances of playing for Wales the following weekend. Who was next in line for the national call-up? None other than Owen himself. Perk became so exasperated that he suggested the two of them settle their differences in the car park after the match.

Mike Ruddock played against Pontypool seven times and only finished on the winning side once: 'They were a yard ahead of everyone else physically and mentally and they found a way to hurt you whether you were in contact with the ball or not. Ribs, fingers, ankles . . . They were wearing you down in every aspect of play, always wearing you down. They made contact just after the ball had gone an art form and they were always testing your will to fight back in those situations. "I'm looking forward to doing battle with you."

'We knew we had more talented backs than Pontypool – Malcolm Dacey, Brynmor Williams, Tony Swift, Mark Wyatt and others – but we lost to them more often than not because we got worn down up front and couldn't match their drills, discipline and durability. We had Clive Williams [a two-time British Lion], Jeff Herdman and Gareth John, Barry Clegg and Geoff Wheel, Trevor Cheeseman and Gareth Roberts – all great individual forwards – but we couldn't match them collectively. At training we emphasised ball skills, passing and aerobic sessions – interval running and sprinting. We didn't train for dogging it out in the scrums or in the rucks and mauls. We had no collective drills for those situations.

'We had a saying at St Helens when we played Pontypool: "If we can hold the first scrum, we can win the game. If we show no weakness and don't give them a sniff, we can win it." It happened once, I think. We held that first scrum and Dacey kicked us down the hill into the corner by the leisure centre. I had a really good feeling running down that hill, but when I got to the lineout I found we had no hooker! Perk had put one through the scrum and laid him out. Paul Hitchens, I think it was, and in those days you didn't have a hooker on the bench. So Paul didn't know what day it was and we scarcely won a lineout all game . . . So much for the good feeling.

'I'd first learned about the Pontypool culture from my first coach at Blaina, a tough-as-nails ex-Pooler flanker called Denis Wright. I'd played number 8 for the Blaina Youth team, but Denis was keen to move me to blind-side flanker when I started training with the first team squad. I thought, "I'm going to get some real technical coaching here. Denis obviously has a cunning plan up his sleeve." Instead, he said, "If their scrum-half tries to come round on our ball, stamp on his foot as hard as you can!" Unfortunately, the first time I went to put Denis's advice into action on the field, my studs got caught in the laces on the half-back's boots and he took the opportunity to boot a one-legged Ruddock right in the bollocks!

'Denis's advice on lineout work was equally cunning. As the opposition scrum-half went to pass, I was to drive into his exposed ribs as his hands followed the delivery. "Hopefully you can put 'im off with broken ribs then, see . . ." added Denis philosophically. "If 'e dive-passes, run over his hands and break those instead." I tried this later in the season against Aberavon on Clive Shell and it did not make me flavour of the month with their back row.' (Mike Ruddock)

As a referee, Corris Thomas observed how well organised Pontypool were in 'playing to the limits of the law': 'Pontypool were very clever and well organised about when and where they applied their illegalities. It's like that with any good side, and it's particularly true of the top international sides like the All Blacks. Whenever they had a lineout throw, Pontypool had a "point man" whose main role was to comment on my positioning and give his teammates exactly the information they needed to implement their methods without fear of retribution!

'It was exactly the same with New Zealand. They would step across the lineout and block out the opposing jumpers in an area where I couldn't see it clearly. But I have to say I never had a real problem either with the All Blacks or with Pontypool as a referee. I looked forward to refereeing them and they were easy games for me.

'I refereed a cup quarter-final between Newbridge and Pontypool in 1982. Newbridge won it 3–0. A typically tension-packed valley derby, it was. One of the scrums towards the end of that game went down and I thought to myself, "I'm sure Pontypool collapsed that scrum." However, I got so excited that I awarded only another scrum to Newbridge when it should have been a full penalty to them!

'The following week I bumped into Dennis Hughes, the Newbridge captain, in the middle of Cardiff. He said to me, "It's bloody lucky you heard Pricey in that scrum and didn't give them the penalty."

'I replied, "Whatever do you mean?" and Dennis said, "Graham Price told his forwards as the scrum packed down, 'OK, let's take this one down, boys, it's our turn for the penalty!'" Later on I discovered that I hadn't awarded Pontypool one single penalty in the Newbridge half for the whole of the second period!' (Corris Thomas)

In Pontypool's golden era there was a clear line drawn between the genuinely hard men of the game, such as Dai Morris of Neath and our own John Perkins, and the cheap shot artists.

As Graham Price remembers: 'The Pontypool forwards,

especially in the '70s, were as hard as a miner's toecap. We were never big, but we had heart. John Perkins, "the Perk", was a perfect example. Only 6 ft 1 in. and 15 stone, but the dominant lock of his era in Wales. All the so-called hard men were not hard men, in my opinion. They were either bullies or hit-and-run merchants who would check the ref wasn't looking, take their shot and bugger off out of there. Perk was the opposite: if he was going to take a shot, he was also going to stand up and take anything that was coming back at him. "Never back down" could have been Perk's motto and it applied to other genuinely hard men like Gloucester's Mickey Burton.

'I remember once Robert Paparemborde telling me how – on some invitational tour – Perky had literally thrown himself in the way of a blind-sider intended for the French prop and taken it himself. While Perk was rolling around dazed on the ground, "Papa" was thanking him and smiling. The Basques play with a huge sense of family and he knew the value of what Perky had done, even if the Perk was probably regretting it!

'The Perk would put his body on the line for the whole 80 minutes for the team; he never shirked a job that had to be done – while the hit-and-run merchants would be out of the game on the fringes, awaiting retribution for their felonies! They knew they'd marked their own card and you'd be looking for them, so they kept out of the way for the rest of the match.

'Perky would give as good as he got – "I've got two stitches in me for every one I've put in someone else," he'd say – and it was true. I can remember taking him up to the hospital in Nevill Hall, Abergavenny, after he'd been kneed in the kidneys from the opening kick-off in one game. To me, he was real Pontypool. He was red, white and black to the core.' (Graham Price)

Terry Cobner takes up the story: 'Perk didn't really care about anything except rugby. He must have had six or seven jobs while he played for Pontypool. He was a miner at the Big Pit, he was a chippie, he was a travelling sales rep and he was a teacher. The minute any of them interfered with his rugby, or even threatened to do so, he'd let it go.

'When he was a rep, he had a call from his manager: "Perk, there's a bloke down in Llanelli who's eager to do a deal. Get down there and close it." So Perk put his blazer on and his Pontypool tie and jumped in his car. When he arrived, they started talking about rugby and it went on for hours. Finally, Perk said, "So, what do you want to order?" The bloke was taken aback and replied, "Oh, I don't really want to order anything now, I just wanted to talk to you about rugby. Come back in the spring." Perky was fuming: "What do you mean, come back in the spring? I'm not a f***ing cuckoo!"' (Terry Cobner)

The Perk was not the tallest second row by any means, but he was the person to whom we threw when in trouble. He was an agile jumper at the front and he was as tough as they come, with a left jab that he used as a clubbing tool to test the will to fight of all-comers throughout the 80 minutes. But he'd prefer to call that lob to the front of the lineout early in the game, whack his opponent in the bollocks as he soared to make the catch and *then* get on with the job of winning the ball in peace and quiet for the rest of the match. That was the protocol.

If anything, it appeared that international rugby was going to pass John Perkins by when he finally gained his first cap as he was about to turn 30 years of age in 1983. Fortunately, he had a strong ally on the 'big five' selection panel: Terry Cobner.

Terry recalls: 'When the "big five" used to select their Wales teams, it would always be over a silver service dinner at the Angel hotel in Cardiff. Rod Morgan, the chairman of the panel, would get out his Parker pen and make an initial proposal for every position. He would invite each panellist in turn to make a case for the player they wanted and then it would be put to a vote among the five of us. Once we'd gone through all fifteen positions, each panellist would be allowed one challenge to the line-up, one player that they felt was either especially worthy or unfortunate to be excluded.

'Having had the experience with Junna, when he hadn't won a Welsh cap despite being on the bench on so many occasions, I challenged the selection to get John Perkins into the team. John Dawes and Rhys Williams were looking at their watches as I kept on challenging until they finally put him in out of exhaustion. It was like that radio quiz game *Just a Minute*, I challenged so many times! I called Perk over to Fairwater school to give him the good news; I think he was expecting the worst, as he'd got into some trouble up at Gloucester the previous week. When I told him he was in, he started crying, then I started crying, and then we hugged. If anyone had come in, they would have thought we were a couple of gay boys.

'Perk and Staff Jones both went in against Scotland for the second game of the 1983 Five Nations after we'd only drawn against England in the first round at home. My first thought was "F**k, what have I done?" when "the Bear" Milne squirted both Staff and Perk behind him out of the very first scrum, but after that things settled down and it ended with Perky stealing a Scottish lineout throw and Staff scoring a Pooler try in the corner! We won the game 19–15.' (Terry Cobner)

Nothing exemplified John Perkins' attitude better than an article he wrote for the Gloucester–Pontypool game programme in November 1992:

Any rugby player who has played at Kingsholm will have experienced the unique atmosphere generated as the teams assemble for a scrum or lineout in front of the popular enclosure ['the Shed'] teeming with Gloucester supporters baying for blood. '*Kick the buggers back to Ponty, Glaws!*' the call would go up, barely discernible above the general hubbub of a fiercely partisan crowd intent on willing Gloucester to victory.

Armed in my day with players like Mike Burton, John Fidler, Mike Nicholls [and later Steve Mills] and Phil Blakeway, Gloucester were more than adequately equipped to satisfy the Shed's demands. Mind you, it was generally recognised that we were no choirboys either, and a Pontypool–Gloucester game was always a case of 'Greek meeting Greek'!

As forwards, we must all have suffered from a perverse form of sadomasochism, since we seemed to derive pleasure from booting and being booted. Not that we didn't have a code of honour though – oh no! It was all right for us forwards to brawl – it was part of our game – but if a fight broke out among the three-quarters, we would look on in absolute disgust. 'Where'd you get that loony from, Burto?' I'd enquire of Mike Burton. 'Take no notice of 'im, Perky. He'll be on his way back to Matson if he don't mend 'is ways.' Burto and I could then resume punching and kicking lumps out of each other, undisturbed by such minor annoyances.

Getting that picture in your mind's eye of your opponent and doing whatever you f***ing well could to upset him, both before and during the game; battling him face to face and wearing him down with or without the ball. Two stitches received for every one handed out. This was chapter and verse in the Pontypool bible (as long as you weren't a back). It was a winning formula on the field in the amateur era and there was no better exponent of it than John Perkins.

Did total physical commitment overspill on occasion into raw violence? Yes, inevitably it did. I always recall reading a letter Steve Flower's dad sent to the *Western Mail* and being quite shaken by it. I still have the clipping at home because

Steve was a contemporary of mine in the Gwent constabulary. I had got to know him quite well and we'd played a number of games for the police in the same team together.

Steve Flower was a promising back-row forward who played for Newbridge around the time of the Chris Jarman incident. In his letter, his father described seeing his son 'kicked in the face by one Pontypool player and then punched by another one' at a game at Pontypool Park on 29 December 1984. The return match was just over one month later. I was on the bench for Pooler that day and I watched as Steve threw an elbow into Eddie Butler at one lineout and Eddie replied with a neat but comparatively innocuous uppercut. Steve suffered a severe concussion after that game and was forced to retire from rugby completely after experiencing 'a buzzing in his head' which only disappeared after an operation to remove a brain tumour. However, in 2004 he suffered a stroke which resulted in partial paralysis; five years later Steve was dead, aged only fifty. It was a tragedy.

Strangely, those first two games against Newbridge were not particularly violent; they were par for the course in 1984–85. A third end-of-season game between the same teams was far, far worse. Three or four players were hospitalised after that match and it was Pontypool, ironically, who took the bull by the horns and cancelled fixtures between the two teams, which may indeed have been a case of 'getting your retaliation in first'.

Ray Prosser was always as proactive in defending the club from charges of dirty play then as he was as a player protecting his own: 'Of course, rugby is a vigorous game and we have played it in a vigorous manner. But we have stopped short of being dirty. I think it's a case of giving the dog a bad name. I sometimes think to myself what my old mother told me many times. "Raymond," she said, "always remember it's better to be envied than pitied." And she's right. When you get these unfair allegations hurled at you, it's only other people's way of trying to pull us down to their level. We are not a dirty team.'

A report in the *Sunday Times* of 1983 is perhaps the best and most balanced rebuttal of criticisms that Pontypool's play was over-robust:

> By force of personality, Ray Prosser has created a distinctive style which is successful, based on a furious forward commitment which is awesome in its power and selfless dedication. It is so strenuously aggressive that it is often mistaken for violent intent . . . The legacy of that reputation, much of it unjust, nowadays has been inherited so that others are frequently the aggressors, as in the wild west someone somewhere still feels the need to test the old gunslinger's reputation . . . If comments about their style are often derogatory, it should be borne in mind that rugby should have no limits to its appeal. It is up to other teams to prove that a different style might be better.

Ultimately, Pontypool were simply better at doing what needed to be done in the '70s and '80s to win games and a lot of people in rugby didn't like it. Unfortunately, the Pontypool code of honour was a recipe for disaster both on and off the field in a professional environment: the puritanical will to wear the hair-shirt would cost the club dear when rugby began to change and money became involved in the game in the 1990s. Those were the days when the sadomasochism became simply masochism and the number of wounds received by the inner fabric of the club off the field multiplied, just as those being dispensed on it dwindled.

CHAPTER 6

LOOKING OUT FROM THE TOP
OF THE MOUNTAIN

Ray Prosser's new model Pontypool finally cracked the nut with its first Welsh Championship and Merit Table win for 14 years in the 1972–73 season. Terry Cobner was carried off the Gnoll shoulder-high by a bodyguard of Neath players after Pooler beat the Western valley All Blacks 19–7 in the final game of the season. Terry had earlier run 60 yards for an interception try to seal the game, his 16th try of the season and a record for a forward at the time. The season had revived enthusiasm for the game in the Eastern valley. Of the £4,547 in gate receipts for the entire season, £2,000 had been taken in April, with huge attendances for the three back-to-back fixtures against Nuneaton, South Wales Police and London Welsh over the Easter weekend.

Five members of the Pontypool pack went on to represent the Monmouthshire side to play Japan in the autumn of 1974: Cobs, Graham Price, Bobby Windsor, Mike Harrington and Bill Evans, with Ivor Taylor in the centre for good crash-tackling measure. Pontypool's regional representation had extended to six forwards and two backs by the time of the 1976 match against the touring Wallabies, with a complete tight five and

Terry Cobner up front, and Ivor Taylor and Keith James in the three-quarters.

Cobs received his long-awaited summons to the full Wales squad in time for the 1974 Five Nations tournament. He scored a try on his debut against Scotland naturally enough, in a game Wales won 6–0 at the Arms Park. He was followed into the Welsh national team by Charlie Faulkner and Pricey during the following Five Nations, which meant that Pontypool forwards now composed half of the Wales pack.

If there were negatives at the time, they were brushed aside. London Welsh broke off fixtures with Pontypool in November 1973 (to be followed by Northampton the following season and Swansea in 1977) after what the Exiles perceived to be an over-robust match at Old Deer Park, and there were a pair of home-and-away bloodbaths against the French side Agen. After beating Pooler heavily at home in the summer, Agen optimistically brought over their own ball for the return match, with the French touch judge doing everything in his power to maximise its use. He even hid the local ball behind his back after one lineout! The disappearance of the Agen variant into the 'bleachers' for good sparked a spill over of the violence on the pitch, with the supporters of the two sides enthusiastically wading into one another in the stand.

On the field the main concern was the difficulty Pontypool had in replicating their success in league or Merit Table games in the cup competition. Their first realistic opportunity occurred in March 1974, in a semi-final against one of the acknowledged cup experts in Wales, Llanelli. The game was played at the Talbot Athletic ground in Aberavon and ironically it was the failure of ever-dependable Robin Williams to convert a Bobby Windsor try near the end of the match that cost Pooler a chance to draw level at 16–16 and win the match on tries scored. Llanelli went on to repeat the dose ten months later when it defeated Pontypool 18–9 at the quarter-final stage, the West Wales backs having just enough ball to break the stranglehold of the Pooler pack and the honorary 'ninth forward' scrum-half Dennis John.

In 1976, it was Swansea who put an end to Pooler's cup hopes at the semi-final stage. In a game notable for the career-ending injury suffered by Mervyn Davies, the great Swansea and Wales number 8, it was the absence through injury of Terry Cobner as their on-field 'brain' that prevented Pontypool from capitalising upon their crushing forward superiority.

It was as if Pooler were cursed in the cup. In the 1979 competition, the original third-round clash against Cardiff scheduled for 13 January had to be postponed because of a hard frost on the pitch. As the new date (10 February) approached and the arctic weather conditions persisted, the pitch was covered by new nylon sheeting supplied by the ICI factory built on the site of the old Ordnance workers' housing area. By Saturday the sheets had been covered in snow to a depth of 11 or 12 inches. It was like a repeat of the 'great snow' of 1947 in Pontypool, where snow had fallen for three weeks solid in February and boys had been spotted tobogganing straight off residential roofs onto snowdrifts that had climbed up to the eaves of the houses! Birds were found in Pontypool Park, dead and enshrouded in ice. As the anonymous local poet 'Chware Teg' had put it then in verse:

Have you ever been at Varteg with the needle three below,
Or on Garn when drifts are piling ten feet high?
Have you ever drawn your belt in with the kids a-starving slow
And *No Nuthin'* in addition to *No beer*?

Although food rationing no longer applied as it had in 1947, and the aim was now 'merely' to win a rugby cup match, 32 years later both the Torfaen Council and an army of volunteers stepped forward as one to clear the pitch and its surrounds and the road up to Pontypool Park.

Snow and sheeting alike had to be cleared in the teeth of a blizzard; goal and touchlines had constantly to be redefined with sawdust during the course of the game. Four thousand spectators turned up more in hope than expectation, but weather forced play to be abandoned after a mere half-hour. Pontypool, hampered by injuries to Charlie Faulkner and Bobby Windsor, lost the second attempt at a replay by 23–12.

Pontypool had lost to Cardiff in the cup the previous year, too, as Eddie Butler recounts: 'We always maintained that high level, we were always at 90–95 per cent, which left us vulnerable on the special one-off occasions, to the teams who could spike for a cup game, for example. Their sharp spike could puncture our high, flat line of performance.

'We knew we could win over the long haul in the Merit Table or league-type competitions, although we were only ever the unofficial champions of Wales. Would the WRU have assisted at our coronation? God forbid. They would have fainted at the prospect.

'I remember Cardiff beating us in the cup on one of those "spikes" on 14 January 1978. We must have had about 80 per cent of the ball and for a good half of the second period we could have established "base camp" in their 22 and been confident that no one would have disturbed it – the game was that one-sided.

'Gerald Davies scored four tries, running uphill and through the paddy field, on those few occasions when they broke out of defence. He must have touched the ball four times in the whole game . . . In fact, *they* must have touched the ball four times all game!' (Eddie Butler)

As a referee, Corris Thomas also witnessed the pattern of

Action from the 1951 tour match between Pontypool and South Africa. Don Hayward looms large at the lineout tail. (Courtesy of Ray Ruddick)

RIGHT: Ray Prosser gets to grips with a Wallaby tourist in typically robust fashion during the 1957 tour match. (Courtesy of Ray Ruddick)

BELOW: Eddie Mogford et al.: Eddie is standing centre stage, above Brian Gregory. Mel Stiff, Mike Harrington, Adrian Hearne and Laurie Daniel are among those who accompany them. (Courtesy of Ray Ruddick)

The cradle of Welsh rugby in Gwent, West Monmouth school – Gwent's answer to 'Hogwarts'. (© John Grayson)

Dawn breaks over the cruel, beautiful Grotto. (Courtesy of Alun Carter)

ABOVE: Clash of cultures: Graham Price, John Taylor and Mervyn Davies are all barely visible in this club clash between the two dominant influences in the Welsh game, London Welsh and Pontypool. (Courtesy of Steve Maggs)

BELOW: The final heartbreaking 100 yards to the top of the Grotto. (Courtesy of Alun Carter)

ABOVE: Pre-season training was a serious business at the club. Here Junna Jones and Pricey lead the pack, with Chris Huish and me concentrating fiercely on the challenge of the Grotto ahead.
(© *South Wales Argus*)

ABOVE RIGHT: Pontypool's greatest captain, Terry Cobner, was the man principally responsible for the revival of the Lions' fortunes up front on the 1977 tour of New Zealand. Here he is tackling All Blacks great Ian Kirkpatrick.
(Courtesy of Ray Ruddick)

BOTTOM RIGHT: 'The Doc', Peter Lewis: An unerring 'boot' and worthy successor to Robin Williams.
(Courtesy of Ray Ruddick)

The view as you came up the steps and onto the 'blood-twmp'. The Bank could be populated by as many as 20,000 fans for a big match. (Courtesy of Alun Carter)

The view of the ground from the 'bob' bank. (Courtesy of Alun Carter)

LEFT AND BELOW: The Bank: It contributed to one of the most uniquely panoramic settings in Welsh club rugby. (Courtesy of Alun Carter)

'Aby' – Mike Goldsworthy – was a much better fly-half than he was given credit for. Here he's beating Gary Pearce with a shimmy and a show of the ball.
(Courtesy of Ray Ruddick)

LEFT: England v. Wales, 1980: Graham Price demonstrates his perfect scrum technique against Fran Cotton in the 1980 game against England.
(Courtesy of Ray Ruddick)

BELOW: Pontypool's all-international pack is well represented, as John Perkins feeds from a lineout in the 1984 tour match against Australia. Junna, Pricey, Staff Jones, Eddie Butler, Jeff Squire and Mark Brown peer through the mist in a game Pooler lost 18–24.
(© *South Wales Argus*)

Pontypool team photo, 1985–86
Back row (l-r): Peter Lewis, Graham Price, Alun
Carter, Jeff Squire, Kevin Moseley, Mark Brown,
Roger Bidgood, Staff Jones, Anthony Llewellyn
Front row (l-r): Goff Davies, Bobby Windsor, Chris
Huish, John Perkins (captain), Peter Thomas, Bleddyn
Taylor, David Bishop, Mike Goldsworthy

'Madman' Chris Huish shows typical Pooler
determination as he leaves a black-and-amber arm
flailing on the turf. (© *South Wales Argus*)

Kevin Moseley rises high above Ian Jones during the
All Blacks 1989 tour match, with yours truly blocking
out all evil-doers. The human cathedral on the Bank
rises in the distance. (© *South Wales Argus*)

The 'Bish': Pooler's star of the '80s pushed the club to new heights on the playing field and was sometimes the cause of controversy off it. Here he is, sitting next to Mark Ring, another prominent Pooler ex-international back.
(© *South Wales Argus*)

Dai Bishop, set to be launched off the back of a scrum by Frank Jacas – a very dangerous moment for any defence.
(© *South Wales Argus*)

Ambushed in Ireland by Foley's coaches and the black stuff! (Courtesy of Ray Ruddick)

After a home win over Swansea (27–4) on 11 January 1992, Pontypool went top of the top division for the first and only time.

Back row (l-r): Alf Mutlow, Sean Hanson, Lyndon Mustoe, Neil Jones, Dean Oswald, Mike Wall

Middle row: Dai Williams, Eddie Mogford, Hadyn Wilmott, John Perkins, Stewart Jardine, Mike Crowley, Lee Mruk, Gareth Taylor, Gareth Lintern, Staff Jones, Goff Davies, Norman Cox, Graham Howden, Malcolm Jones, David Pegington

Front row: Sean White, Martin Jones, Robert Lewis, Ivor Taylor (match secretary), Chris Huish (captain), Garvin Howells (chairman), Lee Jones, Andrew Dibble, Martin Brown

An open-top bus tour of the town in 2003 after the club became Welsh National League One champions. The trophy belongs to a local pigeon-racer.

Leighton Jones (first row standing, centre), son of Junna, leads the celebrations of Pontypool's end-of-season 2009 win over Cardiff, which was crucial to the club avoiding relegation. Club historian Ray Ruddick is in the crowd of faithful supporters behind them. (Courtesy of Ray Ruddick)

Peter Jeffreys, the club's financial saviour after a ruinous court case against the WRU. (© *South Wales Argus*)

almost complete Pooler control up front interrupted by long-range breakouts by the opposition backs; the mild schizophrenia of Pontypool's success in the league and their relative failures in the cup; their invincibility on Wednesday nights and vulnerability on some crucial Saturday afternoons.

'It was an unforgiving place to be, but I always felt it was worse on those Wednesday nights than it was on Saturday afternoons. There was a palpable difference in the atmosphere. Eddie Butler once told me he didn't think Pontypool always had the extra edge they needed for those crunch weekend games.

'I remember a game between Pontypool and Bridgend on one of those Wednesday nights. Pontypool were in total control up front, but it was still a close game coming into the final minutes; Pontypool were leading 13–8, I think. They had a lineout on the final play of the game, only a few metres from the Bridgend line. I was ready to blow the whistle the next time the ball went dead.

'Somehow Bridgend won the lineout. Chris Williams spun it out to JPR in the shadow of his own posts. Somehow JPR worked his way upfield and somehow the ball ended up in the hands of the Bridgend prop Meredydd James, who scored in between the posts. I remember the look on Meredydd's face quite clearly; he looked like the boy who'd just escaped from the sweet shop with some penny blackjacks! So now it was 13–12, with an easy conversion to come, and I was looking over my shoulder with some concern. I was a good 50 metres away from the tunnel!

'The goal was duly converted and I blew the whistle and ran for my life. Pooler supporters were flooding onto the field, screaming in my face; I could see the wild eyes and the contorted mouths spewing out the abuse. I tried to ignore it, but then one of them grabbed hold of me, and I thought, "Oh, Jesus . . . what do I do now? Say 'Un-hand me, sir' or 'I'm a chartered accountant' . . ." No. That wouldn't work.

'Salvation, when it came, arrived from an unexpected quarter. Suddenly Bobby Windsor was alongside me, throwing the "supporter" who had manhandled me to the ground. His arm moved around my shoulder and I can still remember the strength of his grip as he towed me along: "You 'ad a bloody good game, you b*****d!" he said out of the corner of his mouth as he marched me all the way down to the tunnel, with the supporters now forming a respectful cordon around the both of us.

'I cannot describe how grateful I was for his actions at that moment, and I've never forgotten the impression. Moments like that stay with you for a lifetime. But it was typical of the Pontypool volte-face – ruthless and brutal on the field but entirely social and fair-minded off it. Even a man as utterly implacable and cruel as Bobby had that sense of social conscience – I guess that's the phrase – once the game had ended.' (Corris Thomas)

Pontypool's rugby version of bipolar disorder continued to develop in rude health. Every newly acclaimed regional or national team representative was balanced by a new shunning, some new cancellation of fixtures by a club that considered their play over-robust; every championship or Merit Table success counter-pointed by some last-gasp cup failure in games it seemed impossible for Pooler to lose; every on-field cruelty matched by an off-field sense of duty to club, region and even (on occasion) officialdom unrivalled in the domestic Welsh game of that era.

With the capture of Jeff Squire from Gwent rivals Newport at the start of the 1978–79 season, Pontypool were able to field five forwards playing in the current Wales pack. Yet in the summer following the same season, that same 'jewel in the crown' was to lead the Pontypool team off the field before half-time in the final game of a controversial club tour of the

West Coast of the USA. That action incurred a ban of three years from all touring by the Welsh Rugby Union.

The strength-in-depth within the playing squad grew progressively towards the end of the '70s and the beginning of the '80s. Although the front row got most of the plaudits and received a fresh injection of blood with the Jones boys – Staff and Steve replacing Charlie and Bobby – the real area of strength was fast becoming the back row. Eddie Butler had joined the club in 1976 and would in time replace Terry Cobner as Ray Prosser's on-field 'brain'. Squire and Chris Huish joined two years later.

Graham Price comments: 'In the '70s we had a very limited squad, so if all of our international players were missing we couldn't replace them with anything like the same quality. In the '80s we had far more depth, and there were lads who would have walked into most other first-class sides playing for us. They stayed at Pontypool because they loved the culture. We all stuck together and some of those battles between the 1st and 2nd XV packs on the training ground were memorable.

'There would always be a space for a "heavy" Kevin Edwards, a huge young man who eventually made a name for himself with Cardiff; but for a long time he chose to stay at Pontypool Park with the wind whistling around his ears from Perky's punches in training. Likewise number 8 Mostyn Davies and our centre Hayden Wilmott, who I well remember squaring up to the Perk in training one night like a gunfighter in an old western.'

All the while, one of Pooler's great unsung heroes, and one of the best loose forwards in European rugby, Brian Gregory, soldiered on, as Graham Price recalls: 'Our first great back row in my time at Pontypool was formed by Terry Cobner, Mike Harrington and Brian Gregory. Mike Harrington was a bloke who played just under the radar at Pontypool. He arrived about the time that we were really getting our scrum and driving lineout together. He touched down three pushover tries against Abertillery one week; the next, he was in the Gwent side to play the Japanese tourists.

'Brian was one who could have gone on and achieved great things, but he didn't have the necessary ambition. I remember him being called up to a Welsh trial match around 1976 or 1977, but he didn't really want to go . . . We had to drag him down to Cardiff to get him to play. It was at a time when a lot of the "Probables" used to drop out with injuries because they really had nothing to gain from those matches and everything to lose. They were the men in possession of the shirt, after all. The "Possibles", of course, took every opportunity to get really stuck into them.

'One game, "Fingers" [as Brian was known] came on for Trevor Evans, who'd dislocated his shoulder, and transformed the "Probables" immediately by setting up a move that went the length of the field for a try. It wasn't the first time he'd gotten the better of Trevor – the Mervyn Davies cup match against Swansea was another instance – and I'll always remember him scoring two tries on his 250th appearance for the club when we beat Newport 30–13 in 1978. We were all more excited for him than he was for himself, but that was Brian all over.

'Fingers was great value at the back of the lineout. I used to love to roll up on the peel around the end of the lineout, and I knew that if the ball was called to Brian, I'd get my hands on it and be on my way. He would nod at me and say, "I could find you in the dark, Pricey." It was a perfect play for us. It was like we had a psychic link. We scored a classic try from the back of the lineout against Cardiff. He knew that their flanker Bob Dudley-Jones would step out and be waiting for me to come round on that peel, so Brian caught the ball instead, dragged Bob back in towards him and popped the ball back over his head to me as soon as he dipped down to make the tackle! I took the ball without breaking stride and the Cardiff fly-half Gareth Davies was all that stood in my way. I was so low to the ground running that he'd have had to tackle the top of my head to stop me, and I went through to score "unmolested", as they say, by the young Cardiff outside-half!

'I helped arrange a veterans match at Pontypool in the early 1990s to fund a Pontypool club tour to New Zealand. Wales already had a Classic team of golden oldies at the time and I was part of it. Allan Martin was the chief organiser of the Classics and he had a lot of the great Wales players of the '70s in his playing ranks, so between us we arranged a Wales Classics versus Pontypool Veterans game.

'Then we had to tell "Benny". I'll always recall the look of apprehension passing across Phil Bennett's face when he was told they'd be playing a game against Pontypool Veterans. This was supposed to be a game to have a laugh in, after all. His chin dropped onto his chest and he went very quiet for a while. Then he piped up, "That Brian Gregory won't be playing, will he? I'm not playing if he's going to be there."

'Fingers liked to appear more laid-back about rugby than he actually was. He always liked to pretend he couldn't be arsed about training, but the truth of the matter is he used to come out running with me quite religiously. If he said he'd be passing by my house at 6.30, 6.30 it would be, on the dot, and we'd take that first step outside the front door together.' (Graham Price)

Pross used to struggle to get Brian to play because he used to keep pigeons and dogs. He loved his pigeons and he loved his dogs, and he loved them both more than his rugby. Although I'm sure the story is apocryphal, Brian also made out as if he was proud of a murky felony somewhere in his past. He wouldn't say what it was, but I recall he came in beaming to training one evening after it had supposedly been highlighted on *Police Five*, the pioneering 'watchdog' TV programme, hosted by Shaw Taylor, with the big square goggles on. It only lasted for about five minutes and Taylor would ask the public for help with specific crime cases. At the end he would point at the telly and say 'Keep 'em peeled!' I loved it. Brian was pleased as punch that he'd been on the telly, or so he said. Whatever it was that he reckoned he'd done, he puffed out his chest and told everyone down at the club about his anonymous appearance on *Police Five*. 'That's me they were talkin' about,' he'd say and nod seriously.

Brian Gregory's double in the '80s was Chris Huish, another unassuming man and, like Brian, the only one in the pack to remain uncapped by Wales. Both were among the great 'unknown' loose forwards of their eras. 'Madman' was not to be trifled with, as I found out during my first ever game of Prosser 'touch' when he bounced me back fully five yards in contact as I went in to tackle him. The 'Blaenavon Bulldozer' used to wrap up the ball in two hands, carry it out in front of him and simply plough people out of the way.

As the ex-England and British Lions flanker Andy Robinson recalls: 'When Chris was on one of his charges, he was incredibly hard to stop. I can remember an incident in a game against Pontypool. Unusually, it was a time when we were winning by 50 points. It was a really warm day and we were running Pontypool ragged when Chris got the ball. He ran through me and then over me. People like him just never gave up.' The back-row players who made the most impact on Andy Robinson were the Chris Huishes and the Roger Powells of this world, because they squeezed every ounce of talent out of their bodies and showed him the mentality and toughness that was needed to play at the top end of the game.

Huish was a hard man in all respects, but if he was an

archetype of the mentality that characterised Ray Prosser's teams, he also possessed the same devilish sense of humour. Once, little Dai Thomas had the temerity to sidestep Chris in another of those games of 'touch'. A few months later, Dai found himself sharing a room with Madman on tour. He recalls: 'Do you know, he didn't say a word to me for five whole days . . . he wouldn't even look at me.' Dai was just beginning to check his underwear to see whether he was giving off the wrong kind of odour and was starting to worry about the impending retribution, when he saw Pross and Chris looking across and laughing at him at one training session. They finally let him in on the joke, but not before he'd had a good long look down the double-barrels of fear!

Hooker Steve 'Junna' Jones was one of the most important single keys in accelerating Pontypool's success in the 1980s. His rugby life began modestly at Pontypool United under the stewardship of Laurie Daniel. When he moved to Pontypool in 1978 he had to spend a frustratingly large portion of his time sitting on timber while Bobby Windsor started in all the big games. But in the '80s, after Bobby moved across to prop, he came into his own. He took on the Pontypool ideals introduced by Pross the previous decade and sometimes I think he may have understood Pontypool and the Pooler ethos even better than the great man himself.

Junna had originally marked his card as part of an outstanding (and unbeaten) Pontypool United side that had scored over 1,000 points in 1973–74 and contained several players who had played for Pontypool RFC proper. They had fought their peers to a standstill on 30 September 1974, only going down 12–3 to a converted try in the final quarter in one of Pontypool's toughest contests of the season.

Bob Dawkins recalls: 'When Junna came out of the Youth team, he came from Twmpath school and they had been unbeaten for two years or so. A lot of the boys from that side knew that they wouldn't get into the Pontypool set-up because of the remarkable level of competition, so instead they opted for the United club. I was captaining United at the time and my first thought was, "How am I going to control these boys?" Number one on that list was Junna, who was an absolute wild man.

'We played a very good Moseley team featuring Barry Corless, John Finlan and Jan Webster and we had seven boys fresh out of the Pontypool Youth team. We absolutely slaughtered them and I was gobsmacked. How could a team of Youth graduates beat such an experienced and impressive team as Moseley?

'The bloke who epitomised it all was Steve Junna Jones. I used to make a bee-line for the referees after games, and I couldn't believe the number of times that the refs would make reference to our hooker. "He was the difference between the sides," they'd say. Not the scrum-half or the fly-half, who you'd normally expect to make the difference in games, but our hooker! It was Junna who would spark the whole side.' (Bob Dawkins)

Terry Cobner first came across Junna when he was in the Pontypool Youth team: 'That Pooler Youth team was almost as successful as the 1st XV. Steve wasn't a big man, but he was extremely fit – at Wales sessions Junna and "Spikey" Watkins would regularly be miles ahead of everyone else. And absolutely fearless: I used to shut my eyes sometimes when he went into contact! When he was up against Bobby in training in the early days, Bob would bump him and run over the top of him, but Junna would bounce straight back up for more; there was no quit in him. He had a great attitude to the game. I'll never know why he didn't get a Welsh cap – probably because he couldn't keep his hands in his pockets against Gloucester.

'When he first came to training, Pross didn't know his name, so he called him "son", as he would do with anyone he didn't know. Ray wanted to give the Athletic some lineout practice at the end of one session and he called Junna over.

'He said, "What's your name, son?"

'Junna replied, "Aubrey."

'Pross went, "Oh, right." And Junna was always Aubrey [to rhyme with 'strawberry'] after that.

'It always provoked a chuckle among the players when Pross would screech in his high-pitched voice from across the other side of the field, "Awwwbereeee . . ." It sounded like he wanted to pick some fruit urgently. But Aubrey and Perk were the two warriors in the '80s, there's no doubt about it.'

Junna represented my gateway into the Pontypool club in the 1983–84 season and his premature death at only 55 years of age came as quite literally a body blow. I remember it was a Sunday morning, 9 September 2007. The phone rang and I had to take the call upstairs in the office. It was Neil Waite, the former Pontypool Athletic prop and committeeman. 'Al, I've got some bad news. Junna has passed away.' I hadn't seen him for a number of years, but the impact was still like a forceful punch to the stomach. I felt that something had been taken away from my life that could never be put back.

Junna looked after me like an older brother. Away from Pooler training, it was Junna running the weights session or dispatching us on runs down the canal bank and up over the Cwdy Lane; driving us up those hill sprints to the Lamb Inn on Penyrheol, with a golden pint waiting at the end of it. It was Junna who looked out for me on the field and led me astray off it, with a grin on his face. At the time I joined the club he *was* Pontypool RFC.

I'd first noticed Steve Jones in my teens. He would be running the streets of New Inn and Griffithstown with his great friends Dai Leighfield and Neil Waite. The 'Three Musketeers' trained together for years before they became the basis of a training group that included nearly every new player who came to the club. Away from official training sessions at the Park, this group would meet and train up to four times a week and would regularly swell to as many as fifteen in the summer. Junna took an interest in all forms of athletic training and would spend time at the local Pontypool boxing club. John Harris, who won medals at two successive Paralympic Games in the mid-1980s and who, in 2012, was chosen to bear the Olympic torch through the streets of Blaenavon, was asked by Junna to come and give us advice on weights. He also introduced the likes of Kevin Moseley and Roger Bidgood to the benefits of strength conditioning. Junna quizzed sports students on sport science. Ultimately, the sessions he devised would be both gruelling and specific.

Junna was one of Ray Prosser's 'loveable rogues'. When I was driving the van for Colin Thomas, the local builder-merchants, as a teenager, he would always encourage me to pull up on Princes Street for regular cups of tea and sandwiches. After a while I began to notice that the van was always a little bit lighter after the tea and sandwiches than it was before I had parked up and I started to wonder who was getting the better end of the deal!

In my 20s, I joined the Gwent constabulary and was based at Blackwood station. I would still visit Steve and his wife Mavis on my days off, as my dad was teaching in Africa at the time, so the Joneses became my adopted family. On one particular day in the middle of summer I heard loud guffawing and laughter as I neared the front door of his end-of-terrace house. Steve and his brother had observed my arrival and were arguing whether they should let me into the house.

From outside the front door, I could hear a voice saying, 'He's a copper now, will he be OK?'

'Yes,' came the reply. 'It's Spring, for God's sake. He'll be fine.'

As the front door finally opened, I was assaulted by a huge blast of heat. All the gas appliances in the house had been turned to maximum output – the fire in the front room, the gas central heating, the cooker . . . the lot.

The two brothers were both laughing like idiots and offering their hands for a pair of imaginary handcuffs. 'Take us away, Spring, and lock us up!' they said, then collapsed onto the ground, unable to contain their laughter.

I looked ahead glazed, as I always did when I moved into 'anti-criminal' mode. As one of Gwent's worst-ever policemen, it took me a while to cotton on.

Junna had managed to reverse the input of the gas pipe into the meter and had rewound the meter reading to the point it had occupied about two years previously. With the pipe properly reconnected, the brothers were desperately trying to run the meter back on towards a more plausible reading before the arrival of the official gas man!

In the mid-'80s, a nightclub opened on the Clarence in Pontypool. It was called Duke's and it attracted many of the players late on a Saturday night or after a game on Wednesday. On one particular Saturday night, the bouncers that marshalled the front and back doors had taken Mark Jones out the back and beaten him up good and proper. What they did not know was that his big brother, accompanied by the majority of the Pooler team, was still in the club. It proved to be a big mistake.

Word got back to Junna. His eyes lit up with that intense, faraway look I knew so well and he asked me to prime the rest of the boys before he called one of the bouncers over.

'Do you like beating people up?' This initial salvo could mean only one thing. The bouncers mustered behind their man and the Pooler players gathered behind Junna. Steve hit the bouncer squarely on the chin and laid him out, at which all hell erupted. The police arrived and I managed to lock the fire-exit door just after asking Police Sergeant Karen Cherrett for an extra five minutes 'to sort out a private matter'. Karen was suitably obliging and the war inside followed its natural course – unfortunately for the bouncers.

Steve's wife Mavis died of a brain haemorrhage in 1989. It was an extremely tough time for him. When he later met Liz and they settled down together, he was determined to start a family – in fact, many families. Together they fostered several children in the late '90s and early noughties. One of the incoming boys, who had developed a tendency to thieve, was given some advice in typically forthright Pooler fashion by Steve: 'Son, listen carefully. Liz and I are going to look after you well. Remember that, because if you steal anything from us, I'll cut your f***ing hands off. Do you understand?'

Steve Jones's approach to life was a result of his early departure from its mainstream. He was part of the 'rubbish' drifting around Pontypool and the inner desperation that came from that terrorised many an opponent on a rugby field. Along with John Perkins and Kevin Moseley, he upheld the principle of 'the boot' in the '80s while the rest of us kept our heads down, did our jobs and reaped the benefits.

At the same time, it was that same desperation that allowed him to give himself fully to every endeavour he undertook, every child he fostered and every player he mentored, with every fibre of his being. He knew only one way to train and to live: flat out – whether it was running or weightlifting or fathering a kid who had no home.

He became a different animal on the rugby field, playing with an enraged energy and a genuinely nasty edge; it was Junna who was responsible for the cancellation of fixtures with Bristol after he took out one of their players in one particularly unsavoury incident on the pitch. His on-field persona had no knowledge of the humble, welcoming individual who would offer his hand to his battered opposite number in the bar immediately after the game. To the best of my knowledge, the two Junnas never made each other's acquaintance. Cigar in one hand and pint in the other, the eyes of 'good Steve' would gleam brightly as he talked – the emotional energy that only a couple of hours before had threatened to take an opponent's head off would now be leading all his rapt listeners in a sing-song. The head would start to rock, the knee would start to bounce and we all knew there could be only one finale – Kenny Rogers' 'Ruby'.

As his rugby career came towards its close, Junna's body was a mess. He had problems with his knee, he had problems with his neck and he was forever in Eddie Mogford's treatment room up on Merchant's Hill. Anyone would have paid money, and a lot of it, to listen to those two exploring the outer limits of 'unforgiving humour'. They were two peas from the same pod, and they meant the same to Pontypool rugby club.

There were also a number of underestimated but effective Pontypool backs in the '80s, such as Leigh Jones, Lyn Faulkner, Peter Lewis and Goff Davies. Leigh should by rights have been playing for Llanelli, but he used to make the 150-mile round trip to training without complaint. Roger Bidgood and Keith Orrell, who took over in the centres during Pontypool's best-ever season (statistically speaking) in 1987–88 probably upped the quality even further – not to mention wing Bleddyn Taylor, who joined the club from Neath, a move he described as 'out of the frying pan, into the fire'. Leigh and Lyn, and then Keith and Roger, followed the example of Ivor Taylor as powerful crash-tacklers in the centre – and everyone gave Ivor a wide berth when he got involved in a game of 'touch' during training.

Goff 'Sheets' Davies was one of the finest spot-tacklers I've ever seen; he broke up many a wide passing movement before it had even been considered by the opposition by taking man and ball together. All were tireless chasers of the endless rain of high kicks put up by our halves and that gave us the territorial control we wanted.

With the ever-increasing depth of quality in all rows of the scrum and the outside backs, an energetic new spark plug in Steve Jones and a 'brain' to get his messages across in Eddie Butler, all Ray Prosser really needed to complete his vision of the Pontypool game-plan was a scrum-half: a 9 who could set up his back row, do most of the kicking and navigate his team up and down the field.

We'd never been entirely settled at the position in the '70s and Pross would tend to go through half-backs like tissue paper at a funeral. The best of them would probably have been Dennis John and Derek 'Chunky' Thomas, who had emigrated with his family to New Zealand.

The big point of difference between the Pontypool sides of the '70s and '80s was undoubtedly one man: David Bishop. We had never had a player of such talent in the position – or one who could exert such complete dominance over the game. It would be no exaggeration to say that the 'Bish' added a gilt-edged quality we'd never had before or have had since.

Having talked to Richard Hill, the ex-England scrum-half, I know there was a period in the mid-'80s when David was rated by his peers as the best scrum-half not only in the British Isles but also on the planet. Unfortunately their opinion was not shared by the Wales selectors of the time, who more or less reflected the official view of Pontypool's success. By that stage, Pontypool had been pigeonholed as 'rebels without a cause' and nothing could change that perception.

The Bish joined Pooler as a 21 year old after playing a couple of games for Ebbw Vale. His career had been temporarily frozen by a three-year prison sentence after an incident in Cardiff city centre and there was a lot of interest in him when he resumed playing. Charlie Faulkner, by now the coach of Newport, was trying to bring him down to Rodney Parade and there was already an agreement in place to that effect. However, a call from Pross promising Dai a run-on spot in the team to play the touring Australians was enough of a carrot to swing the balance towards Pontypool. Ray made the call only two weeks before the Wallabies game on 4 November 1981, so he couldn't have shaved it any finer! He also knew that David had been told by a Welsh age-group selector as a 15 year old that he 'would never be big enough to play scrum-half' and that pressed all the right buttons with Pross. It chimed with my own experience in the '50s: developing players who'd been told they'd never make it into bona fide internationals had long since become Ray's favourite pastime and a way of thumbing his nose at an undiscerning establishment.

True to Pontypool form, triumph and disaster were easy bedfellows in David Bishop's first season. The club won the Whitbread Merit Table for the fourth time, at the cost of the Bish breaking his neck in a match against Aberavon at the Talbot Athletic ground only three and a half weeks after the Australia game. At the time, the Harley Street specialists doubted whether he would be able to walk again, let alone play rugby. True to Pontypool form, David Bishop was back in harness for the 1st XV only 11 months later, marking his return to top-class rugby against Maesteg with a try in an emphatic 30–3 win! He was even more dominant against Gloucester in the next Wednesday night game, driving the team on towards a massive 52–15 victory against traditionally awkward opponents.

I know Dai used to wear a small bottle of holy water, blessed by the local priest, around his neck for every game after he came back from that horrendous injury. I don't know whether it helped us break the cup curse that had bedevilled Pontypool during the previous decade, but I'm convinced his presence as a player made all the difference in the world. In the 1982–83 season we beat our bogey team Cardiff in the cup quarter-finals – our first win in five attempts against them – before overcoming a very strong Bridgend side in the semis and seeing off Swansea in the final on 30 April 1983. As Arthur Crane et al. reveal in their history of Pontypool RFC, *Pontypool's Pride*, the whole community got behind their team in the week leading up to the final:

> Cup fever gripped the town of Pontypool on the eve of the final. Pontypool Chamber of Trade decided they should mark the club's first ever appearance in the final with shop displays in Pontypool colours and they also painted on their windows messages of support most suited to their particular line of business. 'Swansea have had their chips' was the slogan on Terry's fish & chip shop, while the John Woodward shoe shop message was 'Pontypool will walk it'. The warning from Hughes & Son stationers was 'Bishop leaves them stationary!'

The Bish dutifully fulfilled the final prophecy with a display of tactical kicking and link play with his forwards that rightly earned him the Lloyd Lewis trophy for man of the match. Pontypool had won their first Schweppes Welsh Cup final by 18 points to 6 and it was as much a tribute to their strength in depth as it was to their new star at scrum-half. Staff Jones had stepped down from the team in anticipation of his selection on the British and Irish Lions trip to New Zealand in the summer of 1983 and Eddie Butler had to withdraw on the eve of the match to be replaced by Martin 'Horsehead' Jones at lock. Loose-head Bobby Windsor, the replacement for Staff

Jones, suffered a match-ending leg injury after only ten minutes, which invoked the cry that had so worried Steve Peters – 'Get the Bear ready!' Mike Crowley came off the bench as third choice to give one of the most promising young props in Welsh rugby, Gareth John, a torrid time in the tight.

Even in the moment that all of Ray Prosser's team plans had ripened, however, the fruit still tasted bittersweet. Ray Prosser's wife Nancy, who had been suffering from a terminal illness for many years, had passed away only four weeks before the final was played. Terry Cobner had generously stepped in to coach the side while Ray took a leave of absence to be by her side for the final few months.

Not even Dai's sending off early in the 1983–84 term could prevent a spectacular season of success in the league, although it did probably cost Pooler a repeat of their cup success. The championship reached a stupendous climax that year when Pontypool beat their perennial rivals Newbridge 43–6 on 16 April 1984 to surpass the world record of 1,454 points in a season set by Pontypridd eight years previously, only to be overhauled by Bridgend in their last game of the season at Penarth. When Pontypool came to face their old nemesis Llanelli in the final match, they needed 44 points to overtake Bridgend and 'win it all'.

Eddie Butler takes up the story: 'The game that is etched on my memory is the match against Llanelli on 30 April 1984. We had just broken the world club record for points scored in a season two weeks before against Newbridge – we'd scored 1,461 points at that stage. Then Bridgend, who eventually finished as runners-up in the table, came past us on the rails in the very last weekend of the season by beating Penarth by over 100 points!

'So the scene was set. We needed both to beat Llanelli and score 44 points to reclaim the record. We were feeling a little bit apprehensive. After all, it was Llanelli and they always delighted in spoiling our parties, and it was a hot dustbowl – which suited their style of running rugby.

'Anyway, we were like a steam engine that day – unstoppable. My back-row partner Chris "Madman" Huish got two tries and I touched down for another. It was 30–6 at half-time.

'Inevitably, it was the Bish who put the icing on top of the cake in the second period. We cruised past Bridgend's new world record with twenty-five minutes to spare, and the Bish scored another two tries to pass the club's individual post-war record of thirty-seven tries in any one season.

'We won 54–16 and once again the cathedral dissolved off the Bank, the monkeys in the trees jumped down onto the pitch. They stayed there for what seemed like hours afterwards, wildly cheering announcements that cars were blocking the car park.' (Eddie Butler)

The 1st XV's playing record that season was 46 wins, 2 draws and only 2 losses from the 50 games played.

At the end of the season John Billot described David Bishop's value to Pooler as 'what Wild Bill Hickok was to Abilene – a one-man army'. The wildness was, however, never far from the surface. If the bittersweet nature of the pill to be swallowed was characteristic Pontypool RFC medicine as a whole, nowhere was it more concentrated than in the career of the Bish from that point onwards. There was no fairy-tale ending.

Despite winning his one and only cap against Australia in 1984 – and scoring the only try the Wallabies conceded against the home nations on that tour – one year later Dai was back in trouble again, this time for punching Newbridge lock Chris Jarman in a ruck and breaking his jaw. Jarman brought a private prosecution against the Bish and the WRU handed him an 11-month ban, which gave Robert Jones the time he needed to establish himself as the long-term replacement for Terry

Holmes at scrum-half in the Wales team and condemned Dai forever to 'one-cap wonder-dom'.

By the 1987–88 season, Dai had given up the unequal fight. After kicking the winning penalty goal out of the mud to seal Pontypool's cup win over Swansea (Robert Jones included), he could think of nothing better than presenting his ample backside to the watching Welsh selectors in the main stand.

The only predictable thing about the Bish was his unpredictability. It was even impossible to know when he'd start and finish training! Graham Price experienced that unpredictability first hand in the Pooler training sessions: 'The Bish lived according to his own set of rules. He would come out late for training and he'd go back in early, leaving the 2nd XV scrum-half to fill in for him at the end of the session. Towards the end of a game on a Saturday he'd still be trying to break out of his own 25 instead of nursing the forwards back upfield as he was supposed to do.

'The Bish didn't always carry out orders and rarely conformed to expectations of him by others. He was his own man and went his own way, even if that way led to self-destruction. But he was great to play with. When we ran that lineout peel, on a good day I knew Dai would be on one of my shoulders like a red, black and white bee, buzzing around for the next opportunity. I could almost hear his hunger and his impatience in my footsteps! When I gave him the ball, he'd take off like a rocket, even from our own 10-metre line.

'But the Bish had two heads, and his commitment depended entirely on which one he brought to the game. At other times I'd be looking to link with him from that peel and he'd be nowhere, he'd just go AWOL and I couldn't find him anywhere. Left shoulder, right shoulder, he was nowhere to be seen.

'After the game, when you picked up the *Western Mail* on a Monday morning, you never knew where Dai Bishop would be making the headlines – the back page or, just as frequently, the front page . . . He was completely unpredictable.' (Graham Price)

The ex-Great Britain rugby league coach Phil Larder, who went on to become the defensive coordinator for England's 2003 World Cup-winning union side, says that nothing much changed after Bishop moved to league in 1988: 'David Bishop was part of the Great Britain rugby league squad that played France in 1990 in a two-game series. I remember the teams lining up for the national anthems and I noticed that David wasn't singing. The others were giving it plenty, but not David. So I buttonholed him afterwards: "David, why didn't you sing the national anthem?"

'He replied, "I can't sing that crap, it's not my anthem . . ."

'So, for the next game, I gave him a set of headphones – I think it was a Sony Walkman. What people don't know is that David was listening to *"Hen Wlad Fy Nhadau"* while everyone else was singing "God Save the Queen"! And, what's more, he was singing it, too!

'I guess that's David to a tee. He always went his own way and he absolutely never stuck to the approved script.' (Phil Larder)

David Bishop would return to Pontypool as a coach in the dark days of the 1990s, as an assistant to Bob Dawkins: 'Recently, David Bishop was voted the best Pontypool player of all time in a poll. Gareth Edwards was undoubtedly a great player, but the Bish could do things on a field that I haven't seen from anyone else. I coached Pontypool with him in 1996 and he was very easy to work with – unlike Mark Ring.

'It all came to an end for me in 1996. My wife found out that she had breast cancer and I remember getting this overpowering feeling, in the middle of a training session, that I couldn't go on a moment longer . . . I turned to Bish and said, "I can't carry on." He put his arms around me and gave me a kiss. He understood totally. That set the tone for all our meetings since then; there's always been that warmth and understanding between us.' (Bob Dawkins)

Although we managed a 'three-peat' of Whitbread Merit Table wins between the 1983–84 and 1985–86 seasons, I began to feel that we were weakening in the latter half of the '80s – or others were catching us up. Or probably a bit of both.

Eddie Butler's unexpected early retirement after the tour of Canada in May 1985 hit us hard. When Terry Cobner had stepped aside in 1981–82, it was Eddie who filled the breach as Prosser's on-field organiser and the man who translated the coaching message to the rest of the team, and he did it all without missing a beat. In his three years as captain, we had won the Welsh Cup for the first time, we'd won the club championship twice and lost only fifteen of our 160 matches in that period.

Both Cobs and Ed were the rugby intellects Pross needed at the head of his team. They were great students of the game as well as being fine footballers; they were both adaptable, able to handle different playing responsibilities and able to think their way through a game. Eddie had played a lot of rugby in the second row and Cobner had even turned out for the 1st XV very effectively as a centre. When Eddie announced his retirement at the ripe old age of 28 because of his new work commitments with the BBC, it left a yawning gap in the leadership of the side.

John Perkins had taken over a lot of the responsibilities of club captain in Canada, sometimes even cutting Ed short in the process, but he wasn't the same kind of leader that either Ed or Cobs were. Perk could blow the whistle and get even the most timid of souls to follow him over the top of the trench into a hail of gunfire because his personal example was so strong.

He could lead by example and he was such an ardent disciple of the Prosser way of doing things that sometimes he bore a greater resemblance to Pross than the man himself. But at that stage of his career, Perk was not an independent rugby thinker, although ironically he became one after his playing days were over.

The final season for the Prosser/Taylor coaching partnership was also 1986–87, so it truly was the end of an era. Although the club had enough left in the tank to win one more club championship the year following their departure, Ray Prosser was not a man you could easily replace. He had an experience of rugby that was global and it was reflected in his coaching style; he had an experience of Pontypool as a rugby club that was unique in both its longevity and its success.

Ray had travelled to the far side of the world and brought back the 'Golden Fleece' of his playing/coaching philosophy with him. His ability to pinpoint leaders who could implement his strategies (Eddie Butler and Terry Cobner) and sparkplugs who could drive the team forward by a sheer act of will (Steve Jones, John Perkins and Bobby Windsor), allied to the host of talent unearthed by his scouring of the Gwent valleys and developed through the purgatory of the Pooler training environment, made for a potent winning combination. From now on, without its two heads but still with its boots on, Pontypool would no longer be the same force in Welsh rugby.

CHAPTER 7

THE TIMES, THEY ARE A-CHANGIN'

I joined Pontypool and played my first game for the 1st XV in 1983, having captained the Wales Schools Under-18s side the previous season. Less than a year later, with a typically Pooler sense of irony, I got my first job with the Gwent police constabulary. I stayed with the force for the next six years and left at the same time I left Pontypool to go down to Newport. My one and only reason for joining the constabulary as a fresh-faced 19 year old was that it allowed me to pursue my real dream – of playing for my home-town club. It was a shame I couldn't admit it.

I remember my interview with the deputy chief constable, Bill Rostron, so vividly. His directness was unnervingly similar to Ray Prosser's. He was an ex-Welsh guardsman with a military bearing who somehow always looked taller when he was sitting down; his back was ramrod straight in that leather chair. Bill was responsible for discipline and recruitment in the Gwent force. I had gone to school at West Mon with three of his children and Bill came straight to the point without wasting questions: 'Carter, you know Hugh and Mark, don't you?' Hugh and Mark were his two sons, one of whom was my contemporary, the other in the year below.

'Yes.' I felt a bead of perspiration appearing on my brow involuntarily, although I couldn't be sure whether it was as a result of the sun beaming through the immense glass windows of the police headquarters in Croesyceiliog or my own growing sense of anxiety.

'If you were on patrol one Saturday evening and spotted Hugh and Mark drunk and disorderly in the centre of Newport, what would you do?'

The anxiety grew as I struggled for the right answer. I could now feel the bead of perspiration running down my face, from the top of my head.

Bill's eyes narrowed, as he loomed above me. He was still seated, but it felt like he was standing. 'You would let them go, wouldn't you?'

'Uhh . . . No, I'd book them.' I had no idea whether I believed my own answer as the roasting, inner and outer, continued.

'Of course you would! They're your friends. Now wipe your brow, boy!' Bill barked.

I felt like I had been rumbled by Bill's interrogation, my true motives laid bare. I didn't really want to arrest anyone, least of all my friends, and I never had the sense of conviction as a policeman that I had as a rugby player for Pontypool. In the circumstances, it was no wonder I went on to become one of Gwent constabulary's worst-ever policemen. The thirty-year career of my grandpa, Donald Jenkins, in the Monmouthshire force, may well have been one factor in persuading Bill Rostron to give me a chance against his better judgement. More importantly, Bill was a fan of Pross and Pooler, and that swung his vote my way irresistibly.

The coalminers' strike was in full flow when I was posted to Blackwood police station after completing my period of training more or less successfully. Blackwood sat in between a number of nearby collieries, therefore it was an epicentre of the strike turbulence. Oakdale, Markham and Britannia Pengam had a significant historical root in the area. Britannia, the country's first electrical colliery, was established in 1910, the same year as Markham, while Oakdale had sunk its first shaft three years earlier in 1907. Between them, the three collieries were the main employers in the Rhymney and Sirhowy valleys, with a workforce of almost 5,000 men. By 1989, the year I decided to move down to Newport to play my rugby, all three collieries had closed.

The miners' strike hit Wales particularly hard because all of the 21,500-strong workforce subscribed to it in November 1984 and saw it through until the bitter end in March 1985. The miners knew that Wales was virtually a single-industry economy and that all the local communities had grown up around the collieries, so they struck as if their lives depended on it.

One colliery, the Tower at Hirwaun, famously survived when the workforce bought out the owners after a protracted struggle in 1995, and it continued production until 2008. In May 2012, the six million tonnes of anthracite that remained on the surface began to be worked as an opencast mine, with the coal going by train to the Aberthaw power station.

The purchase of the mine gave the 239 miners who bought into it by pooling their £8,000 redundancy packages a great sense of self-empowerment. Many of them had worked in the outside world in low-paid production-line jobs where 'you had to put your hand up to go to the toilet' and they hadn't enjoyed the experience.

Despite the doom-and-gloom predicted by the 'experts', year on year the mine recorded profits, secured major contracts and quickly became the biggest employer in the Cynon Valley. It held the fabric of the community together. As the leader of the buy-out, Tyrone O'Sullivan, said, it at least offered some proof positive that ordinary people could control their own lives. None other than the Welsh First Minister Rhodri Morgan acclaimed the buy-out as 'a pivotal moment in national self-confidence that paved the way to devolution'.

As one Hirwaun miner told *Red Pepper* magazine: 'You stood together. But if you go outside, you'll see men struggling on their own. Underground you wouldn't see a man struggle, you wouldn't have to ask anybody to give you a hand, they would see you struggling and they come and automatically give you a hand.'

In other words, the values that made Pontypool RFC great in the 1970s and '80s were identical to those that made miners of the valleys want to protect their jobs and the communal solidarity they represented in 1984–85. You worked bloody hard – sometimes harder than seemed humanly possible – you earned every penny you got and saw the results of your labour; both during and after the shift, you stood together as one. This blue-collar ethos stood in stark opposition to the vision of the future the Chancellor of the Exchequer Nigel Lawson expressed when he told the House of Lords Select Committee on Overseas Trade in 1983: 'There is no adamantine law that says we have to produce as much in the way of manufacture as we consume. If it does turn out that we are relatively more efficient in world terms at providing services than at producing goods, then our national interest lies in a surplus on services and a deficit on goods.'

Whatever a 'surplus on services' meant, it did not create any surplus in the area around Blackwood: it created nothing but deficits. All the talk from supporters of the free market of releasing labour from 'unproductive' state-sponsored jobs into new high-waged employment turned out to be hot air. Twenty years on, studies revealed that less than half the mining jobs had been replaced in the coalfield areas and all the economic regeneration of the mining communities had occurred through various forms of public funding and support from local authorities, not through the free market. The cost of this regeneration was estimated at £28 billion as long ago as 2004.

In the meantime, the UK still consumes over 66 million tons of coal, more than it did back in 1985, but well over two-thirds of that coal is now imported. The Tata steelworks in Port Talbot imports 2.5 million tons of coal every year on its own, while sitting on a 47-million-ton potential drift mine site in Margam, which could both ensure its supply, cut its costs and create more than 500 jobs in the area.

The socioeconomic pattern that existed before the mining communities developed in the Gwent valleys in the early twentieth century has reasserted itself, with a very low proportion of the labour force in work, low wage levels, high incidences of disabling long-term illness, poor housing and poor patterns of education attainment. Employment growth in South Wales has occurred exclusively along the M4 corridor, not along the northern rim of the old coalfield areas. Margaret Thatcher's policy of eradicating the mining industry in South Wales has turned out to be a far bigger and more costly 'folly' than any of the towers built or rebuilt above the Grotto in Pontypool Park. Her decision to 'sell off British coal' had a profound effect on both the mining communities and the employment base within those communities over the following years – and it had a pronounced effect on the type of rugby player produced in the valleys.

More immediately, it affected the shift strength at police stations throughout South Wales during the strike itself. In Blackwood, the normal shift strength of seven officers dropped down to three. Many officers were absent, literally fighting against miners at various pits around the country to ensure those who wanted to cross the picket lines to work gained entry. The Welsh police invariably ended up in the coalfields of Nottingham and Yorkshire, where there was no chance of seeing a familiar face in the picket lines full of working men who Thatcher chose to see as 'the enemy within'.

When I first started at Blackwood police station, I was in the charge of an ex-CID officer from Maindee in Newport called Jon Young. Jon's unit had been disbanded and he had been put in charge of my training. He was on a mission to find as much action as possible for me and the education began at Britannia Pengam colliery. Britannia had been used as a training colliery and there were two huge 'tips' of surplus coal stacked up that were considered unsaleable. These small mountains proved to be too much of a temptation to the impoverished striking miners who lived in Bargoed, Cefn Forest and the surrounding areas.

The tips were extremely dangerous because they could give way at any moment, engulfing a child who happened to be playing on them or indeed a miner who had come down to replenish his fuel supply at night. It was to Britannia colliery that Jon drove, looking to find a first arrest for his new protégé. Having to arrest a striking collier blackened from head to toe by coal dust, taking some useless coal from the tip to keep his family warm at night, was not a career highlight – in fact, it was quite the opposite. The miner in question had sacks of coal loaded up next to Pengam Road, which ran alongside the colliery, and the station sergeant did not take it well when sack after sack of coal had to be brought into Blackwood station as evidence. It was a complete mess inside and outside. I felt as little sympathy with my role when I made that first arrest as I had when I first faced Bill Rostron in the sunlit hothouse of Croesyceiliog HQ. I had no idea what I was doing and I liked the job even less that day as a result of the job I'd been asked to perform.

On subsequent visits to Britannia with the same objective, I would use a shortcut I had found through the undergrowth and make sure I blew my police whistle, which each bobby carried with him, well before any of the officers were within range of an arrest. It alerted the ant-like masses down on the coal tips. As soon as the loud peep rang out, anywhere between a dozen and two dozen darkened 'ants' could be observed scuttling away or sliding down the tips and into hiding. It was like picking up a stone and witnessing the frantic scurry of activity underneath it. But it at least eased my conscience and allowed me to believe I'd played some small role in postponing further humiliation for those miners.

Fortunately, there were some moments of light relief to brighten the life of a 'doomed policeman'. After a Wales versus Ireland match in 1985, we stopped a van being driven in Cefn Forest by an Irishman from Tipperary. When I opened the driver's door, he literally fell out of the seat into my arms in an alcoholic coma. Being from the Republic, he had to have his case put forward before the magistrate post-haste and Jon Young was forced to phone Tipperary police station on Sunday evening to verify his identity.

The officer on the other end of the phone confirmed that he knew the gentleman in question personally and went to find his sergeant to clarify his driving licence details. When he returned, he said, 'We t'ink he might have a provisional . . . but he's a feckin' good driver, you can take it from us. We've seen him driving down the main street!'

Like most of the working population in Wales, I found myself getting ever closer to the M4 with each new posting. After five months in Blackwood, I was transferred to Cwmbran Newtown, inconveniently situated between Pontypool and Newport. The town itself was mostly new housing with a new migrant population to match, lured closer towards the M4 artery by the promise of subsidised house prices and jobs. It came as quite a shock after my experience of the strong valley community in Blackwood.

My beat was the town centre, which had a pedestrianised area that made it a shopper's paradise for both those who intended to pay and those who didn't. Shoplifting was the main crime. There were no collieries here, but there was a powerful sense of the tedium and alienation the miners strove so hard to avoid by staying underground. Shoplifting, alcohol and drugs – and even suicide attempts – were the order of any day for a bobby on the Cwmbran town-centre beat.

There was a teenage glue addict who I had been told to look out for. Away from sniffing bags of adhesive she could be quite a sensible girl, but when 'high' she was real trouble. My sergeant at Cwmbran, Adrian Davies, was a man of Pontypool and a big supporter of the club. He was accompanying me one night when she was in the town centre with her plastic bag. Adrian and I cornered her and I confiscated the bag, which had several tubes of glue squeezed into it. She went crazy trying to get it back. We disposed of the bag and thought that was that.

Prior to the end of my shift at 5 a.m. the girl reappeared in the lobby of the station asking for me. When I came out, her eyes were ablaze and she pulled out a knife. I reached for the wooden truncheon that was hidden in a long inner lining adjacent to my right pocket. I could not retrieve it quickly enough and a Keystone Cop sequence ensued, as I ran laps around the station, desperately trying to feel for the lace attached to the top of the truncheon, all the while being pursued by a crazed teenage girl.

She was sentenced to a couple of years' detention and sent letters of apology to the station. While in the detention centres, she was a different person, then when she was released again it never took long for her to misbehave. On a Friday prior to a game against Glamorgan Wanderers, Adrian Davies had agreed I could finish early at 3 a.m. At 2.45 an alarm went off at the stationery store in General Rees square, much to my annoyance. I arrived to see her standing high above us on the roof of the House of Fraser building. She was screaming, 'I'm going to jump!' I was very familiar with this pattern of behaviour, as she'd made numerous 'suicide attempts' previously, so Adrian asked me to talk her down.

'Go on, then. Jump! You're wasting our time and yours just staying up there, and it's the quickest way down,' I shouted.

Forty-five minutes later, she walked down the stairs, as per usual.

The Cwmbran station was literally split down the middle in rugby terms, with half of the officers supporting Newport and the other half supporting Pontypool. Luckily, both my shift sergeant and the inspector, Roger Tuck, were Pontypool supporters. The banter in the station was in-your-face and it could be provocative; it became a part of your motivation, knowing that walking into the station after the game with a victory would make life so much easier.

Roger Tuck lives in New Inn and has now retired from the police force. He was at the core of a large segment of Pontypool supporters who used to meet in the Rising Sun in New Inn. In his retirement, he has become a landscape painter, drawing attention to the many areas of natural beauty in and around Pontypool.

Roger would adopt typically canny Pontypool-type practices to bring felons to justice. To give one example, I recall an occasion when we had caught a bloke who we knew had been responsible for a series of burglaries in Cwmbran. The problem was that there was little circumstantial evidence available. We needed a confession before we were obliged to take him off the hook and throw him back into the water. CID had interviewed him and there was no positive result. Time was running out and he would soon have to be bailed and released.

Roger got wind of this and knocked heads with me. It turned out he had come up with a cunning plan. Our 'silent' burglar was locked up in Cell 3. He was well able to hear what was happening in the long corridor that ran alongside the eight cells at Cwmbran station – there was a 'peek' hatch, but it was not big enough to put your head through and see out – so I grabbed hold of Roger in the charge office and he started shouting and bawling, making all kinds of noise and protestation. He then started slapping the walls of the corridor, shouting, 'No . . . stop . . . no. Argh . . . let me go. Ugh . . . you b*****ds! This is police brutality!' He grabbed hold of the door to Cell 2 and slammed it back and forth a couple of times before collapsing on the floor still moaning and groaning.

'Let that be a lesson,' I shouted harshly, slamming a door shut. I stood patiently at the end of the corridor and listened to the bravura performance that was to follow.

Roger continued to moan, to the extent that the man in Cell 3 became concerned.

'You all right, mate? What have they done to you?' His face was pressed up flat against the peek hatch.

'Orgh, argh . . .' Then came a quiet gasping: 'My ribs . . . I think they're broken . . . Argh.'

'The b*****ds.'

'Yes, the b*****ds!' Roger repeated, hammering the final nail in the coffin of the unsuspecting inmate of Cell 3. Confident that he had established the necessary rapport, Roger then asked quietly, 'What are you in for?'

'I've done over a load of houses in Thornhill, but they haven't got anything on me. The stash is in a lock-up and they've got f**k all out of me in interview.'

Roger straightened up and walked to the door of Cell 3, then introduced himself. 'Hello, I'm Roger Tuck, chief inspector.' He calmly introduced the custody sergeant, who had just recorded the previous conversation. The bloke was so stunned he just 'sang like a canary', his confession to some 20 offences flooded out of him and soon after a garage full of stolen property was recovered.

Each police recruit underwent a probationary period, or a period of assessment, lasting two years. After you had successfully negotiated this period, it was very difficult to lose your job. A short while after I was confirmed as a bona-fide police constable in the Gwent constabulary, a call made to Cwmbran station took everyone by surprise. The secretary of John Over, the chief constable, requested that I attend a meeting with him in person. This was highly unusual practice, as Bill Rostron, the deputy chief, normally dealt with disciplinary and internal matters, and so this stimulated a lot of talk on the grapevine within the station.

So it was back to the scene of one of my least favourite memories: the large office at the end of the headquarters building at Croesyceiliog. Careful not to crease or mess up my best dress tunic, I took a seat in the secretary's room, which separated the chief from his deputy. John Over began by congratulating me on getting through my probationary period. Then somehow the progress of my career in the constabulary was tied in to the fact that I was playing at Pontypool RFC.

'There are a good many players in that team who are known to us,' he said, 'and it may not be in your best interests to continue playing with them. There are plenty of good, respectable clubs within the force area that you could play for.'

The interview occurred around the time of Chris Jarman's prosecution of the Bish in the law courts and after another prominent Pontypool player, Frank Jacas, had been expelled from the force. It was a short meeting and a one-way conversation, and I formed the impression that John thought it would be a good idea if I took my playing boots down to Rodney Parade.

I was dumbfounded nonetheless. It took me a while to pick my jaw up off the floor. At the time I couldn't make the connection between my job and my playing rugby over the weekend for Pontypool. The wiring just wasn't there back then. However, the interview did give me access to the alternative view of Pontypool, from the vantage point of the big city on the M4. In Cwmbran station, I was on the cusp of the city and the valley, and I'd had first-hand experience in 1984–85 of how the valley communities built around heavy industry were under siege.

John Perkins was a miner at the Big Pit and both Staff Jones, who worked at My Lady Windsor, and Garin Jenkins were born in Ynysybwl. Garin was the last miner to ever play for Wales when he won his first international cap in 1991. All were men of Pontypool. All were part of a rich but dying seam of naturally hard men who benefited both the valley clubs and the national side. They were the last of their kind. When the destruction of the mining communities in the Eastern valley really began to have an impact in the late 1980s and early '90s, there was no one to take their place.

For me personally, the beginning of the end came during a turbulent domestic period when a girl from Malpas turned my life upside down. We had married young and too quickly, on the spur of the moment, in the style of one of those Las Vegas 'overnight' weddings. Life was demanding enough with a full-time job and every spare minute spent training or playing rugby, then as soon as the bands were exchanged I was apparently expected to give rugby up and commit to a life of domestic bliss.

Steve Jones had just been made captain of the Pontypool club and, with my life in turmoil, I committed a heinous crime in the eyes of the Pontypool hierarchy: I trained and played two games on permit for Cardiff Rugby Club. I didn't make the first move; the invitation came at the prompting of Bob Norster. Once he got wind of Norster's phone call, Junna turned up at Cwmbran station with a Chinese meal one Saturday night to persuade me to return! Although not officially 'on duty', the shift was eager to take advantage of the free meal. I returned with my tail between my legs at the end of September after a couple of weeks spent *hors de combat*. During the course of the season, I went on to miss some big cup matches, but the end-of-season British Combined Services and Police tour to New Zealand would renew my enthusiasm for the game.

In October 1989, Pontypool had a marquee fixture with New Zealand. John Perkins had taken over the coaching reins from Bobby Windsor during the 1988–89 season and so was in his second year as coach. It was clear from this point forward that all my energies should be concentrated on playing number 7 or open-side flanker; it was the position in which I was best suited to develop at the higher levels of the game.

Up until that point I had played in every position in the pack – partly because of the old amateur system, where one forward replacement had to cover all eight positions up front in case of injury. Steve Jones's knee had finally packed up in a game against the Llanelli Scarlets. The back five of the pack that day were Hadyn Moreton, Kevin Moseley, Richard Goodey, Frank Jacas and Mark Brown. I noticed a wicked grin pass over Ivor Taylor's face. He leaned towards me and rasped, 'Son, it looks like you are going on at hooker!'

Coming on for the last 30 minutes against a very tidy Llanelli front row of Anthony Buchanan, Ceri Townley and Laurence

'Ollie' Delaney was a disturbing prospect to me. It was all quite friendly, and I was even beginning to enjoy myself, until Llanelli had a scrum only five metres from our line. Pricey looked over and said, 'We are not going backwards.' Under pressure, the scrum went down and I can still remember Staff's advice as it collapsed: 'Don't fight it, go with it.' I was bent in half and I thought my neck was going to break. Welcome to the dark world of the front row.

That incident was typical of a season in which I could simply not get comfortable in the 1st XV, and certainly not at my favoured number 7 spot. It was only the attraction of playing in the New Zealand game that kept me going in 1989. Although I continued to train hard in company with my good friend Steve Jackson, an uncompromising Blaenavon and Pooler back-rower who is one of the most upbeat people I have ever met, the spectre of a doomed marriage and a doomed police career culminated in my severance from both in August 1989.

The 1989–90 season started well, with away wins against Gloucester and Newport, with the latter game going particularly well for me. We beat Swansea at home, but I picked up a hip injury early on which rendered training over the next month difficult. I needed to play for the Athletic about ten days before the All Black match in order to confirm my fitness and convince Perk I was fully ready to play in that game. It was too early for a full 80 minutes, so I gambled on an all-out training session on the Saturday before we played the Blacks the following Wednesday. I got through the session, but when I looked at the team on the message board in the usual way after training, my name was not on the list. Perky had opted instead for a big pack, with a bloke named David Churchill in the second row, Richard Goodey moving back to number 8 and New Zealander Dean Oswald shifting across to the open-side flank. He had never played there before.

Pontypool were routed to the tune of 47–6 at the Park.

I saw the writing on the wall and thought to myself: 'This could go on for the next six or seven years.' I wanted a chance to prove myself at a higher level and there seemed to be little prospect of me getting that exposure at Pooler, so when an advertisement appeared in the *Western Mail* towards the end of 1989, I found myself replying to it. The ad reminded me that there was a world far, far beyond the confines of Pontypool Park:

> *Rugby player wanted for Second Division French side Stade Olympique Millau, 2nd Row or Number 8. Apply to PO Box . . .*

I knew it was the right moment to get away from the claustrophobia of Pontypool and open my mind to a new vista of possibilities. Only three weeks later, I found myself standing on the tarmac in front of three large gangster-like Frenchmen at Fréjorgues Airport, Montpellier. The drive across the Causse du Larzac up onto the plateau was spectacularly dangerous, the conversation necessarily limited. The deal was done and the next eight months were spent in glorious exile in this idyllic spot in the south of France. I was given a studio apartment and a Peugeot 305 as part of the deal and a job in the most aromatic village in France.

Roquefort-sur-Soulzon, home of Roquefort cheese, sits on the side of Mount Combalou. This small village is the only place the cheese can be matured, amongst the caves and fissures of the mountain. According to local legend, a love-smitten young shepherd enjoying his lunch on the Combalou plateau once spied a beautiful shepherdess in the distance. Leaving his flock, he hid his meal – ewe's milk curds on rye bread – in a nearby cave, damp and cool. When the shepherd returned after several fruitless days searching for the object of his love, he found his picnic much changed in character. Mould had blanketed the bread and deep green veins marbled the curds. The starving shepherd could not resist the uninviting prospect.

'*Mais c'est bon!*' His cry rang like a bell around the nearby valley, as the depth and piquancy of the new and unexpected flavour tantalised his palate. And so the greatest cheese in the world was born.

Traditionally, the cheese-makers of Roquefort-sur-Soulzon leave their loaves of rye bread in the caves for six to eight weeks – a little longer than the shepherd – until they are consumed by the mould. The interior of the bread is then dried to produce a powder. The smell of the mould spills out of the caves – it is the dominant aroma of the entire valley; it embraces you and your clothes as you approach the village and does not release you until you are at least 10 km distant.

The intoxication with my new life and the apparent lack of interest on the other end of the phone from Junna during our regular chats only reinforced the current of my thinking. Although I knew Pontypool was still in my blood, I knew just as clearly that it was not a part of my rugby future. The ambition to play for Wales still burned strongly; when I returned home with my Breton friend Yann Kerroux in tow – Yann had introduced me to Jacques Brel and folk music from the north-west – Paul Turner was the first to contact me. Paul and I had grown up alongside each other in Edward Street, Griffithstown. Through Paul I met up with Gareth Evans, the former British and Irish Lions centre, at Newport Rugby Club. They had just been relegated and were looking to rebuild with Gareth in charge. It was an opportunity to show Perky and Pooler what I was capable of, and I had a point to prove. In August 1990, I departed the French dream and landed in Rodney Parade fully charged and ready to go.

The one game that had whetted my appetite was Pontypool

away early in September on a Wednesday night. For weeks, nothing else occupied my mind except for that game against my old club. I walked down through the town and the park on the way to the ground. There was a raging anger born of a Pontypool upbringing and the fact that the number 7 jersey on my back was now black-and-amber. On the night Paul Turner kicked eight penalties, as Pontypool were undone by a better 'boot', and Newport won their first game at the Park for well over a decade, 30 points to 9. I stood in the middle of the pitch and gave the main stand the bird at the end of the Pooler match – a gratuitous gesture that was nonetheless a real indication of my state of mind at the time.

I was 'playing angry' and the fury continued throughout the following season; it was one of the reasons why I was capped against England and Scotland at the beginning of 1991. The other reasons were Roger Powell and Glenn George. Roger had played open-side throughout his career and was one tough bastard. He looked after me closely and, as a coach, he developed my game at number 7 hugely, with a stream of accurate and revealing technical advice. Ironically, his suggestions dovetailed neatly with the conversations I'd had with Mark 'Shaft' Brown over the previous years at Pontypool. Glenn was just an inspiration, sometimes infuriating but always finding a way to charge you up in one way or another. He was Newport's answer to Chris Huish as 'Mr Consistent'.

As the true implications of the changed socioeconomic climate in the valleys began to make themselves felt in people's ordinary lives, more and more players from the traditional coalfield areas were lured down to the big city. Eventually, the trickle became a torrent. While I felt I had proved a point by winning at Pontypool Park, and winning my Welsh caps with Newport, the movement of other players such as Kevin Moseley, Roger Bidgood, Lee Jones, Andrew Dibble and

Andrew Peacock from Pontypool to Newport over the next couple of seasons also helped prove it for me. With an international-quality tight-head prop in Lyndon Mustoe already playing for Pontypool, the club had a ready-made front three of Dibble, Peacock and Mustoe that would have been a worthy successor to its forebears. Andrew Peacock was by repute the strongest scrummaging hooker ever to play for the club, including Bobby Windsor, but both he and Andrew Dibble moved to Newport to ply their trade in the '90s. It was a symbolic moment.

Roger Bidgood was the first big player to follow me down the valley. He was a Caerphilly boy who, like me, had also previously bought into Junna and the Pontypool way. Kevin Moseley was already a capped Wales lock when he made the journey south to 'the Port' soon after, while David Llewellyn was another key player who came down to play at the scrum-half from Ebbw Vale. He was a Trefil boy and very handy with his fists. His uncle had been in the Parachute regiment and taught him how to box. Pound for pound, he was as powerful a player as the Bish. Paul Turner's ability to manage a game from 10 proved to be an ideal foil for Dai's talent on the break.

The game that brought Glenn and me onto the radar of Welsh national coach Ron Waldron was the match between Newport and Neath at Rodney Parade on 29 December 1990. At the time Newport was still a Division One club, while Neath were the acknowledged kings of the Premier Division, having put together an outstanding 51-match unbeaten run against Welsh opponents. It was Moseley's debut game for Newport. Neath clearly were not expecting the physicality of the reception that awaited them that evening. We had three big locks in the team, with David Waters playing at number 8 in between Glenn and myself. When their biggest player, a young second row called Andrew Kembery, started making a nuisance of himself at the lineout, clambering over Kevin Moseley's back, he didn't realise the mistake he was making. Moseley just shrugged him off and, as he fell through the lineout, Dai clocked him from no more than six inches with a real peach, turning his shoulder and putting all his weight through the punch. Poor Kembery fell like a Californian Redwood. He was already spark-out before he hit the ground. Dai had already scored a try in the game and his replacement, Bassaleg boy Nigel Callard, touched down for another to make the final score a decisive 19–7 to Newport. The sending off of the Neath flanker Martin Morris for a challenge on Paul Turner also turned out to be a significant moment; along with the hand injury suffered by Richie Collins, it meant that Wales's two first-choice flankers were out of contention for the start of the 1991 Five Nations. That opened the way for Glenn and me to start against England and Scotland on the back of that victory over the Welsh club champions.

These were memorable matches of the kind I had missed out on up at Pontypool Park. For once, I was part of them. Newport made me feel welcome and they made me first choice; they gave me a platform for my international aspirations and the money I was getting from the club – which I hadn't received because of Pontypool's rigid 'no payments' policy – helped me get through college in relative comfort.

It was the valley towns that felt the economic decline triggered by the pit closures in the '80s most keenly. Some became ghost towns. The migration south towards the M4 by the workforce was echoed by the same movement of players who would under other circumstances have stayed at their home-town clubs. Nearly all the valley clubs were in the same position – Ebbw Vale, Abertillery, Newbridge, Cross Keys and others. The socioeconomic decline and the rugby decline ran exactly in parallel.

The league fixture between Pontypool and Newport on a bone-hard pitch in January 1992 probably signalled the death knell for the club. It was one of those nights where the crowd extended up the great bank on the east side of the ground and well up into the trees. As Pooler had lost their previous fixture against Newport, everything was set up for a brutal Pontypool backlash. In the event, it was something of a damp squib: a scrappy, ill-tempered 7–7 draw. Paul Turner came up to me afterwards and said, 'I don't know why, but somehow I think that game will be the finish of Pontypool.'

I believe that there was also a subtle lowering of standards at the club in the mid-'80s, which began to make both myself and others feel uncomfortable.

The Bish didn't conform to the values or standards we set at Pontypool and had to be put in his place once or twice, notably by Haydn Moreton on the plane over to Canada in 1985. I felt that the change in our values started with our attitude to the Bish. He was late for matches and often late to the start of training.

Over the course of time, the need Pross evidently felt to make provision for David Bishop's star quality eroded the democratic ethos the club had always stood for. If you make an exception for one man, however talented, where do you draw the new line in the sand? The level playing field had been lost, that one exception was enough. The Bish was capable of winning matches single-handed on the field, he was that good a player, but off the field his impact was just as profound. Although professionalism was the real issue, it was the first crack in the structure, the first deviation in the code by which Pontypool RFC had lived and died.

On one occasion I was warming up in the changing room next to Dai Thomas. He was changed and raring to go when the Bish ambled in five minutes before kick-off. Despite being fully prepared to play, Dai was told to change back into his clothes so that David Bishop could play instead of him. The action, however well-intentioned, sent out the wrong message to the other players about the need to meet a consistently high standard of behaviour on and off the field.

What happened to Dai Thomas also had a curious echo in Terry Cobner's own experience. Although there are a number of apocryphal stories of the team bus sweeping past Terry's house without stopping to pick him up, the mechanics of the rift between Cob and the club he loved so much were rather more prosaic.

He recalls: 'I wish I'd played one more year for Wales and one year less for Pontypool. Looking back on it, it is a matter of regret to me that I didn't follow that course. I could have played in the match that Wales lost 13–12 to the All Blacks at the end of 1978 – Paul Ringer played instead of me and I ended up coaching the forwards. Rod Morgan, the chairman of selectors, had called me in to coach the forwards in the week leading up to the match. That was the afternoon when three All Black forwards dived out of the lineout and Roger Quittenton chose to penalise Geoff Wheel instead. But I should really have been playing that day, not coaching the pack before the game.

'However I was voted onto the "big five" selection panel from outside the committee at the same time John Bevan was elected coach, and he asked me to take care of the forwards. So that was my pathway forward for the next four years and I enjoyed it immensely.

'My relationship with Pontypool had deteriorated. I left the club under a cloud. I'd fallen out with them, although there was, in all honesty, some fault on both sides. I'd been training poorly for some time and my heart wasn't really in it. Whether I should have told them I was no longer good enough, or they should have told me, is a moot point. Someone should have said something. I just wanted to get a chance to wave to the Bank before I left.

'The straw that broke the camel's back was a game where I was coming back from a cheek-bone injury for the Athletic side against Berry Hill – a nice gentle re-introduction! My idea was to play one match for the Athletic and one final home game for Pontypool, so that I could say a proper goodbye to the club and the supporters.

'Glyn Charles rang me to say that the game had been postponed from the Saturday [the pitch was waterlogged] to the following Wednesday night, but that the team would remain the same. So Brenda dropped me off on Wednesday before the game – I always liked to arrive early so I had plenty of time to prepare – and I started to get changed.

'A committeeman came in and said, "What are you doing?" and straight away my sixth sense was tingling; I knew something was wrong. I said, "I'm getting changed to play." He replied, "No, you're not. We're taking a look at a young boy from Newbridge tonight." He was not to be budged, so I put my clothes back on and walked out into the torrential rain.

'Brenda had already gone back home and I had to walk all the way back to Abersychan. It was a miserable and humiliating end, one that chilled me to the marrow. I couldn't believe they would do that to someone who had captained the club for over ten years during the era of its greatest success – and that boy who came down from Newbridge was never seen again, at least not at Pontypool Park.' (Terry Cobner)

Pontypool's outlook proved to be nowhere more brutal than in its treatment of its own favourite son. The timing could not have been more unfortunate, with Cob standing in as coach while Ray Prosser sat at the side of his wife Nancy's hospital bed. In the long term, I believe Pooler's alienation of Terry

Cobner cost it dear because he was one of the few men at the club with the necessary vision and drive; he could have helped it steer a course through the clashing rocks of professionalism successfully just over ten years later. When Eddie Butler left unexpectedly at the end of the 1988 season, the effect was magnified. I think most of the intellect and vision that could have negotiated the period of change to come left with them.

As rugby moved into the '90s and professionalism became inevitable, law-making changes also increasingly began to favour the team with the ball in hand, moving the game away from the Prosser philosophy inch by inch.

As Mike Ruddock points out: 'Outside the forwards, the other impressive aspect of Pontypool's play was what would now be termed their kick-and-chase game. They kicked accurately and their forwards were quick to chase and they hunted as a unit. As a loose forward, I found myself running backwards for large portions of the game. I couldn't target their half-backs. It was a very simple plan, but it was very demoralising for the opposition. Games against Pontypool tended to be ones when I spent a lot of time doing what I least enjoyed – trying to stop driving mauls or rescue ball from retreating scrums or save situations where we hadn't handled their kicking game well.

'The pasting I took in those matches against Pontypool influenced my coaching outlook forever afterwards. When I first started coaching, I was much more Pontypool than Swansea. I used to look for ways to tighten all the nuts and bolts first and my coaching outlook only began to change as the laws of the game changed during the '90s.

'For example, the change in the law that enabled the catcher to call a mark in the air rather than having to wait until he came back down to ground had a huge impact on the way a side like Pontypool wanted to play the game. It may have looked like a small tinkering, but in reality kick-chase teams had to rethink their whole approach as a result of it.

'Another small-but-significant change was the law allowing the man who went down on a ball that had been kicked through to bounce back to his feet before he could be engaged by the chasing team.

'Both changes protected the defensive team against the kicking game and neutered two important situations where Pontypool would be banking on hurting you by smashing beyond the defender and testing his will to fight back when the dose was repeated.

'Little by little, the advantages of playing the Pontypool way were eroded and it became less and less attractive to kick the ball away. As a coach watching these transformations taking place in rugby union, it nudged me closer to Swansea and Stan Addicott, although I never forgot my roots in Gwent.' (Mike Ruddock)

A kind of defiant bloody-mindedness had been the most invincible feature of Pontypool under Ray Prosser and Terry Cobner in the '70s and '80s. Cob, however, proved to be progressive and open-minded as a coach, recognising that at international level and in times ahead the Pontypool way would have to evolve to keep pace with the times.

Perk and Pross, by contrast, wanted to keep doing the things that had worked so well in the past, even though Rome was already beginning to catch fire around them. As a club, Pontypool was always right on the limit, punching well above its weight, and that made it very sensitive to the slightest change of circumstances. The changed socioeconomic climate in the valleys and the disruption of the heavy industry/grammar school rugby power-base in the mid-'80s – West Mon would turn comprehensive in 1982 – along with subtle changes in the law-making of the game, plus the loss of intellectual property represented by the departure of Eddie Butler and more especially Terry Cobner, were crucial to Pontypool's future as a club.

The cracks did not start to appear until Ray Prosser had called time on his epic coaching stint at Pontypool Park, however, after 18 years of almost unbroken success.

CHAPTER 8

THE NIGHTMARE '90s AND THE DAWN OF PROFESSIONALISM

The 1990s did not prove to be a happy decade either for Pontypool or for Welsh rugby as a whole. Aside from one rather startling success under the English-based coach Alan Davies in 1994, Wales failed to win any Five Nations championships. Moreover, 1994 was the only year in which Wales finished with more wins than losses, with the overall record between 1990 and 1998 (before the arrival of Graham Henry) reading Won 10, Lost 25 and Drawn 1. For the first time, Wales were the poor relations of the Five Nations, suffering the indignity of whitewashes in three championships between 1990 and 1995. In the two World Cups of 1991 and 1995, they could only manage two victories and failed to get out of the group stage on both occasions.

The low point came in Cardiff on 6 October 1991, when Wales lost to Western Samoa at the Arms Park. It was the first time in the competition's history that a seeded nation had been beaten by a non-seed, and it happened in the 'cathedral of rugby' in front of their own people. Ironically, Wales came a glaring second-best in the area where Ray Prosser had erected the totem of Pontypool strength – mental hardness built through physical conditioning. The Pacific Islanders played with a pace and dynamism that Wales could not match, as Robert Armstrong reported in *The Guardian*:

> As Wales found when they toured New Zealand three years ago, injuries proliferated largely because they did not have the requisite body hardness to withstand fierce though legitimate contact with the Samoans. The lock Phil May dislocated his shoulder, and Richie Collins and Tony Clement were also forced to retire with severe shoulder bruising. All will receive specialist treatment at a Brecon unit today.

Armstrong's colleague Frank Keating added prophetically:

> Some sixth sense must have inspired the Welsh management, weeks ago, to book the whole squad into the Penoyre Rehabilitation Centre for Sports Injuries near Brecon today. Some will be booking in for bed and several breakfasts, poor Wales.

It was a dark time for Welsh rugby at club level, too. In 1990–91 the Welsh Rugby Union had decided that the simple club-organised systems which had worked up to that point – the Whitbread Merit Table and the *Western Mail* Championship – were no longer sufficient to determine the best team in Wales. They arbitrarily split the top clubs in Wales into two leagues of ten clubs each. The sponsors of the Merit Table, Whitbread, had invested more than £64,000 in the amateur game in Wales over ten years by the end of the 1984–85 season. As Whitbread's managing director Gerry Walton put it, 'It's all part of putting something back into the community. The community in Wales is very important to the beer industry because they are the people who consume our products. We know that the clubs appreciate our financial contribution even if the general public are largely unaware of it. At Whitbread we all enjoy going to watch the matches and being part of the rugby community, so we don't look at it as purely a commercial operation . . . We have a very formal contract with the clubs; it's done on a handshake once every three years! That's the way it always has been and that's the way we hope it will be in the future – a gentlemen's agreement.' The days of gentlemen's agreements and the supra-commercial bond between sponsor and sport were sadly coming to an end.

The 10/10 split into two divisions also had some unforeseen negative consequences in respect of the traditional fixture list. As Graham Price says: 'We lost it back in the early '90s. Up until that point, there had been an unofficial Whitbread Merit Table and a *Western Mail* Championship. That was as good as having a league. So when the Welsh Rugby Union decided to take a more active role in managing the table and turning it into a league, all they really had to do was give it another name and maybe develop the sponsorship to give the clubs more funding.

'The union had kept out of club rugby previously. They organised the cup and the internationals, which were great, but they let the clubs organise their own fixture structure. We had no meddling back then; the clubs organised the championship and Merit Table fixtures. It was successful, relevant and very meaningful to all the clubs involved.

'Things started to go wrong when the union got involved directly. In their wisdom, they split the old Merit Table down the middle. They put ten clubs in the first division and ten in the second division. But the clubs retained the same fixture list, of course, and they continued to depend on relationships that had been forged over decades. At Pontypool, for instance, we'd still play someone like Abertillery – who were in the league below – on a Wednesday night. With the new structure, the league game on the Saturday had become the be-all and end-all so both teams would pick a weakened side, effectively a 2nd XV, for what had always been a great local derby. The matches became meaningless and instead of getting 10,000 or 15,000 people in on a wet Wednesday night, the crowds started to stay away. People slowly got out of the habit of watching midweek rugby and some of the local derbies were devalued.' (Graham Price)

As Ray Prosser told me himself at Pontypool market: 'People would come to watch Pontypool play Abertillery or Cross Keys rather than watch Wales playing the Springboks! There would be 20 people on every 16-seat bus on the way to the game. The buses would break down and they'd have to phone the depot to get an engineer out to repair 'em at the road side! I remember on one evening they literally tore those nice Sally gates down. There were so many people pressing to get in, the gates just came off their hinges. That was back in the mid-'70s.'

From Bob Dawkins' point of view: 'In the days of "The *Western Mail* 18" or the Merit Table, it would be the games between Pontypool and Newbridge or Abertillery that mattered. You couldn't get into the pubs or the fish-and-chip shops for the solid phalanxes of supporters from both sides. I used to tell my wife, "You can't drive a car down Pontypool high street on Saturday. Take the Twmpath road instead." The high street would be swamped with people going to the game in the afternoon and the whole town would come alive. It was a great day to be a shopkeeper or a publican.

'It wasn't just a game of rugby, especially where those local rivalries were concerned. The same was true in other valley towns like Pontypridd or Maesteg, I'm sure. When the game went to leagues, and later turned professional, something died in the game in Wales. It was certainly the beginning of the end for meaningful, top-end rugby in the valleys. What was 10,000 on a Wednesday night or Saturday afternoon is now 300 people. No one has any feeling for the regions, and what is more no one has any feeling left for their own clubs because they've been gutted by the big boys higher up the food chain. Now the shops – that were so vibrant – have been boarded up and you'd be hard pushed to tell whether there was a game on that afternoon or not by the number of people in the high street. I tell my wife, "You don't need to take the Twmpath road any more." It is a tragedy.' (Bob Dawkins)

Although it appeared to be a subtle change, when the union split the league into two divisions of ten teams each I believe it was an important precursor of things to come. The union had demonstrated for the first time a real interest in controlling league rugby in 1990–91 and at the same time a worrying blindness to the importance of traditional fixtures and regional networking. Fewer people wanted to watch the traditional derbies because the best players weren't playing in them and at that point it started costing the club more to put on a game than they were making back through gate receipts. On the community level, people began to get out of the habit of watching rugby games and regarding them as major social occasions – where they would go to the rugby simply to meet up with their mates and have a pint afterwards. So the process of unpicking the club fabric had already been set in motion, one thread at a time. It weakened the community within Pontypool and it broke down the links between Pontypool and its catchment area – the clubs that were part of both its heritage and, in previous years, its feeder system.

When the league structure became formal, the reality of *shamateur*-ism became more obvious. A club such as Newport, which had always been quite strict about compensating players for expenses and nothing more, suddenly began to offer players 'terms' both to keep existing talent and to attract players from other clubs to Rodney Parade.

Graham Price comments: 'It affected the Pontypool way quite severely because we had never paid players to play. The response from the committee was, "The day Pontypool starts paying its players is the day I'll be leaving." That was the popular refrain. After Pontypool toured New Zealand for about a month in 1992, on returning to the UK 15 players left the club. Ironically, it was supposed to be a development tour! All we ended up doing was developing players who then left for greener pastures. We were left with a 2nd XV for league matches and started shipping water in the league to the tune of 50 or 60 points per match.'

From the inception of leagues in 1990 to relegation in the 1994–95 season, Pontypool slipped steadily down the league table one place at a time, from sixth in the first year – the only 'amateur' season during the '90s when they finished with more wins than losses – to seventh the following term, eighth in 1992–93 and ninth in 1993–94. Bobby Windsor, Mark Ring and Bob Dawkins shouldered most of the coaching burden in the early '90s, as Dawkins recalls: 'Bobby Windsor was one of Pooler's greatest sons as a player, but as a coach he was not a very good communicator. He was a hard and ruthless man on the field but strangely sensitive and indecisive off it. It was difficult at the best of times to rely on Bob and he found it particularly hard to tell a player that he hadn't been selected to play. Even quarter of an hour before the game he would be afraid to tell him he wasn't starting!

'Bob had asked me to come in and help with the Pontypool backs while Mark Ring was away on holiday in Spain, but he didn't tell "Ringo", who was a kind of player-coach at that time! I think Bobby was afraid to tell him, too. Ringo was not best pleased when he got back to find me there taking sessions . . .

'Bobby wouldn't turn up to games if he thought we were going to get potatoed. He'd make an excuse not to come. I think he was so used to the conveyor belt of talent that used to run through the club from generation to generation during the '70s and '80s that he couldn't quite believe it when players stopped coming to Pontypool and the talent dried up. He just buried his head in the sand and wouldn't look.

'I would say that Bobby was a good coach of good players, but he didn't really know what to do with the ones who needed a lot of help. I worked my bollocks off in that final season [1993–94] trying to work out plans to avoid the big drop-out of the top division because I was running scared that I would be associated with a relegated Pontypool team. We won our final three games of the season, against Newbridge, Dunvant and Cross Keys, and I slept for a solid fifteen hours that Saturday night! I've never felt so relieved in my life . . . but it didn't stop us getting relegated the following season.' (Bob Dawkins)

Only a few short months after Pooler were demoted to the second tier of Welsh rugby, an even more traumatic event occurred on the global scale. On 26 August 1995, the International Rugby Board declared rugby union an 'open' game and therefore removed all restrictions on payments to players and coaches and all others associated with the game. The main impetus for the change came from the southern hemisphere, in particular from Australia, where an ongoing war over pay-television rights in rugby league had been waged between the rival concerns sponsored by Rupert Murdoch (News Corp) and Kerry Packer (Seven Network) since the early '90s. News Corp had been buying up the rights to broadcast a wide range of sports, including the Premier Football League in England and the NFL in the United States, in order to launch its pay-television platform, which started as BSkyB in the United Kingdom.

It was inevitable that the quarrel over rugby league should soon spread to its sister code in Australia. Much as he had done with cricket, Packer formed the breakaway World Rugby Corporation (WRC) to sign up the leading South African and New Zealand Test players and it was only the hurried formation of SANZAR – a body representing all three major southern hemisphere unions and backed financially by Rupert Murdoch – that persuaded the players to return to the fold of their home unions. SANZAR proposed a provincial competition, with teams from all three countries, to be called the Super 12, which had in reality been running in one form or another since 1992; an all-new Test-level championship to be called the Tri-Nations was also mooted. Naturally, the new body received a huge broadcast contract from none other than Murdoch's News Corp, to the tune of US$550 million over ten years.

Back in the UK, another of Pontypool's most notable sons was about to return to Wales, not to rescue the fortunes of his home-town club directly but to help oversee and organise the entire structure of Welsh rugby as it entered the professional era. Terry Cobner had taken up a teaching position in 1987 'with a special interest in rugby' at Oundle, one of the most famous private schools in England, having served his coaching apprenticeship under John Bevan with Wales and Ray Prosser at Pontypool.

'I went on to teach at Oundle school for ten years after leaving Pontypool and finishing my coaching stint with the national team. The change in culture was huge, and in Wales people kept telling me that I'd be back within a month. In fact I found it alien but very refreshing; it allowed me to breathe away from the goldfish bowl that was and is Welsh rugby. I went from sploshing around in my wellington boots at Fairwater to a finely manicured £30,000 per year school [the cost for a boarder]. They had nine rugby pitches, a 400 m cinder running track, a heated 50 m swimming pool, twenty-four tennis courts, eight squash courts and a shooting range.

'All I had to do was to go into the "Cloisters" and pin up a list of boys required for rugby, for training sessions four days per week with a game every Saturday afternoon. It ran like clockwork, with none of the rougher Pooler edges! The boys would all be there, waiting for me at 2.30 on the dot, warmed up and keen as mustard. It was superb. I taught them what I knew about rugby and I learned from them at the same time – it was always a two-way street. The 1st XV went through the season unbeaten in 1989. I wish I could have bottled some of what I'd learned and sold it back in Wales! I would have made a fortune.

'I finally took the proverbial "poisoned chalice" and became the Welsh Rugby Union's first professional Director of Rugby in 1995–96. I firmly believe I was appointed to the job 18 months too late because the wheels of professionalism were already turning, and turning fast. Vernon Pugh was the chairman of the IRB at the time and I had huge respect for him. He was an intellectual, but he could put the hobnail boots on when necessary, especially in negotiations.

'But Vernon was thrown over a barrel by the southern hemisphere in August 1995 because they'd given him an ultimatum: "We're turning professional. Come with us or accept a schism within the game." It was a done deal. Vernon chose the first option, even though he was well aware that the northern hemisphere wasn't prepared for the coming change in any shape or form. In the south they already had the Super rugby competition in place, and the fixture list that went with it; they had the players centrally contracted, they had the broadcasters and the sponsors already positioned. We had nothing.

'When the game turned professional, everyone in Wales thought they'd have to start paying players overnight. Clubs went into overdrive and some went bankrupt; players were being paid to train, never mind play! There were no structures in place and we needed to buy ourselves some time in order to build them well before the fanfare announcing the arrival of professionalism in the north. If necessary, we should have bitten the bullet and remained on an amateur footing until we knew we could handle the transition.' (Terry Cobner)

Jason Smith was a prominent legal representative for players and coaches at the time. He now specialises in advising businesses on start-up and long-term planning 'best practice': 'I got into it at the time the game turned professional; up until then players hadn't needed agents to represent them. As soon as the floodgates opened, it was sheer madness. It happened overnight and there was nothing planned or progressive about it. Every rugby union player suddenly had the same thought: "I am a rugby player and I need to get paid for what I do, therefore I need an agent to negotiate the best contract for me." This even applied to players in League Six North or whatever. It was bizarre. There was a gold rush and everyone stampeded to be a part of it.

'Professionalism created a culture where everyone was expecting to get paid, however high up or low down the playing ladder you were. In that sense, the situation was unworkable right from the start. Players became more mercenary and started moving clubs for more money rather than any other reason.

'Rugby union clubs were not set up to run as businesses from the days of amateurism and their administrative apparatus was amateur in outlook as a result. So they quickly began to overstretch themselves and their finances when the gold rush happened. Right from the start I felt it was unsustainable. About five times every week, as I did the rounds negotiating contracts for my players, I used to think, "They're going to go bust." There were no proper business models in place as a rule, although you did get the odd attempt to break away and rationalise rugby as a business from the likes of Cardiff and Swansea when they played in the English Premiership for a season.

'So the basic problem as regionalisation loomed on the horizon in Wales was that too much money was circulating around too little quality and being spread over far too wide an area. Clubs were still streamlining their administrative apparatus, creating business models that should have been there from the beginning and recovering from the mistakes that had been made at the outset when the game turned professional in August 1995.

'Unfortunately, the same ill-conceived pattern was repeated when regional rugby in Wales was introduced before the 2003–04 season, which showed that the essential lessons had still not been learned.' (Jason Smith)

The combination of an arcane amateur administrative apparatus and the socioeconomic decline in the area with the closure of heavy industries was fatal to a club like Pontypool. Terry Cobner, for one, believes that 'once the game went professional Pontypool was doomed. It was just a matter of time because there's never been any real money in the area.'

The administration was so amateur that no one even knew where the gate money went after a game. As Gordon Richards, a stalwart of Pontypool and Panteg cricket club, says: 'Pross would ask, "How many people do you think were there last night, Jockey?"

'I would reply, "I reckon about 10,000, Pross."

'"Yes, that's my thought as well. You wait until the takings have been counted, mind. It will be more like 5,000!"'

Cobs and Pross would constantly bemoan the profusion of entrances to the Park and the recruitment of members of the public who used to volunteer to take the money as supporters came in. The money the club should have been making too often bled away into the cracks. The huge gates that Pontypool attracted never seemed to translate into revenue for the club and, of course, that mattered far more at a time when the club was being run on a professional basis.'

Rumour has it that the majority of the money was distributed in secret among the players, who still could not appear to be paid by Pontypool RFC in broad daylight, but no one knew for sure. It was a typical Pontypool solution. Towards the end of Ray Prosser's reign as coach, the players had been paid in kind by Peter Lawler, a lifelong fan who owned an engineering firm in the area. Peter would find ways to give the players money and Pross would turn a blind eye. But the issue of finance needed to be confronted head-on in the professional era and at Pontypool it wasn't. Key administrative questions, such as whether the club should continue to play at Pontypool Park or move to a new venue, or whether Elm House was the best administrative site, were never even considered, to the best of my knowledge. The club administration turned a blind eye and hoped that everything would continue just as before. The club lacked a man of vision to plot the way forward and a professional administrator to implement that vision.

On the larger scale of Welsh rugby, Terry Cobner well understood the need to get the money available concentrated into a smaller number of fully professional sides: 'At the time [1996–97] we had twelve teams competing in Europe from the base of the Welsh league and every last one of them was getting its arse kicked, whether it was in the Challenge Cup or the Heineken Cup proper. The talent spread was far too thin. So the first leap was from twelve to eight premier clubs – it should have been four, but I think that was too much of a jump to manage for the political interests in Wales.

'There was a special general meeting and when I stood up to speak I could feel the general committee boring into my back, and the clubs boring into my front – they all thought I was hanging myself. But thankfully the motion was passed and twelve became eight, and finally in 2003 the five regions. It was all about what was achievable politically in relation to the money and the talent available. Personally, I didn't care if we went down the route of regions or super-clubs, but politically regions were the only solution. The rest of the game in Wales would never have accepted the super-club idea.' (Terry Cobner)

With more playing resources being concentrated in a smaller number of clubs, the issue of centrally contracting the players to the Welsh rugby union became a more urgent issue. The gradual progression from twelve to eight and then five turned out to be more of a hindrance than a help to the process of uncoupling the players from their club allegiances.

'Central contracts were definitely discussed at the time. Vernon came to me and said, "There are meetings being held in Cardiff and a certain individual is attempting to contract Welsh squad members to himself. We need to get the core of the Wales squad contracted to the union. If we control the players, we will control the game in Wales."

'With the limited funds available, the best we could do was dual contracts, with players contracted to both the union and their clubs, but with the union contract having primacy. We only had enough money to contract those we considered the best eight to ten players in Wales. However, this brought us into confrontation with the clubs and it took the intercession of Graham Henry, who was by then national coach, to surrender the contracts back to the clubs. Graham couldn't see any point in a bitter, long-term fight. Our attempt at central contracting was a failure and it was the one and only time I ever saw Vernon Pugh walk out of a meeting. The amount of conflict generated by the need to control players' contracts was disproportionate, with club fighting union, and then club fighting club for control of a player. It was immensely debilitating, a complete mess.' (Terry Cobner)

From the point of view of Kevin Bowring, the national coach at the time, the debate lacked a necessary third party who could represent the players' interests: 'I was the national coach when the issue of central contracts first arose. The two protagonists were Vernon Pugh, chairman of the WRU, and Peter Thomas, the first of the benefactors within Welsh rugby down at Cardiff, who owned the players' contracts. The battle was for ownership of the players and the right to direct their affairs. At the time there was no independent body to represent the players' interests, so it became a straightforward tug of war. From a player's point of view, they want both. They want to be sure they will have an opportunity to play for their country and they want to be paid for their services on a day-to-day basis at their clubs. At one stage Gwyn Jones came up to me and said, "Look, I'm not playing for either my club or my country at the moment, how can it be sorted out?" So it has to be a tripartite agreement that includes the needs of club, country and players themselves.'

Administrative chaos was matched by increased chaos on the field. With most attitudes within the game in Wales remaining stubbornly amateur, the fortunes of the national team rapidly reached a tipping point. The watershed proved to be the Wales tour of Australia and the Pacific Islands in the summer of 1996. The performances of the Australian teams Wales played on that trip came as a profound shock to Kevin Bowring, who is now the director of elite coach development at the RFU:

'In 1995 the game had gone professional and I was appointed head coach of Wales – the first full-time appointment in the professional era. In the summer of 1996 Wales toured Australia and it was a huge wake-up call for us. It was a real eye-opener to witness first-hand just how far the southern hemisphere had kicked on with the introduction of the Super rugby competition.'

Although it had first started as far back as 1992 in the amateur era, with only six teams, the advent of professionalism allowed the new Super 12 competition to aggressively seek out sponsorship. The Super 12, with four regions from South Africa, five from New Zealand and three from Australia, gave News Corp a unique selling point, a product they could sell on pay television that had no equivalent on the free-to-air market. The income streams guaranteed by News Corp were a huge shot in the arm for Australian rugby union, which badly needed a foothold in the sporting market at home, with strong competing interests in the form of Aussie rules and the NRL. With their playing talent now concentrated in only three regional sides – the New South Wales Waratahs, the Queensland Reds and the newly formed ACT Brumbies – and all their players centrally contracted and participating in a top-notch competition only just below Test match quality, Australian rugby was primed to explode.

Kevin Bowring continues: 'The speed and quality of play that had obviously been engendered by the Super rugby competition in the spring came as a real shock to us when we toured Australia in the middle of June. Although we were capable of scoring 30 points per game, we found ourselves losing by huge scorelines. Super 12 sides were used to playing constructive attacking rugby at high speed and we lost by 69–30 to the new Brumbies franchise under Rod Macqueen. At half-time we were in the game at 24–23 after scoring a great try from a counter-attack by Rob Howley, but we just couldn't live with them in the second period. They were simply too fast and too fit for us.

'We went on to lose 51–41 to Australia "B". We were shipping far too many points outside the Test matches against opponents we would have been expecting to at least contain. In the Tests themselves, we were beaten 56–25 at Brisbane in the first match and crushed 42–3 in the second game at Sydney. So we went through that tour conceding on average 50 points per game even to provincial opponents!

'Terry Cobner was the Director of Rugby in Wales at that time and we sat down and had long conversations about what could be done to improve the quality of Welsh rugby by changing the structure. Terry suggested, and I was fully in support of the idea, that four or five regions were the way forward in Wales.

'When professionalism was first introduced, I think the dominant attitude from the players was, "Give me money to do what I'm already doing." Of course no one really knew how much money they ought to be paying [the players] in any case. The conclusion drawn from the 1996 Australia tour was the very reverse of that message. It was now: "Give me money to do something very different, and very much better than what I'm already doing." It was a difficult transition period and the southern hemisphere had gotten the jump on us with the Super 12. They were already playing a faster and more skilful game than we were capable of. There was no comparison between the two games being played in the north and the south, and I would estimate that we were already about three or four years behind in our professional development.' (Kevin Bowring)

Four years behind was exactly right. The first version of the Super rugby competition had been trialled as far back as 1992 as 'The Super 6'. When Ireland toured New Zealand that summer, they had lost both the Test matches and all three of their games against the top provincial sides – Canterbury, Manawatu and Auckland – they encountered. Against the three provinces they had conceded an average of fifty-three points per game, and that was Wales-in-Australia territory.

The eminent Irish rugby journalist Brendan Fanning recalls trying to get a few words after one training session with the

Auckland coach of the time, one Graham Henry. 'It was pissing down with rain and I had to run across the length of the field to get to Graham. When I arrived breathlessly in front of him, I only had enough strength left to ask him one question, "What do you expect from tomorrow's game?" He turned and replied briskly, "Well, we're just a provincial side taking on a team full of internationals, so I wouldn't expect too much." Then he gave me his trademark grin, and there was a sparkle in his eye. I couldn't determine whether he was being serious or not. I only found out the next day, when Auckland whipped Ireland by sixty-two points to seven!'

Five years later, an Ireland development squad returned to the Shaky Isles to undergo an even more traumatic experience. One of the positive highlights of the tour was a hard-fought but decisive 41–10 loss to the NZ Maori. In his book *From There to Here: Irish Rugby in the Professional Era*, Brendan remembers the players laughing and joking and singing on the team bus afterwards, so happy were they that defeat had come by a relatively narrow margin of 30 points. Then Brian Ashton, the head coach, stood up:

> For f**k's sake, you're a national side, development or not, and you've been beaten by 30 points, and you're f***ing happy? You should be as quiet as mice, going home to your room, sitting in your f***ing room and nobody coming out until we go training.

That summed it up. This was professional rugby.

Although the Welsh Premier league was eventually reduced to eight teams for the start of the 1997–98 season, it did not trigger any immediate improvement in the fortunes of the national side. Wales managed two creditable victories in the 1998 Five Nations tournament, but they also endured two hammerings of fifty points or more, losing 60–26 to England at Twickenham and then being whitewashed 51–0 at their temporary Wembley 'home' on a sunlit April afternoon by France. The defeat against France was enough for Kevin Bowring to be hung out to dry as the ritual scapegoat for failure, despite a respectable 52 per cent winning record as Wales coach.

He recalls: 'It was our best championship since 1994 and I didn't think we were as bad as those two heavy defeats suggested. I wanted to introduce changes. We needed a far more competitive structure and things had to be in place so we could make an impact in the World Cup. I told them it was the most important time in the history of Welsh rugby. The breakaway of Cardiff and Swansea [in 1998–99 Cardiff and Swansea forewent their domestic fixture list and linked up with the English Premiership clubs on a "friendly" basis] benefited those players enormously. The higher standard has allowed them to develop and it just wasn't there in the Welsh League.

'I also drew up a development plan for Welsh rugby, including central contracts for the top twenty-five players up until at least the end of a 1999 season which peaked with a World Cup on our own patch; the establishment of four regional teams to play in Europe; and the appointment of both a financial officer to negotiate player contracts and a full-time assistant coach to help out the head man. The union responded by questioning me. "What are you doing all this for? You should be out there on the field coaching." They made excuses in the short term and put it off until some time in an indefinite future. They said they might have a look at it before the World Cup in 2003. They expected me to carry the can. I couldn't compromise any more. People were making decisions who didn't know anything about the world game.' (Kevin Bowring)

At the same time Pontypool continued to languish outside the top tier of Welsh club rugby, narrowly avoiding their second relegation in three seasons with a final day 14–8 win over UWIC. Once again the fortunes of the national side and the little club up the Eastern valley seemed to be running in parallel, for better or for worse.

Worse was yet to come for Wales. On their summer tour of South Africa after Kevin Bowring's departure, a makeshift management team and a weakened touring squad came within an ace of the ultimate humiliation when Springbok hooker Naka Drotske dropped a pass with no one in front of him in the dying seconds of a 15-try rout. If the pass had been snared, Drotske would have walked in to score and the scoreboard would have ticked over into three figures. As it was, Wales lost 96–13 and were branded 'the worst international team I have ever seen' by Springbok coach Nick Mallett.

Back in Pontypool Park, Ray Prosser would still be walking the Grotto to his favoured spot on the second peak well into his 70s, but now the walks would be taken on his own. No one in Wales was following the example he had set 25 years before, either physically or spiritually. It would take a New Zealander from Auckland to do that, to revive a little of the 'spirit of the '70s' in Wales. His name was Graham Henry.

CHAPTER 9

THE LONG ROAD TO REGIONALISATION

The arrival of Graham Henry in Wales sparked a transformation in the fortunes of the national team. In October 1999, Wales embarked on a ten-match unbeaten run on the approach to the first World Cup of the professional era. The perception of Henry as 'the Great Redeemer' granted him an unusual amount of power (for a coach) to influence the structure of the game in Wales and in 1998 he took on the proposals originally made by Kevin Bowring. Henry came from a background in which he had seen the New Zealand provinces more or less successfully merged into larger regional entities for the purposes of the Super 12 competition. Some of the mergers weren't entirely comfortable: the Blues franchise absorbed the traditional enemies of Auckland and North Harbour, while the Hurricanes were a blend of Taranaki and Wellington. But overall, it worked. Through the Super 12, New Zealand was able to identify its elite rugby athletes and pinpoint the processes that were needed to develop an elite rugby athlete in the professional era far more quickly.

Wales was succeeding, but club performances in the Heineken Cup failed to convince. Only one Welsh club side, Llanelli in 1999–2000, advanced beyond the quarter-final stage in the four seasons between 1998 and 2001. There was little doubt in the minds of the key decision-makers in Welsh rugby at the time – the Director of Rugby Terry Cobner and head coach Graham Henry – that the number of fully professional entities had to be reduced to no more than four regions or super-clubs. The money and the talent in the game in Wales were still being spread far too thinly and, in any case, Terry Cobner had only viewed the reduction to eight clubs in 1997–98 as an intermediate stage to something both better and more radical.

At the same time, the Welsh Rugby Union was hamstrung in its attempts to consolidate the professional base further by the 1997 'Loyalty Agreement' with those eight clubs – Swansea, Cardiff, Pontypridd, Ebbw Vale, Neath, Llanelli, Bridgend and Newport. The agreement guaranteed that at least eight clubs in the Premier Division would enjoy the privilege of being in the highest position in the national club hierarchy – and it presented a rather obvious legal obstacle to making the desired changes in Welsh rugby at the top end.

Opposition to any change in Welsh rugby was reinforced periodically by the findings of reports such as that of Sir Tasker Watkins's working party in 2001, which warned against any reduction in the number of clubs in the Premier Division. Its recommendations included central contracts for international players and an expansion of the new Celtic League, with home and away fixtures. The report emerged from its conservative shell to lambast the prospect of a change to regional rugby:

This has so far received no tangible support, which is not surprising seeing our leading clubs are famous and have been for a century or more. There is surely nothing a few, so called, super teams could do that these clubs could not do as well if not much better. So why destroy clubs which we regard with pride and respect.

The stark reality behind any expansion of the Celtic League was that Welsh clubs – and there were nine of them in the inaugural Celtic League in the 2000–01 season – could not even threaten to succeed in that competition, let alone at the higher level represented by the Heineken Cup. They filled out the bottom half of both the two playing pools, lost more than 60 per cent of their games and neither of the two clubs that qualified for the knockout stage (Llanelli and Neath) advanced beyond the quarter-finals. As things stood, the Welsh clubs could not achieve success in any multi-national club competition and they were not sustainable financially.

Kevin Bowring understood that a fully professional intermediate tier was necessary as a springboard to Test rugby after his experiences with Wales in Australia: 'The question was, "How do we create a higher level of competition in Wales to bring the skills and conditioning values up to that benchmark?" As the national coach, I wanted a better tier of competition sitting just below international level. I was aware of the chasm that would have developed further in those areas had we not conceived a new structure for the game in Wales. We needed a fix quickly and it was not to be found in the league as it was. If you look at the positive effects of regional rugby in Wales, the one thing it has achieved indisputably is success at national level. Since 2003–04 when it was first implemented, we've won three Grand Slams in eight years, the first of which arrived barely two seasons after regional rugby started.' (Kevin Bowring)

Both Graham Henry and Terry Cobner were well aware that there was not enough talent or money to sustain more than at most three professional entities in Wales, as Terry Cobner states: 'There were three points we had to consider after the game had moved into the professional era:

How much money have we got?
How much talent have we got?
What fixture list do we need?

'In terms of money and talent, I've no doubt we only had enough of both to sustain three regions or super-clubs . . . but that wasn't going to provide the fixture list we needed. I'd held talks with [Gloucester chairman] Tom Walkinshaw in England and he made it clear that England weren't interested in Welsh regions. They only wanted Cardiff and Swansea, and that was it. Of course, no one in Wales would have agreed to that, so it was a non-starter.' (Terry Cobner)

When Nick (Bishop) talked to Graham Henry about it, privately he would concede that he believed Wales could only sustain two regions, in terms of the player base and financially.

As Henry says: 'I think there were only about sixty to seventy good players who might have been able to play professional footie in the country, so that would mean two squads of about thirty to thirty-five players each. At the most you could have had three professional teams, but that would have been the outer limit. But the game in Wales was just too political . . . I knew I'd never be able to get the idea of only two regional teams through, even though that was all we could really manage in terms of playing resources. All the big clubs along the M4 would want their share of the pie.

'They would never admit that they had such a limited pool of elite players, even though I'd seen that was the case from the first Probables versus Possibles trial match we'd staged a few months after I became Wales coach. I was there when they created the Super rugby competition back in the mid-'90s in the southern hemisphere, and divided the New Zealand provinces into five regions, so I reckoned I had a better understanding of what being an elite professional athlete in rugby really meant.' (Graham Henry)

An East Wales and a West Wales side, or a three-way division between Monmouthshire, Glamorgan and Carmarthen, should therefore have been the major options when Wales decided to adopt a regional structure, given the money and talent available. But of course these weren't the only considerations: politics and local interests – what Graham Henry used to call 'village-isms' – would intervene on both counts.

The two-region East/West Wales division had a limited but promising history, both teams having played the legendary 1967 All Blacks and the 1973 Australians. Indeed the East Wales side came out of the game against New Zealand with a highly creditable draw in the only tour match where the All Blacks failed to register a victory. They went on to beat the touring Wallabies in 1973 by 19–11. Various amalgams of Glamorgan, Gwent and Monmouthshire, in addition to the usual club combination sides such as Neath/Aberavon and Pontypool/ Cross Keys, had appeared against touring nations throughout the 1960s and '70s.

In December 2001, two main proposals were presented to the leading clubs by the WRU. Both were to some degree compromised by the need to satisfy existing political interests, and both were presented with the important 'rider' that the players be centrally contracted to the WRU, who would also retain the power to move players between clubs/regions as they saw fit. The proposals were as follows:

1. Five franchised super-clubs based on existing clubs – Cardiff, Newport, Swansea, Llanelli and probably Pontypridd
2. Four regions with the provisional titles of West Wales, South-East Wales, Gwent and the Valleys.

Under both schemes, the newly established teams would compete in both the Celtic League and the Heineken Cup, with a ten-team Welsh League operating underneath them in a second-tier competition. The super-club concept came under the most immediate pressure because Bridgend, Caerphilly, Neath and Ebbw Vale were all lying outside it unless some unlikely club mergers took place. The four-region idea received most support, despite running against the spirit of both the old loyalty contract and the new 'joint venture' agreement Bridgend had recently signed with the 'big five' clubs. Nonetheless, Henry said he was encouraged that there was a genuine desire for change in the air, having attended the WRU's previous general committee meeting: 'It was very positive. Everybody is keen to make progress and do what is best for Welsh rugby. This is a rare opportunity for change. If we don't take it, we might as well all pack up and go fishing.'

With an invisible deadline for the agreement to be in place of the 2003 World Cup, the need for a solution became increasingly urgent. When Graham Henry, one of the main movers and shakers behind regional rugby, resigned from his position as Welsh coach early in 2002, that urgency became tinged with desperation.

'Everything is under consideration. Everybody knows we have been looking at the future structure of the game for a long time. We will look at everything, whether that is provincial, regional, franchises or super-clubs. Hopefully, we will have a recommendation to be put to an EGM by the end of the year,' commented the WRU secretary Dennis Gethin early in September 2002.

David Moffett, one of the chief brains behind SANZAR and a previous CEO of the New Zealand rugby football union, was appointed as WRU group chief executive in December 2002. Moffett had a track record of drastic cost-cutting and the revolutionising of the business side of organisations with which he had been involved. In another previous role, Moffett had been chief executive at the National Rugby League in Australia in 1999 after it moved to a 14-team competition. The South Sydney Rabbitohs, Australia's oldest club, had been kicked out of the competition after refusing to merge. Moffett was not a man who believed in gradual change; he was someone who did not mind in the least leaving some very obvious tracks – and not a little blood – in the sand behind him. When he was appointed in Wales, everyone knew there would be casualties.

Moffett was initially tasked with reducing the union's crippling debt of £55–60 million, the majority of which had been incurred by the building of the Millennium Stadium and pushing through the change to regional rugby. Some of Moffett's initial ideas, which included the cultivation of North Wales as a new playing resource, showed what a double-edged sword his appointment could turn out to be. While he was refreshingly free of the 'village-isms' that beset those in Wales, he had a grasp of Welsh rugby geography that was at times childish in outlook.

After much toing and froing, with different and ever more unlikely club mergers being proposed on a regular basis in Welsh rugby's very own version of musical chairs, a final format for the Welsh regions was agreed on 1 April 2003. With Cardiff and Llanelli stubbornly holding out for stand-alone status, the remaining six clubs would merge to form a total of five regions:

- Bridgend and Pontypridd would merge to form the Celtic Warriors
- Neath and Swansea would merge to form the Neath-Swansea Ospreys
- Newport and Ebbw Vale would merge to form the Gwent Dragons

- Llanelli and Cardiff were to stand alone and form the basis of the Llanelli Scarlets and the Cardiff Blues respectively

Whatever idea David Moffett and the club benefactors wanted to implement, I believe that they both needed to commit fully to two essential elements within the new format:

A new point of identity: The new regional identities had to be sufficiently far removed from their club roots to embrace support from the wider catchment areas they were supposed to represent

Central contracts: The players had to be centrally contracted to the union, which could then move players around to create the optimal balance between the representative sides

On point one, there is a definite difference between continuing to represent what you have always represented and pretending to represent something new while remaining obstinately the same.

As Graham Price points out: 'There was confusion between club and region, so that the regions never started from a clean slate. The Blues were too easily identified with Cardiff, and Llanelli with Scarlets, for example. Pontypool fans were first asked to identify with the Warriors, then with the Dragons after the Warriors were dissolved!

'Everyone knew that the Dragons were basically Newport, so they were never going to build any support base further up the valley. Of course Newport will say they've attempted to embrace their catchment area outside the city itself, but they haven't. The truth falls between the stools – and into the confusion. It's there in the name: Newport-Gwent Dragons. No one really knows whether it's Newport or Gwent, so none of the supporters believe in it either. It's a strange bastard child.

'There was a county system in place – albeit not a very popular one – which might have helped solve the problem of disentangling the regions from the clubs. Monmouthshire and Glamorgan had played matches against touring sides in the amateur era, as had East and West Wales, so there were some points of identity beyond the clubs already in existence.

'The alternative was to make Cardiff, Newport, Llanelli and Swansea the representative sides without fudging the issue, sliding all the other clubs back to semi-pro or amateur level. At least that would have been clear in establishing a clear base of support. Even that would have been better than what they did.' (Graham Price)

When the regions eventually came into existence, three of the four entities failed to represent anything other than their past. There was no sense of the new.

Kevin Bowring comments: 'When the regions were first formed, I think only the Ospreys truly embraced a new identity. Llanelli was still obstinately Llanelli, although it was now called the Scarlets; Cardiff was still Cardiff, but it was now called the Blues; and after a brief struggle Newport was still Newport, as in the Newport-Gwent Dragons. Pontypridd, Pontypool, Bridgend, Aberavon, Maesteg, Newbridge and a host of other clubs were effectively left unrepresented, especially after the disintegration of the Celtic Warriors. Pontypool was possibly the most famous of those clubs, with its history and contribution to the second golden era of Welsh rugby in particular, but it was by no means the only one.' (Kevin Bowring)

Jason Smith, a legal representative for a number of players, states: 'The WRU and the club benefactors did not start with a clean sheet of paper. They started by trying to protect pre-existing interests and embrace other people in those interests. You won't convince me that Cardiff and Llanelli and

Newport were thinking about anyone other than Cardiff, Llanelli and Newport when they signed up for regional teams. They were not thinking about a fresh start.

'The identity of the regions was ultimately far too close to the identity of the clubs playing in the next tier down in the Premiership. So you had duplication – Llanelli playing as both Llanelli RFC and the Scarlets, Cardiff as Cardiff RFC and the Blues, Newport as Newport RFC and the Newport-Gwent Dragons. The identities were never completely separated from region to Premiership club.

'There was a stronger impulse to cooperate and make that fresh start between Neath and Swansea, and that's why the franchise took off more quickly than the others. Building a new stadium was part of that dynamic. Leighton Samuel said he wanted to, but he never did it at the Warriors. Most of the Welsh club stadia weren't up to the standard required for a regional franchise, and they would certainly not have attracted significant sponsorship. I remember taking my son to Rodney Parade and the toilet was a trough. He looked at me and said, "Dad, where's the toilet?" and I could only helplessly point at the trough.' (Jason Smith)

The two- or three-region proposal would therefore have helped create those new identities and convinced the clubs not directly involved in mergers that there might be something worth supporting in the new structure. It would also have provided sufficient opportunity to play, with potentially sixteen home-and-away fixtures in a Celtic League composed of three Welsh, four Irish and two Scottish regions, plus six group matches in the Heineken Cup. That would have given a total of 22 matches, compared to the 16 played by professionals in the Super 15 in the southern hemisphere. The other obvious rationale for the two- or three-region proposal lay in the fact that, as both Terry Cobner and Graham Henry well knew, there were not more than about 70 top-end players in Wales at the time. They could have been split straightforwardly into two squads, or supplemented by a mix of a dozen or so of the top foreign imports and next best Welsh players and divided into three. Either way they could have provided that effective intermediate step to Test match rugby.

The following two squads would have accommodated all the best available talent in Welsh rugby at the time quite comfortably.

West Wales

Front Row: Paul James, Duncan Jones, Iestyn Thomas, Adam Jones, Ben Evans, Rob McBryde, Matthew Rees, Huw Bennett

Second Row: Chris Wyatt, Rob Sidoli, Brent Cockbain, Deiniol Jones

Back Row: Scott Quinnell, Jonathan Thomas, Andy Lloyd, Dafydd Jones, Richie Pugh, Martyn Williams, Emyr Lewis

Half-backs: Dwayne Peel, Mike Phillips, Stephen Jones, Ceri Sweeney, Gavin Henson

Centres: Sonny Parker, Scott Gibbs, Mark Taylor, Matthew Watkins, Leigh Davies

Back Three: Shane Williams, Dafydd James, Mark Jones, Gareth Thomas, Barry Davies, Garan Evans.

East Wales

Front Row: Gethin Jenkins, John Yapp, T. Rhys Thomas, Mefin Davies, Gareth Williams, Chris Horsman, Chris Anthony, Andrew Lewis

Second Row: Craig Quinnell, Ian Gough, Andrew Moore, Luke Charteris

Back Row: Richard Bryan, Jason Forster, Nathan Thomas, Nathan Budgett, Michael Owen, Richard Parks, Ryan Jones

Half-backs: Gareth Cooper, Ryan Powell, Iestyn Harris, Neil
    Jenkins, Nick Robinson
Centres: Andy Marinos, Tom Shanklin, Jamie Robinson, Hal
    Luscombe, Jonny Bryant
Back Three: Craig Morgan, Kevin Morgan, Nathan Brew, Nick
    Walne, Gareth Wyatt, Rhys Williams.

The issue of foreign imports was something that would have
been addressed by a commitment to a maximum of three
regions, too. In the first season that the Welsh regions played
in the Celtic League, there were ten non-Welsh qualified players
at the Blues, seven at the Dragons, six at the Scarlets and three
apiece at the Ospreys and Celtic Warriors. That's a grand total
of 29 players – virtually a region by itself – playing in sides
that are designed to produce and develop talent for the Wales
national team. It didn't make much, if any, sense.

Kevin Bowring considers some parallel examples in England:
'It's far easier to invest in playing talent early when there are
lesser numbers to consider – and no foreign import complications.
I can give you a good example of that. In 2008, Joe Simpson
was nominated for the IRB Young Player of the Year award
after the 2008 Junior World Cup, ahead of Australia's Will
Genia.

'Genia was already playing Super rugby for the Reds and in
2009 he duly ascended to the Wallaby squad for the 2009
Tri-Nations, as it was then. He came off the bench in the first
four games before starting against the Springboks in Brisbane
and the All Blacks in Wellington.

'Joe Simpson only became first-choice scrum-half for Wasps
in time for the beginning of the 2009–10 season and played
for the Saxons in the 2009 Churchill Cup. These were two
very different pathways, with Genia able to come to the
forefront very quickly because of a simple regional structure

which "belonged" to the nation's past. At that time there were only four Australian franchises, including an embryonic Western Force, and two native Aussie-qualified scrum-halves in the Reds squad.

'Wasps had two other 9s with international experience ahead of Simpson in the shape of Irishman Eoin Reddan and Kiwi Mark Robinson. Both had already played international rugby for their countries and obviously couldn't be considered for England. So Joe's pathway was blocked for a significant portion of time.

'Young George Ford has also found his pathway blocked at Leicester, although this time by another Englishman in Toby Flood. Owen Farrell and George played side by side in an outstanding England Under-20 team that could have beaten New Zealand in the final of the 2011 Junior World Cup. One went on to play for England the next season, the other got stuck on the bench for his club side and lacked the same number of opportunities to express his talent at the top level. A simple regional model sitting well above the club game, with players centrally contracted to the host union, gives you the ability to control and expedite the development of players like that.' (Kevin Bowring)

The Ospreys were the only one of the new regions to experience success on and off the field immediately after the formation of the regions and it was because they committed to a new point of identity wholeheartedly. Their commitment was illustrated by two of the most meaningful signposts:

- The building of a new stadium
- The abandonment of the club name

The Ospreys went beyond the Gnoll and St Helens to ground-share with Swansea City FC at a new all-seater venue, the

Liberty Stadium, on the banks of the Tawe. They were also the first to drop the club title 'Neath-Swansea' from their name in May 2005. The Dragons went the opposite way, insisting on adding 'Newport' to theirs.

Jason Smith continues: 'When I advise businesses, either at the start or when they are in transition, I always emphasise the importance of communication – communication with staff, suppliers, customers, etc. – but there was very little evidence of that communication in the regions. They didn't communicate with their projected support base and as a result they tended to alienate it. Newport was supposed to work in conjunction with Ebbw Vale, but it alienated its partner and by extension the rest of its support base in the valleys by insisting on the inclusion of NEWPORT in double-size font [twice the size of "Gwent"] in the regional title.'

Kevin Bowring comments: 'There's a question arising when you choose to retain a club name, as the Dragons did, whether you're truly trying to connect to other parts of your regional catchment area. Did the Dragons connect with Ebbw Vale, for example? Was the connection fostered and sold? The truth is that this work was not done and the traditional breeding grounds of Welsh rugby, like Pontypool and Ebbw Vale, suffered as a consequence.' (Kevin Bowring)

The success of the Ospreys in attracting support from well beyond their traditional catchment area was derived from their willingness to drop the Neath-Swansea name. Not only did it enable them to attract a wider base of support, it also gave them other concrete financial advantages, for example in the sale of replica rugby jerseys. The Ospreys jersey sales back in 2006–07 were second only to Munster in the UK, with 45,000 shirts being sold that season. At the time, the marketing director of Kooga (the designer and manufacturer of the Ospreys jersey), Bill Newton, considered it to be a sales phenomenon. 'Once again, the Ospreys shirt has continued to defy belief and sell in huge numbers. It sells well right across the country, in Scotland, London, Cornwall, the North West – there isn't anywhere that it doesn't sell.' No fewer than eight different sponsors had their names emblazoned on the Ospreys jersey, bringing over £500,000 worth of revenue into the region's coffers. All in all, no fewer than 70,000 items of Ospreys/Kooga material were sold in a season during which the region won the Magners League and reached the EDF Cup final at Twickenham.

The Ospreys attracted sponsorship and support from well beyond their traditional pastures. You could see Ospreys jerseys on the high streets of towns anywhere in west or central South Wales and there were stories of coaches travelling out of Dyfed, Scarlet heartland, to watch the Ospreys play in Swansea. They weren't afraid to embrace an identity that was neither Neath nor Swansea, although it was rooted in both. As a brand and a marketing concept, it's far easier to sell to a wider audience when you're not confined by the geographical boundary of a particular town or city.

The Scarlets followed the Ospreys' lead in the autumn of 2008, dropping the Llanelli name and within a couple of months moving into their new Parc Y Scarlets home.

Even an iconic West Wales rugby 'father' such as Derek Quinnell recognised the need to separate the identities of the club and the region clearly. 'It will be much simpler for the region to be known as the Scarlets and our Premiership side to be Llanelli – it makes sense. The name "the Scarlets" embodies everything that is great about the rugby region as a whole, takes away any confusion and is simpler all round.'

The Parc Y Scarlets was completed in time for the start of the 2008–09 season and has become a focal point for the improvement in attendances in the Scarlets franchise – and their will to move out into the community they represent, which goes as far as the Heart and Soul Kitchen, built within the stadium, which provides a natural setting for players and fans to interact. The idea was to make the game one small part of the Parc Y Scarlets match-day experience and people have bought into it, with the Scarlets' average gate standing as high as 10,335 in late 2012, making them Wales's best-supported team at the time.

It's hardly a coincidence that the most successful regions in terms of playing achievements and improved attendances are the Scarlets and Ospreys. Over the past two seasons, the Ospreys' average RaboDirect PRO12 attendance is 9,000 per game and the Scarlets' 8,600, well above David Moffett's minimum viability target of 8,000 per game. By contrast, the Blues have attracted an average gate of 7,800 and the Dragons a meagre 5,600, both below Moffett's minimum guideline. The Scarlets and Ospreys, therefore, cumulatively attract 20 per cent higher attendances than the Blues/Dragons and they have won the Celtic/Magners/Rabo leagues five times between them, where the Cardiff Blues have won the Amlin European Challenge Cup just once. Although it's all relative, they have been the ones to drop the club names and fully commit to their new stadia, thereby embracing their regional status more fully.

By contrast, the Blues and Dragons have yet to drop their names and move to new homes, escaping the limitations of their city-bound 'start-point'. The Cardiff Blues were unable to make their ground-share with Cardiff City Football Club work and the club announced a return to the Arms Park in May 2012. The Blues' average attendance at Cardiff City stadium had gone as low as 7,200 in 2011–12 – well below David Moffett's 'magic' 8,000 regional success guideline – forcing the Blues to return to their home stadium. It was, however, another clear 'red flag' that the franchise had not committed fully to the regional concept. The failure to jettison the club name and the reversion to the Arms Park are an indelible shorthand for Cardiff remaining obstinately Cardiff.

Jason Smith believes that the identification of region with club could have been avoided if the regions had been presented as franchises at the outset, with central contracts as the main plank in any tender. With a franchise system, you could:

- Offer five-year franchises based on tender
- Invite coherent business plans to support those tenders
- Involve the benefactors as shareholders in the franchise
- Attract new sponsors
- Centrally contract the players

The key issue was undoubtedly central contracts. Central contracting has been associated with all the successful regional models worldwide, whether it is Ireland in the northern hemisphere or Australia and New Zealand in the south. The two go hand-in-hand. It's the host union that has to run a regional system, so it's only logical for the players to be contracted to that union.

Jason Smith says: 'Central contracts are also more efficient because the host union pay the player to play whether it is a Test match or a club game in the Rabo 12. If the region pays the player, they are doing so whether he plays for them or not, whether he's away with Wales or part of their match-day 22. They may get some compensation from the union, but ultimately they are not getting value for money. That increases the probability that the player will be seen more as a financial asset, which in turn means he is more likely to end up in France or England. If you're in business and you pay £XX for a machine and you're told you'll only have it for half the time you need it, you wouldn't be too happy. You'd think twice about buying the machine in the first place. Nonetheless this is what is happening with some of the Welsh Test-match players.

'As an agent and players' representative at the time [2003–04], I got to see the kind of contracts the players were offered by the clubs. Quite frankly, they were pathetic from a legal point of view; they were not worth the paper they were printed on. For example, there was never any attempt to approach the issue of a player's image rights sensibly within the contract; no one knew who owned those rights and whether the contract included payment for them. This in turn created problems at point of tax or national insurance. Academy contracts didn't provide for time allotted to continued study. Jamie Roberts, for example, was studying to be a doctor at the time he received his first professional playing contract.

'Nothing was thought through. Everything was rushed and half-baked. Shambolic and unprofessional would be the words for it.' (Jason Smith)

If you control the players' contracts, you control the market and you control the wage structure, as Ireland have proven so clearly over the past few years. No one in Ireland leaves the country because they all understand the wage structure and they're all contracted to the IRFU. It takes an astronomical offer, like the one Jonny Sexton recently received – reputedly £750,000 per season – from Racing Metro, to drag them outside that structure.

Philip Browne, the IRFU chief executive, said that ultimately it had not been in the best interests of Irish rugby to compete in a bidding war to keep Sexton in Ireland, simply because the structure was made for all to benefit from its even-handedness, not just one individual. 'Ultimately we had no option but to take the decision that it would not be in the best interests of Irish rugby to chase the reported financial incentives being offered. We have always recognised that some of our players will be targeted by overseas clubs with offers which, quite simply, are not within our orbit.'

Central contracts would have granted the union control over the market for players as well as the power to designate one of the regions as a 'development region'. As it was, the regions were in competition with each other internally to secure the services of the best players, which naturally pushed the price up and made a 'poor man's market' even poorer. It had a huge negative impact on the regions' development by eating into finances that could have been used to develop new facilities or a beefier marketing strategy. The failure to start afresh on a blank sheet of paper – to centrally contract the players and control the internal market – was key to the union's failure to promote regional rugby as it might have wanted. What actually followed was a wage spiral fuelled by the pay demands of the top players.

As ex-Celtic Warriors coach Lynn Howells explains in his autobiography, *Despite the Knockbacks*:

> We went way over budget to sign up Gareth Thomas and Dafydd James, at the time probably the two highest paid players in Welsh rugby. Both were on well in excess of £100,000 a year . . . Gareth Thomas, the chief executive at the Celtic Warriors, knew that the financial situation would become untenable. He had produced financial forecasts which showed we were heading for big debts.
>
> The squad costs were horrendous. As their share of the WRU funding each month, the Warriors would receive £137,500, but the wage bill alone was £200,000. Also the WRU money arrived in the club's bank early in the month, but the salaries went out one month in arrears, so there was always a scramble to cash the cheques in case the money ran out.

Jason Smith was a legal representative for Gareth Llewellyn, Colin Charvis and Alix Popham. He cites the example of Mike Phillips, one of the top Welsh stars, whose salary spiralled out of control as he hopped from region to region: 'Mike Phillips was a classic example. Mike moved from his home region at Scarlets to the Cardiff Blues for more money, and when the Ospreys offered him a better deal he moved to the Liberty Stadium two years later. You can't blame the player for that, he has to secure his own future, after all.'

As Rob Howley, the Blues coach at the time, put it: 'The Ospreys have come in and gone way above the market value. Mike really can't say no, can he?'

Howley went on to explain the common-sense truth: 'It would be totally unfair to go way above and outside the wage structure just for one individual player. We have to respect the likes of Martyn Williams, Tom Shanklin and Gethin Jenkins, who have earned their deals.'

From a financial standpoint, from the point of view of regional rugby as a whole, it made no sense at all. Every move Mike Phillips made 'bubbled' the market further and raised the ceiling for the top players. It ate away at funds that would have been earmarked for other equally crucial aspects of the regions' development. It also probably cost each of the regions £150,000 per annum in agents' fees because agents are always at their most active in a free market.

The lack of market control also created a log-jam in certain playing positions. Lynn Howells explains: 'A number of players were not actually playing. Teams were stacking up players in certain positions to strengthen the depth of their squads . . . That doesn't help players in the national squad who might be getting only 20 minutes here and there. But coaches of the regions had to think of their region first and they had to have a big squad.'

When Mike Phillips moved to the Ospreys in 2007, it created an imbalance in the playing squads that would have been naturally corrected by the draft system built into central contracting in New Zealand. The Cardiff Blues were left without an international scrum-half at all after Phillips' departure. The Ospreys, meanwhile, had an ex-All Black starting, in the form of Justin Marshall, with Mike Phillips now backing him up from the bench. And when Marshall left to play in France, the Ospreys replaced him with another New Zealander, Jamie Nutbrown.

The regions were created to provide a stepping stone to the higher level of rugby and the Wales national squad for players like Phillips, but in practice this was not the case because of the free market. The ability to buy in a big foreign import such as Justin Marshall and the coaching need to 'warehouse' international-quality players two or three deep in key positions spoke against it. The union lost its capacity to move people around for the better of Welsh rugby when it opted out of central contracts in August 2003.

The opposite side of the coin to foreign imports is the creation of a youth pathway via academies. The relationship is direct and it is reciprocal – as one wanes, the other waxes. So the emphasis on foreign imports delayed the development of academies. An ex-Springbok or All Black fills the gap that might otherwise be filled by a promising young home-grown player.

Now that the regions don't have the money to pay the top foreign players to come and play in Wales, they have been forced to develop their academies; the impact on Welsh top-tier rugby has been entirely beneficial. With Kahn Fotuali'i moving from Ospreys to Northampton for the 2013–14 season, the last foreign superstar has disappeared from the Welsh regional scene. It was a symbolic moment. Now the young Welsh academy hopefuls will have to play because there is no one else.

They won't threaten anyone in European competition, or even the Rabo 12, but the national squad will benefit.

That's the outlook now. The regions will become 'farm' teams for their richer French and English brethren, who will monitor them as hotbeds of young talent, knowing that they can pay them top dollar – or at least a better dollar than they will receive from the regions. Like Argentina and Samoa, the Wales national team will go on improving, even with more than two-thirds of its starters plying their trade in English or French club rugby and their young players being developed in foreign leagues. At domestic level, there is no prospect of anything other than a steady decline. As the top players leave Wales, there will be fewer and fewer star attractions for the already threadbare support bases. The club game won't be able to help because the free market has already stolen its soul.

Jason Smith adds: 'A lot of the young Welsh players have come through an academy and don't know any other job; they don't have any other skills except rugby. Therefore they have to maximise their earning potential before retirement comes around 33 or 34 years of age. The French clubs are offering the top Welsh players their pensions from this standpoint, financial security for them and their families when their rugby playing days are over. Not everyone can be a coach or a TV pundit, and it's not easy to start your professional life again from scratch in your mid-30s. It would be foolish for them to refuse the opportunities that the French clubs are offering.'

As Gethin Jenkins recently said, 'I just hope something gets sorted out that will benefit players in Wales. At the moment they are being forced to leave. It's all right paying off the Millennium Stadium debt, but if players are leaving then you have no product.'

The French club salary cap is set at just over £8 million per team and that includes a favourable ruling whereby 30 per cent of a player's income is ring-fenced as 'image rights' and not subject to income taxation. Wales's regional salary cap is set at £3.5 million, with players fully subject to taxation law. Every Welsh player has gone to France for the money: £175,000 per year in the UK equates to £250,000 in France, plus the favourable tax situation. It's a 'no brainer' for any top Welsh player. Wales cannot compete without locking down the contractual situation and offering external incentives, as the IRFU have done with their players.

Jason Smith continues: 'Nothing succeeds like success, as the old saying goes, and many young people are more attracted by the success of Swansea City FC and, more recently, the newly promoted Cardiff City soccer team than they are by the ailing, failing regions. The regions have never been in good financial shape – ever – and now I know they are very, very close to the edge. The Scarlets were in terrible shape a couple of years ago, the Ospreys have offloaded all their "galacticos" and the complexion of their side has changed completely. The Dragons are propped up by the WRU's 50 per cent shareholding. The regions have never been in a healthy financial state and now it's worse, given the current economic climate.

'The WRU and the regions need a long-term business plan and they need it now. George North will, I believe, be seen in retrospect as a tipping point. When Northampton offered him a huge salary increase to go to Franklin's Gardens, it triggered the whole debate about central contracts again. Basically, the WRU were the only people in Wales who could have afforded to match Northampton's offer, but naturally they wanted a sweetener – in other words, control of the player via a central contract. If the North situation had gone down this route, the others would have fallen like dominos. But, make no mistake: the WRU is the only player Wales now have in the open market they engineered back in 2003. They are the only buffer between top Welsh rugby talent and the cash-rich French and English clubs, and if they can't offer a player enough incentive not to go, nobody can.' (Jason Smith)

In December 2012, the results of the first serious inquest into the state of the regional game in Wales was published by the accounting firm PricewaterhouseCoopers. Most of their conclusions were in line with the reasoning already indicated. The report concluded that the four regional businesses were not sustainable on a stand-alone basis, without continued contributions from benefactors to prop them up to cover what it termed 'the funding gap'. At the time of the report, that gap was approximately £3.8 million per season. It had previously been covered by club benefactors such as Peter Thomas, Tony Brown and Mike Cuddy.

At the same time, the report gave due warning that the support from benefactors was drying up fast due to the economic downturn in the UK and their disillusionment with 'a relationship of conflict' with the governing body.

Key points to emerge from the report were:

- Not all regions were able to provide us with an up-to-date business plan
- Acceptance by the regions that they cannot compete financially with English and French clubs and have focused instead on developing younger players
- A more positive change in the WRU-Regions relationship is required, with a management board to help enforce it

The WRU and Regional Rugby Wales earlier this season therefore agreed to the formation of the Professional Regional Game Board to oversee professional rugby in Wales. It had four union representatives and four from the regions, with Mr Justice Sir Wyn Williams installed as an independent chairman with voting rights. The board, established in December 2012, has at the time of writing yet to hold a single meaningful meeting.

In the meantime, the Blues, Scarlets, Ospreys and Dragons reached an agreement to stop any centrally contracted Wales player from appearing in their teams. There is a mounting suspicion that the union is prepared to let the regions fall into the large financial black hole they have dug for themselves. The WRU reported a record £63 million turnover, including a £2.4 million profit in the year ending June 2012, with the repayment of the Millennium Stadium debt apparently 30 years ahead of plan.

David Moffett says: 'In chasing the debt repayment, they are keeping the game poor, not only at the professional level but also at the club level. It just doesn't make any sense to keep the game poor just so that you can say, "Well, we'll be debt-free by 2020," or whatever it is.'

The stage has very obviously been set for revolution rather than evolution. Wales has turned into a northern hemisphere version of Australia rugby-wise, with its traditional passion for the game threatened by other sports (league and Aussie rules in Australia; football in Wales), while it tries to fund an over-ambitious regional design.

Jason Smith agrees: 'Wales has turned into Australia, the only difference being that the Australian regions are franchises and the players are centrally contracted to the ARU. This means that, like the IRFU, the Australian rugby union pays its players very well not to leave Australia, so departures are rare birds. The only players who do leave tend to be players on the fringe. A couple of years ago Stephen Moore was eagerly sought after by a number of French clubs, but he didn't go to France because he was rewarded handsomely for staying in Australia. But there is the same need for success at national level to sustain growth at the lower levels. Without a successful profile in the Wallaby side, fans will turn to their contact sport alternatives – the NRL and Aussie rules. The revenue generated by the national team's success funds the regions, not vice versa.'

Australia basically has always had enough players to fund two highly competitive provincial teams – New South Wales and Queensland – sitting just below the top tier of international rugby. With the advent of Super rugby, they have managed to create and sustain a third viable franchise based around Canberra, the Brumbies. But the creation of a fourth and fifth franchise – one in Melbourne to represent South Australia and another in Perth to represent Western Australia – is simply a flight of imagination. There are no more players in Australia to justify those fourth and fifth franchises than there are in Wales. Two is a solid reality, three is the attainable dream for the ambitious. That is the realistic limit and it still needs to be funded by a successful national team because the regional level will not be generating huge gate receipts with fewer fixtures to fulfil. And, of course, in Wales it would mean the regeneration of the club game below that, with the likes of Newport and Cardiff dropping back to the second level with greater playing resources available than before.

Kevin Bowring comments: 'Regional rugby has benefited the Wales team. Four championships, including three Grand Slams, in the space of nine years are a testimony to that. There is, however, not enough money in the game in Wales to afford four regions, so the likelihood is that the fourth region – probably the Dragons – will either be "demoted" to the status of a development region or abandoned altogether. That will be "natural shrinkage" towards Terry Cobner and Graham Henry's original idea that Wales could sustain two or three regions at most. It would also shrink playing opportunities at the higher level; however, with a significant layer of the top players leaving Wales to play in France and England, it may not matter.

'Wales needed the Millennium Stadium, of that I've no doubt. The Welsh people needed a cathedral of rugby at which to worship, and they deserved it. Rugby is the national sport. So the debt incurred was a necessary one, although it did cripple other aspects of Welsh rugby, such as player development, for the best part of ten years. Of course, I was the coach at the time when we began playing our home fixtures at Wembley. How can I ever forget that?' (Kevin Bowring)

In national terms, I believe we have about 28 top-class international players. We can put out a full match-day squad of twenty-three, plus probably five others, and that's it. We have enough quality to compete at international level unless we have an atypically long injury list – as in the autumn of 2012 – but we do not have enough quality to be competitive across four regions, so nothing much has changed from 2002–03 in that respect, except that the quality player pool has probably shrunk slightly. We only have about one-third of a regional squad that is top notch in quality terms, and that's not enough to compete with the French, the English or, for that matter, the Irish Heineken Cup sides.

For the regions, an Anglo-Welsh league may well be the best way forward, with all four Welsh regions being involved in a two-tier, twenty-four club Anglo-Welsh competition, with two starting in the top tier and two in the bottom segment. However, this would admittedly create a problem for our Celtic cousins in the current Rabo 12 league and it would not be ideal from that point of view. But we have to increase the intensity of our domestic competition. As it is, the Welsh regions currently have far too easy a ride into Europe – you need the dogfight in order to get better.

CHAPTER 10

A CEMETERY IN THE VALLEYS

If you ask Eddie Butler now, he will cheerfully refer to Pontypool Park as the 'cemetery'. It has become a habit, one tinged with a profound underlying sadness at the fall of not only a once-great club but also the valley culture it represented. In a short video documentary for BBC News, Eddie recalled the local derbies between Pontypool and Blaenavon: 'The whole of Blaenavon would march into town from the top of the Eastern valley. The referee would gather the two captains together in the centre of the pitch before the game and ask, "What's it to be today, then, gentlemen – rugby or fighting?" The captains would reply without hesitation, "Rugby, sir." And, with the first shrill blast of the whistle, the fighting would start.

'Now, in the days of regionalisation, things do not spill over so readily – and we're all the better for it. Or are we? Does modern regional rugby have any soul? Blaenavon is now a football town; Pontypool is hanging on by a thread. It is still fighting but is losing on the field and in the law courts. North of the M4, rugby suffers. South of the motorway, it appears to thrive.' (Eddie Butler)

The 'cemetery' extends far beyond Pontypool Park into all the rugby-playing valleys of South Wales, from the Garw and

Ogmore in the west all the way across to the Eastern valley itself. If regional rugby has failed anyone, it is the clubs and supporters in the valleys.

It should not have been this way. At its inception in 2003, regional rugby had promised to keep faith with the valleys in at least two regions: the Celtic Warriors (a 50–50 joint venture between Bridgend and Pontypridd) and the Dragons (a partnership between Ebbw Vale and Newport). The Warriors were intended to not only fuse Pontypridd and Bridgend but also supposedly to represent valley clubs like Maesteg, with similarly proud histories in the amateur era. Despite having one of the strongest playing squads, a generic name and a stated desire to build a new stadium somewhere between the Brewery Field and Sardis Road as factors all in their favour, the Warriors found themselves battling the odds.

There were two main issues. Leighton Samuel, the owner of picture frame manufacturer Décor Frame and the Warriors' chief benefactor, had some doubts about the business model for the region right from the beginning – doubts that were magnified when, following the merger, the full extent of Pontypridd RFC's tax burden became evident. The club owed HMRC around £700,000, which was enough to force it into administration. Leighton Samuel was obliged to hand over the Pontypridd share of the region, which he had purchased for £100,000 from the administrators, to the WRU, thereby inviting the curse of shared ownership – a situation that Samuel would find unworkable.

Second, despite the Warriors' success on the field, Leighton Samuel eventually stopped using Sardis Road in Pontypridd as a venue. Sardis Road had only two-thirds the capacity of the Brewery Field (7,800 compared to 12,000) and lacked permanent facilities for corporate hospitality.

As Lynn Howells, the Warriors coach at the time, points out, however: 'Even the former Bridgend players knew how much of an advantage it was for us to play at Sardis Road. Whether it was the hills, the stands or maybe the wins Ponty had experienced there, there was something about Sardis Road that gave us an advantage and this was now going to be taken away. The players weren't happy, the fans weren't happy and I certainly wasn't happy.

'It was another step, the final step, towards taking rugby away from the valleys. The Dragons had said they would play all their matches at Rodney Parade, so the Gwent valleys had already been denied top-class rugby. Now the same was happening to the Rhondda Cynon Taf and Merthyr valleys. It was the final nail in the coffin and probably the biggest mistake Samuel made.'

The move down towards the M4 lost the Celtic Warriors their representation in the mid-Glamorgan valleys. The identity of the region inevitably became too concentrated around Bridgend once the Sardis Road decision had been made. Leighton Samuel found it increasingly difficult to work with the union in the day-to-day administration of the region and when he was offered a way out on the back of one of the union's regional financial reviews in May 2004, he took it. Even then, the union was unable to directly purchase Samuel's share of the Warriors (valued at £1.2 million), so managed to persuade the other four regions to fund it instead!

Pontypool, like other Eastern valley clubs such as Abertillery, Cross Keys and Newbridge, was supposed to fall under the umbrella of the Gwent region formed by the merger of Ebbw Vale and Newport. The relations between the two clubs were riddled with acrimony right from the start, with fundamental disagreements over the naming of the region (Newport wanted 'Newport' in the title), playing colours (black and amber for Newport, traditional Monmouthshire blue for Ebbw Vale), playing and training venues (Newport wanted to use Rodney Parade exclusively, Ebbw Vale suggested Cwmbran Stadium), and even the composition of the squad. As the Newport chairman, David Watkins, said ominously, 'Regional rugby might not now occur, or not in the way that was thought.'

Eventually, the Ebbw Vale co-benefactor Marcus Russell resigned his position, leaving the way open for the Newport faction to include a double-sized 'NEWPORT' in the regional name, play every regional match at Rodney Parade and divert most of its developmental resources into Newport RFC. In his final statement, Marcus Russell said:

Despite the decision that the name of the new regional side should be Gwent having been made on three occasions, including by mutually agreed independent arbitration, the matter continued to dominate the agenda of the directors of Newport Rugby Football Club Limited to the exclusion of other, vitally important, matters. The situation became so dysfunctional that the management of Gwent Rugby Limited were unable to address fully, and thus able only to make slow progress on, matters such as obtaining corporate sponsorship, developing brand awareness, selling season tickets, drawing up staging agreements, etc.

I am now forced to consider my position. I entered this process with the strong and sincere intention of helping to create a team to represent the whole region of Gwent and to become a real force on the club rugby stage: also to provide the sporting public of Gwent at large with a team with which they could identify. I was initially supported and encouraged in this intention by Tony Brown. In order to achieve the ambitious objectives set for Gwent Rugby Limited, two things needed to be in place:

(i) The whole-hearted support, cooperation and expertise of the directors of both shareholders

(ii) and wide-ranging support for the new regional side from the sporting public throughout the Gwent region.

The business plan which was drawn for Gwent Rugby Limited, and registered with the WRU, is wholly dependent upon the above key success factors being achieved. In the event, neither of these essential prerequisites for success has been forthcoming. Almost from the outset of the implementation phase, Tony Brown, together with certain other directors of Newport Rugby Football Club Limited, have opposed any of the progress required for the success of Gwent Rugby Limited in protest against the name Gwent, and, later, Gwent Dragons.

Furthermore, an analysis of the sales to date of Gwent Dragon season tickets shows that only a small percentage of the sales have been made to rugby followers who were not season-ticket holders of Newport RFC last season. My initial belief that the sporting public of Gwent would welcome, and support, the notion of a top-class rugby side representing the whole region of Gwent and playing out of Rodney Parade was ill-conceived. It is now my strong view, given the above circumstances, that such viability and success can best be achieved if the infrastructure of Gwent Dragons is subsumed into the existing operations of Newport RFC. This being the case I am forced to come to the conclusion that I have no constituency which allows me to continue to pursue my original aim.

Russell's statement might have been echoed, with minor modifications, by thousands of supporters across the Gwent valleys, and it was voiced concretely by two-thirds of the legendary front row.

Graham Price says: 'I remember going down to watch the Dragons in the early days and everything was Newport. All the dominant personalities down there were still more or less the same as they had been in my playing days, so nothing had really changed.'

Bobby Windsor – 'the Duke' – takes up the argument: 'You

go down to Rodney Parade for Dragons games and the supporters are shouting, "*New-port*" I am Newport born and bred, but I have lived up here in the valleys and I've seen how rugby people feel about it all. There would be much more enthusiasm in the valleys if it was a true Gwent side. If it was the Monmouthshire Dragons, they would support it. But as it stands, there's nobody up here supporting the side we should be supporting because it's seen as a Newport team, which causes a lot of resentment. It's not just Pontypool that's in trouble. It's the whole of the Gwent region.' (Bobby Windsor)

With Russell's resignation, the original holding company was dissolved and resurrected as Dragons Rugby Limited, with 50 per cent shareholdings for Newport RFC and the Welsh Rugby Union. As of 26 March 2013, the book value of the company was *minus* £2,482,463. This represents an increase in debt over the past nine years of almost £1.8 million. Despite that undoubted financial failure, and the clear evidence that the region has not embraced the progressive attitude of the Ospreys and Scarlets in jettisoning the 'club' name and moving to a new stadium, there are still diehard factions like the Newport Action Group that firmly believe that Newport's old identity only needs to be restored in a regional cloak for the franchise to be successful. They would like the name changed to Newport Black & Ambers, a reversion to traditional black-and-amber colours and a new badge to reflect the changed 'regional' responsibilities. Maybe they are right. But then there would have to be an admission that they represented nothing more than themselves – nothing more than Newport – and that was not the original intent behind the shift to a regional structure.

The refusal of the Newport group at the Dragons to extend themselves outside the big city limits, coupled with the dissolution of the Warriors, left valley rugby unrepresented and trying to survive outside the regional mainstream. While the head of the game in Wales began to flourish, with the national team winning their first Grand Slam for 27 years in 2005, the body suffered.

Kevin Bowring, the head of elite coach development at the RFU, sees it as a failure of what he calls 'connection and extension': 'Was there another solution outside the regionalisation of rugby in Wales? I don't know. But clearly the grass roots needed to be nourished and the sense of identity and belonging fed. In my missionary work now for the RFU, it's something Stuart Lancaster [head coach of England] and I emphasise: the need for "connection and extension": connecting and extending the work with the national team to the grass roots of the game. So the question for the regions is, or should be, "How do we connect and extend towards that historical depth of feeling, that passion embedded in clubs like Pontypool, Pontypridd, Bridgend and Maesteg?"

'We need to recapture that – whether it's in Wales or England – in order to find that continuity with the past, in order to be real again. Otherwise we are just a poster in a car park or an unused season ticket. How do you develop a group of self-aware, self-reliant players who feel responsible for that continuity? By arriving at a five-star luxury hotel or country club and tossing your car keys to a porter for him to park your car up? I don't think so.

'When I think of men who represented those values in the past – in my past – I think of men like Dai Morris at Neath. A miner, a blue-collar worker who did hard physical work for five days a week and worked just as hard and physically on the field on a Saturday afternoon or a Wednesday night, who turned up to training regardless of the weather without complaint. Nothing for show with Dai Morris, but I wouldn't like to be hit by him. It was like being run over by a tram carrying dug coal in the mine.

'This gap grew wider with the advent of regional rugby in Wales. Supporters in the crowd didn't necessarily watch one of their own trotting out onto the pitch to represent them on Saturday afternoons – men who worked in the local community like Dai, or John Perkins for Pontypool. So the sense of belonging isn't really there.

'The great tribal rivalries have diminished with regionalisation. Although we still have Ospreys against Scarlets, or Blues versus Dragons, there is not a local derby waiting around the corner every other weekend – or for that matter the Valley versus Big Town conflicts we used to get when Swansea played Neath, Cardiff played Pontypridd or Newport visited Pontypool. I recall watching Aberavon and Neath fighting out a bitter three-all draw one week, then joining up to play as a combined side against the All Blacks the next. Men like Brian Thomas and Billy Mainwaring, who had been the best of enemies, played arm-in-arm alongside each other for the greater cause.

'Ironically, the main success story to come out of the initial stages of regionalisation was the Celtic Warriors franchise, which was about as close to a valleys franchise as you could get. They had a good player base, they had that sense of identity and belonging that the others lacked and they'd been successful. They had split games with Wasps, who at the time were probably the best side in the Heineken Cup, but they were the first to go when the financial pressure came on.' (Kevin Bowring)

Bowring's summary of the situation is corroborated by those who volunteer their time to keep the clubs running at the grass roots of Gwent rugby – as coaches and referees, as pitch-markers and kit suppliers and managers of the fourth XVs and age-group sides. They have a concrete, day-to-day understanding of how the newer generations of rugby players are growing up without any feeling for the traditions that surround both the valley clubs like Pontypool and indeed the national game as a whole.

The majority of clubs now struggle to field teams at Colts level from 15 years upwards. Part of the issue is the skimming-off of talented teenagers into the regional academies and development programmes. While the support and training these youngsters receive at the academies is by general consensus excellent, every day spent at an academy is also a day spent away from the local club that nurtured them from the very beginning and where they learned their rugby; every day spent studying nutrition or physical development in the gym is also a day spent off the 'natural curve' of learning the skills necessary to play rugby through competitive matches. The volunteers will tell you that the skimming-off process also means the more limited players left behind at the clubs become exposed: they have to play more matches beyond the range of their ability, get knocked around and leave the game. The structure of the club is eroded, as the number of players affiliated to it steadily shrinks.

Promising young players are fast-tracked through to the regional development programmes before they have completed their apprenticeships at their clubs, and once they get there they are not encouraged to give anything back to the communities where it all started for them. The process is not reciprocal. As a result, they have little sense of the tradition of which they are a living part. How can there be any 'connection and extension' when youngsters are driven through to the head of the game so single-mindedly? Their education is not spreading outwards, rather it is spiking upwards. The governing body urgently needs to find pathways for its emerging players that also represent an investment in the club from which they grew – to take with one hand, but also give with the other.

The situation is the same in reverse. Centre Gareth Maule is Pontypool born and bred; he played for the Wales Under-19 side and the Dragons regional Under-20s before moving on to the Scarlets at the end of 2006. In 2005–06, while he was in the Dragons squad, he was 'seeded' back to Ebbw Vale rather than Pontypool to gain more club experience. At the time, both Ebbw Vale and Pontypool were struggling in similar circumstances in the bottom half of the Welsh Premiership, so there was no compelling reason not to send him back to his home-town club and 'extend' to the grass roots there. Gareth will still come back to take a long walk through the Park with Pricey and watch Pooler on his weekends off from the Scarlets, but the region still chose to seed him with Ebbw Vale as a player.

A move back to his home-town club is one Gareth himself would have relished. He is a young man who is very aware of the local tradition and sense of history that surrounds him and he is keen to participate in it. He knows that Pontypool belongs at the top level but also that regional policy needs to feed tradition in order for it to be reinvigorated: 'When you go anywhere in the rugby playing world and say you're from Pontypool, people automatically start naming the great players, the front row. I'm sure Mike Hook can get them back to where they should be. I've been up helping at Pontypool United with the juniors, so my phone is always on and I'm happy to help in the area.'

A club cannot build its own success story or maintain its traditions when its investment in young players is capped off prematurely or when its own sons are sent to another club to which they have no connection.

Roger Lewis, CEO of the Welsh Rugby Union, declared in an open letter in 2012: 'A winning Wales filling the Millennium Stadium is the power which drives the whole of Welsh rugby forward.' Nothing could be further from the truth, at least in the valleys of Wales. The head cannot drive the rest of Welsh rugby forward if it cannot 'connect and extend' through its arms and legs effectively, if the arms have become too atrophied to lift themselves and the legs have forgotten how to run.

It is the same everywhere outside the blessed M4 belt, not just in Gwent. In February and March 2013, two articles appeared in the national press from the pens of eminent rugby journalists Donald McRae (in *The Guardian*) and Peter Jackson (in *The Rugby Paper*) offering insights into the plight of clubs such as Bridgend and Maesteg in the era of regional rugby.

McRae met Derrick King, the chairman of Bridgend, who is in no doubt that 'the union would like fewer clubs. Of course they would never admit that, but there's no doubt. Pontypool were demoralised. I felt very sorry because they're a legendary club. They took the union to court but lost a pretty bitter case. It's crazy. We should be supporting club rugby because that's where our identity was forged. But that identity has all but gone. We can only talk about the past now – or worry about the future.'

At the top end of the Llynfi Valley in Maesteg, they are lucky if they can find 15 men to play on a Saturday afternoon. 'The season before last was dreadful,' their chairman David Morgan tells McRae. '[In October 2011] we lost 149–14 to Cwmllynfell, but we started the match with fourteen players and by the end of it we were down to ten.'

Maesteg coach Richard Webster described the situation to Peter Jackson: 'We were due to play Heol-y-Cyw and I phoned the WRU to say we couldn't play the game because we didn't have a front row. I wanted it postponed. They said it had to be played as arranged. I couldn't get them to see the bigger picture of a club fighting to survive. What does losing by 60 or 70 points do for morale? All I wanted was a bit of help. Instead they stuck by the rulebook and said we'd be thrown out of the competition and fined £500.

'I said if it came to that I'd pay the fine myself because

Maesteg RFC couldn't afford it. The club give me petrol money, but I refuse other expenses. I leave work early and there are times when I could do without it. It's not for the love of the club, because Maesteg is not my home town. I do it out of respect for the players who have helped me. I still have a passion for the game.'

Maesteg is a mirror image of Pontypool in the Eastern valley. In the amateur era, it was the social and sporting hub of a group of satellite clubs that included Maesteg Celtic, Maesteg Quins and Nantyffyllon, in the same way that Pontypool was the centre pin for Pontypool United, Garndiffaith, Cwmbran and Blaenavon. But the damage is not confined to the valleys, or even to clubs who are still attempting to ply their trade north of the M4. On the south-east coastline lies Penarth RFC, a perennial fixture in the Merit Table of the '70s and '80s, but another proud club that almost slid into oblivion at the turn of the millennium. Their current chairman Mike Gooding was in charge of affairs when the club's own professional crisis arrived. Speaking to David Roberts of the *Western Mail*, Gooding commented: 'There was a time when I thought we had had it – I couldn't raise a team, we were £70,000 in debt and nobody seemed to care. The Inland Revenue was knocking on our door, claiming thousands of pounds of unpaid taxes, most of it on wages paid to players. We lost 13 players to neighbouring clubs after we were relegated to Division Five East, mostly because they offered up to £100 for a win, and I couldn't see where I was going to get a team from.'

Two days before the start of the 1999–2000 season, Penarth were due to travel to Blaina for a Division Four match and they were six players short. It was looking like the end of the road for the 'Donkey Island Butcher Boys' after 120 years.

'The easy thing would have been to ring Blaina and call off the game, tell the WRU we were shutting up shop and walk away. But Penarth Rugby Club has given me so much fun and enjoyment throughout my life I couldn't let it die. I got on the phone to Bob McPherson, one of our former captains and coaches, had a meeting with him in the pub on the Friday night and somehow managed to scrape together fifteen players to take to Blaina.

'I went [to Blaina] fearing the worst and I headed straight to their secretary when I arrived . . . To my amazement, he said his club had lost 16 players over the summer, he had struggled to raise a team and had also thought about calling off the game. Their situation mirrored our own! We went out and won the match by a record score, 72–7, but then only won one more match all season. It got so bad that I had to play twice [on the same day].' (Mike Gooding)

Fortunately that match against Blaina proved to be Penarth's 'dark night of the soul' and they have made steady if modest progress upwards from that point on. Now they nestle comfortably in mid-table in the Swalec Division Three South-East and their financial situation has stabilised on what is basically an amateur footing. The issue of a host of clubs left unrepresented in the regional era is, however, recurrent. It could be seen as a manufacturing defect in the overall design of regional rugby in Wales.

Bob Dawkins says: 'While I understand that the union can only afford so many regions, in my opinion there was no need to undermine further that point of identity in the valley communities which was provided by clubs like Pontypool. The "top 18" all represented centres of population. No one can pretend that Llanelli, Swansea, Cardiff and Newport now represent those population centres, whatever their "catchment areas" are supposed to be.

'So when I hear Roger Lewis talking on the TV, I find myself wanting to hear something I can understand, for the union to do something that helps the valley clubs reclaim that point of identity in their communities. The strongest structure in the world is a pyramid, a structure that has a wide and stable foundation and one that won't fall over whatever the weather. What we've done is to erode the base of the pyramid.' (Bob Dawkins)

In concrete terms, the playing depth across the base and mid-section of the pyramid has suffered quite dramatically. As Terry Cobner pointed out, there are only 28 Test-quality players in Wales. Beyond that there is a large drop-off in quality, as Wales's Autumn internationals in 2012 proved. When Wales lose key players, such as tight-head Adam Jones, scrum-half Mike Phillips or full-back Leigh Halfpenny, they have no one of equivalent quality to replace them. In fact, there is something of a black hole in the playing resources behind those three. The erosion of depth has taken place on the most basic of levels. If you compare Wales's tight-head prop forward stocks now with that time in the '70s and '80s, when there were many more active population centres and the valley clubs were thriving, you quickly discover that there is no comparison to be made.

If Graham Price got injured in the '70s or '80s, there was always someone who could come in behind him and do the job for the national team. In the '70s, there was Mike Knill at Cardiff or Rhys Morgan at Newport. None other than the giant Frenchman Gerard Cholley had indicated in 1976 that Knill had given him one of his hardest matches after coming on in the first half for Pricey. Rhys Morgan was one of the great unheralded assets in Welsh club rugby – just ask any of the front rows over the Severn Bridge if they looked forward to their encounter with Rhys. They didn't. When I played second row for Pooler, you could feel the force and angle of Rhys Morgan's engagement from right over the other side of the scrum, it was that powerful. People forget that Rhys was a great footballer, too – he kicked 126 points when he first broke into the Newport 1st XV in 1975! Yet both Mike Knill and Rhys Morgan only won one cap apiece for Wales; in today's game, they would have accumulated forty or fifty each.

In the '80s, Wales were even better off for tight-heads than they were in the previous decade. Apart from Rhys Morgan, who was by now a fully mature campaigner down at Rodney Parade, there was Ian Eidman at Cardiff (who eventually replaced Pricey in the Wales line-up in 1983) and beyond him there were Meredydd James at Bridgend, Peter Francis at Maesteg, Gareth John at Swansea and John Richardson at Aberavon. There were others such as John Dixon and Brandon Cripps. The base of the pyramid in the clubs was healthy: it generated any number of people who were experienced and could do a more than competent job if called upon.

Ian Eidman was unfortunate to be injured just before the Lions' 1983 tour to New Zealand. If he had been fully fit and able to keep his profile high with the selection panel, I've no doubt he would have made it a 'full house' for Welsh props on that tour since Ian Stephens, Staff Jones and Pricey were already cemented in. As it was, Scotland's Iain Milne went instead.

The point is that – allowing for changes in nutrition and conditioning brought by the professional era – any of those tight-heads above could have replaced Adam Jones more effectively than either the Blues' Scott Andrews or the Ospreys' Aaron Jarvis in the Autumn. No disrespect to either, but they have started a total of 61 regional games between them and have yet to establish themselves as the first choice for their regions, let alone become legitimate options for their country. I'm sure they were never less than fully committed, but at the same time they are still novices in propping terms.

It is the same at scrum-half. In the Autumn 2012 and 2013

Six Nations tournaments, the replacements for Mike Phillips were Tavis Knoyle and Lloyd Williams. The truth is that we do not know whether either of them has what it takes at international level. Back in the '70s, Wales knew they had accomplished back-up to Gareth Edwards in the shape of Ray 'Chico' Hopkins at Maesteg, Clive Shell at Aberavon, Selwyn Williams at Llanelli and Brynmor Williams at the great man's very own club Cardiff. Hopkins went on the Lions tour to New Zealand as the back-up to Gareth, having only played 20 minutes for his country. Brynmor Williams toured the same country in 1977 as the Lions number one option when he had yet to win his first cap! Now the pathways aren't so clear. The Wales coach Warren Gatland is forced to select players in that position more in hope than expectation.

What of the pathways for young up-and-coming coaches in Wales? With the weakening of the club scene in the country, the experienced coaching talent in Wales is forced to go abroad if individuals hope to develop their careers further. Most of the coaches have gone to the Premiership in England. David Young is Director of Rugby at London Wasps, while Nigel Davies occupies the same position at Gloucester and has assistance from Paul Moriarty; Lyn Jones is the head coach at London Welsh; Kingsley Jones was the head man at Sale before moving to coach Russia ahead of the 2011 World Cup; Sean Holley has recently joined Andy Robinson at Bristol, while Graham Henry's forwards coach Lynn Howells has coached Doncaster Knights in the second tier of English rugby and is now the Romanian national coach. Wales's first Grand Slam-winning coach of the regional era, Mike Ruddock, coached Worcester Warriors before moving to Ireland to coach their Under-20s and steer Lansdowne RFC to the All-Ireland Championship in his spare time. Rowland Phillips is currently coaching Viadana in northern Italy.

They all had to find jobs elsewhere in the UK or in Europe because they couldn't be re-absorbed into either the Welsh club scene or the regions. Phil Davies has only just returned to Wales as the Blues' Director of Rugby after a long spell in Leeds and two years at Worcester. The regions cannot provide enough jobs to keep all the good coaches in Wales and the chasm down to club level means that the clubs don't have enough playing quality or money to justify their appointment. We are losing a huge quantity of valuable intellectual property as a consequence. There's a bottleneck between the top and the bottom of the game in Wales that was created by regionalisation and Welsh rugby can't clear its throat. The top coaching property in Wales cannot flow easily between the regional, national and club levels and it has taken the same path as the top players.

The coaches and the star players are fast becoming the 'wild geese' of Welsh rugby and the numbers migrating are only going to increase. The big difference is that when the coaching talent flies south for the winter, it is unlikely to make the return journey to its homeland.

As Eddie Butler concluded in the BBC documentary: 'The key to the success of regional rugby now is the fifth region – Wales, the national team. Wales have to play more, a minimum of 12 games per year, to finance the regions: more people watching more international rugby, generating more gate money than ever before. That is the contemporary equation.

'Rugby has become an upside-down game, nourished from above, not below. The regions, desperate for money, are losing more benefactors than they are acquiring – Tony Brown at the Dragons, Mike Cuddy at the Ospreys – and they have become more dependent on WRU cash injections as a result.

'The danger is that contact with the roots of the game has been lost. The top has become heavier and more important

– some might argue more self-important – than the bottom of the game and it doesn't take a structural engineer to point out that such structures tend to come crashing down upon themselves.

'Me? I love rugby where the sun doesn't shine – not on the *Truman Show* riviera south of the M4.'

What of Pontypool? The club has endured the same violent see-saws of fortune in the regional era that it survived in the amateur game, though now there are far more downs than ups. After languishing in the bottom half of the Premiership table in the first two seasons after regionalisation, in May 2006 Pontypool finished bottom of the Premier Division and were relegated to Division One East. They were promoted again two seasons later, but finished in the bottom three of the table in the three seasons between 2009 and 2012. There was to be no triumphant return and no heroic upsetting of the odds in the professional era. Every season the club was fighting for its life.

In 2008–09, for example, only an injury-time try in the very last game of the season from Aberavon full-back Marc Bennett sent Bridgend down, and even then the Ravens' captain Gareth Bowen had time to miss with both a penalty and last-gasp drop-goal attempt. Either would have been enough to relegate Pontypool instead of Bridgend. Bridgend had been reinforced by a number of regional 'ringers' for that game – 'not so much Ravens as Ospreys after an overnight transformation that has attracted the attention of the Royal Ornithological Society if only because it makes a mockery of the climax of the Premiership pecking order', as the Cardiff–Pontypool match programme noted – while Pontypool travelled to the Arms Park for a showdown with table-topping Cardiff.

Before the game the Pooler captain, Leighton Jones, the son of coach Junna, led the players down to a corner of the ground where the 1,000 or so diehard supporters had congregated. The whole playing squad raised their hands and applauded their loyal fans and the supporters roared their approval. The galvanising effect of this tiny piece of 'connecting and extending' between club and community was extraordinary, with Pooler going on to win the game 32–15 and scoring four tries into the bargain.

Graham Price recalls: 'After that the supporters were putting together DVDs entitled *The Great Escape* and playing the music on the club website. The announcer would even play the score over the tannoy when Pooler were about to pull off another lifesaving comeback in our home games!'

Pontypool was, however, no longer at the top of the food chain, even among the clubs in the Eastern valley. Where in the halcyon days the likes of Abertillery and Cross Keys had always been feeder clubs to Pontypool, now it was Pooler players who were being poached.

'They didn't even wait until we went down to poach our players,' Graham Price continues. 'I remember two Cross Keys scouts sitting in the main stand, in the committee members' box, and then gaining entry to the hospitality suite to offer terms to our players. They didn't even bother to stay on the Bank; they just stood in the hospitality area negotiating with our players. It was quite literally daylight robbery.'

The club went into liquidation in July 2000. I say 'the club', but fortunately a limited company, Pontypool RFC Ltd, had been created in 1998 to look after its commercial affairs and so its collapse did not affect Pontypool's ability to play in Wales's Division One the following season. A new cash backer was found in the shape of Bob Jude, who owned a flooring company and had previously been involved with Ebbw Vale. Junna Jones had returned to coach Pooler on the field and was the centre pin holding the club together from 1999 to 2005. Under Junna's stewardship, Pontypool were promoted to the Welsh Premier Division at the end of the 2002–03 season, and they even attracted a 5,000-strong crowd for a touring match against the visiting Fijians in November 2002, a game Pooler lost 74–16.

Graham Price points to the disconnect between events on and off the pitch: 'Bob was eager to invest money in new players, but the problem was that he tended to buy them without consulting Junna. Steve would find these new players turning up for training and he'd have to find a place for them out on the field; I think some of them had taken Bob for a ride, we got so little game time out of them. Nonetheless the broad strokes were positive and we climbed back into the Premiership in 2003.

'When David Moffett announced the formation of regional rugby in 2003, it effectively relegated us again! It was like climbing to the top of the mountain only to be told that there was another steeper peak above it, and we knew there was no chance of being included in the club mergers that formed the basis of the regions. The goalposts had been moved again. It meant that all Bob Jude's money had been spent for nothing because his objective had been for Pontypool to become a fully professional outfit.

'Bob Jude never recovered from that blow. He reckoned he was owed money by the WRU. With some justification, the union thought that the opposite was true, but in the upshot it was the club that suffered. It was forced to give up its union subsidy for the following season to avoid dropping six divisions. All the while court judgments against his company, Pontypool Premier Rugby Club Ltd, mounted, as bills went unpaid. Some players hadn't been paid for months, while a special fund-raiser had to be arranged to finance hospital operations for three others. Bob just dropped everything, leaving Junna to hold the baby. I suddenly had to give players a lift to games because the buses were no longer being subsidised. It all happened at a snap of the fingers.' (Graham Price)

The split between the rugby club and the companies created to fund it commercially proved to be as symbolic as it was long-lasting. When the playing squad undertook a tour of the town by open-top bus to celebrate promotion in 2003, they had to borrow a piece of silverware, hurriedly donated by a champion local pigeon-racer! The real trophy had mysteriously vanished at the same time as the club's ex-owner.

After Jude's departure, a new controlling company, Pontypool (2003) Ltd, was established by a consortium of businessmen, with Jeff Taylor, an ex-Pontypool player, at its head.

Graham Price says: 'Pontypool had always maintained a very strong age-group section and Youth side, ranging from the Pontypool Schools Under-11s to a Colts side which produced five Welsh schools internationals in the final year my own son played for them. After that it was Pontypool Youth, which historically had always been a powerful side. The club committee had always funded the age-group sides and the Youth team because they were the future of the club, but Jeff Taylor was unwilling to set aside money for the same purpose, so that aspect of the club's continuity came to an abrupt end.' (Graham Price)

The clubhouse was also sold and, as Mark Ring put it, 'No clubhouse, no soul, I'm afraid.'

By the summer of 2006, Jeff Taylor had quit, selling the company that owned the playing rights to the club, citing the reluctance of management, players and even the supporters of the club to accept change. He left the club debt-free but was swiftly followed out of the door by the Director of Rugby (policeman Gareth Hale, who had neither the rugby knowledge nor the club background of a Steve Jones), two other coaches and twelve players. When the club was put up for sale following the side's relegation from the Premiership, the asking price was just £1. Taylor described his last season as chairman as a 'nightmare of divisiveness', as Pontypool polarised around Taylor and Hale on the one side, and Steve Jones and his son Leighton, the club captain, on the other.

Leighton Jones felt he was being painted into a corner by being appointed captain while his dad was being moved out of his coaching responsibilities: 'I feel under the current conditions and my own state of mind I'd be of little use . . . However, I am and will always consider myself to be a Pontypool boy and find it particularly sad that an environment exists at the club whereby traditional values of respect, trust and honesty are no longer evident.'

A hooker like his father, Leighton went down the road to Newport. Ironically, he was sent off playing against Pontypool on 25 November 2005. He was more deeply Pontypool, and more like his dad, than even he realised.

This was not the end of the story. In 2006, Pontypool (2003) Ltd was taken to an industrial tribunal by Steve Jones and his claim for constructive dismissal was upheld. Junna's role had been changed from head coach to 'development manager'. Jeff Taylor had sent Junna a letter citing his 'management style' and 'current health problems' as reasons for the then board asking him to stand down as head coach.

As Junna had been damned by the company's action on the one hand, Jeff Taylor celebrated his 'great dedication and energy' in words on the other: 'Indeed, without your courage two years ago, I doubt if the club would exist.' It was all somehow typical of a club bewildered by its very existence in the professional era. While the fires were still clearly burning as brightly in Junna the coach as they had been in Junna the player, that passion could seemingly never be rewarded, despite the fact that Junna was by now one of the highest-qualified coaches in Wales. Even after the tribunal's judgment had been made, there was little chance of the recommended £14,200 compensation cheque flopping through Junna's letterbox.

Former chairman of Pontypool (2003) Ltd, Jeff Taylor, said the company disputed all Mr Jones' allegations. When asked who would pay Mr Jones, Mr Taylor said: 'I'd be surprised if anyone does. Any liability would fall on the old company, but it is in the process of no longer existing. New owners Park Promotions, who took over the running of the club two weeks ago, are not liable to pay costs.'

As the club transmogrified through a succession of failed companies, the torch of the Pontypool spirit remained stubbornly the same, without a clubhouse and often playing on park pitches – a flickering anachronism in a time it neither wanted nor understood. When Junna passed away unexpectedly only one year later, at the age of fifty-five, it was as if the spark of that torch had somehow been put out with him. I think everyone knew it at his funeral, that a life larger than the man himself had somehow been extinguished.

There was still time for one more heroic misadventure. Over the last five years, Pontypool have been barely surviving in the Welsh Premiership, finishing 13th out of 14 in 2007–08 and 2008–09, and one place higher the following two years, 2010 and 2011. Pontypool finished the 2011–12 season with two clubs below them in the league – Bedwas and Tonmawr. Coincidentally, they also finished on the same number of points as Newport RFC one place above them.

In April 2011, the WRU announced plans to reduce the number of clubs in the Premiership from fourteen to ten, with the aim of concentrating talent in a smaller number of semi-professional entities. The British and Irish Cup competition had started the previous year and was now the centrepiece for semi-professional clubs in the UK and Ireland. It included twelve sides from the English championship, three 'A' sides from the Irish provinces, three Scottish clubs and the top six teams from the Welsh Premiership. This competition demonstrated in its very first year – and has continued to demonstrate in the years following – the relative weakness of the second tier of Welsh rugby, with twelve of the fourteen semi-finalists coming from England and Ireland over the past four seasons. The writing was on the wall at the cup's inception, with no Welsh club qualifying for the knockout stages.

The proposal to introduce the reforms for the 2011–12 season was rejected by the WRU board as being too early. Clubs who wanted to play in the revised Premiership the following year had to qualify for an 'A' licence based on criteria, sign a participation agreement and also be judged on 'meritocracy' – league results spread across the past six seasons. Under the plan, a minimum of two and a maximum of four Premiership division teams from every geographical region would be represented. The vote among the existing Premiership clubs was unanimous and Pontypool RFC was one of those who signed up to the proposal. The WRU planned to reveal the identities of the ten successful clubs in December 2011.

In November, the WRU changed course and decided to admit another two clubs to make up a twelve-team Premiership. The additional two clubs were Carmarthen Quins and Bridgend Ravens. A WRU statement read: 'Under the new plan put forward by the regions Bridgend RFC and Carmarthen Quins RFC will be the two teams added to the reformed Premiership in order to fulfil the talent recruitment strategy requirements of the Ospreys and Scarlets.' The two clubs to be relegated were the bottom club, Tonmawr, and Pontypool, who finished 12th, ahead of Bedwas, who retained their Premiership status.

This effectively diluted the original intention of the whole plan, which was to concentrate Welsh talent in the second tier in a significantly smaller number of clubs. In the current season, all 12 members of the revised Premiership have competed in the British and Irish Cup in an expanded competition. They won only 28 of their 72 pool games and Llanelli RFC were the only team to advance to the knockout stages. They were promptly knocked out by the Bedford Blues in the quarter-finals.

The addition of Carmarthen Quins and Bridgend to the Scarlets and Ospreys feeder systems also gave the healthier western regions a 7–5 feeder club advantage over the Blues/Dragons in the Premier Division. In the third tier of the national championship, meanwhile, there was a marked geographical imbalance, with nearly half of the twelve teams coming from the Gwent valleys (Pontypool, Blackwood, Newbridge, Ebbw Vale and Bargoed). It is hard to escape the feeling that the attitude of the Dragons as a region – their determination to become a Newport super-club rather than a truly Gwent or Monmouthshire representative – and their ailing financial situation has affected the union's attitude towards them. The Dragons have failed to embrace the region and they have failed commercially. It is, however, the valley clubs who have borne the burden of Newport's intransigence.

As Sir Raymond Jack's court judgment of 11 July 2012 indicates:

> The [WRU] proposals centred on the addition of Bridgend Ravens and Carmarthen Quins to the Premiership, thus raising the number of clubs from 10 to 12. The proposals were specific to those two clubs, but were supported by all four Regional clubs. Bridgend is in the Region of, and closely connected with, the Ospreys, and Carmarthen likewise with the Scarlets. The case made for their inclusion centred on the claim that without them the 'player pathways' to the two clubs would be weakened.

Pontypool is in the Region of Newport Gwent Dragons, but the Dragons did not make a similar case for Pontypool's inclusion.

Despite the fact that so very many players (including myself) have passed between the two clubs during their rugby careers, the relationship between Pontypool and Newport has never been an easy one. The Pontypool club historian Ray Ruddick says that fixtures between the two clubs were cancelled between 1948 and 1962 for reasons unknown. Ray tells the story of a game in 1934 between the two sides which had to be abandoned by the referee. Apparently he had decided to send a Pontypool player off the field, but in those days the captains were permitted to challenge the decision; if the opposing captain felt the decision was too harsh, the referee could reinstate the player at his discretion. This scenario was about to occur, with the Pooler player reinstated, when the Newport touch judge positively flew onto the field, demanding that the expulsion stand! An argument ensued and the referee was forced to abandon the game, with the score deadlocked at five-all.

A similar kind of stalemate characterised the relationship in the regional era almost 70 years later, but Newport now had the power to determine the fate of Pontypool and every other club in the Gwent valleys because they controlled the region. It was 'village-ism' at its worst.

Pontypool being Pontypool looked for the opportunity to push itself to the limit and dispense a stitch or two while enduring five or six in return. They drove matters on to a spectacular legal denouement by taking action against the WRU, challenging the union's assessment of its own 'A' licence criteria in respect of three other clubs – Swansea, Bedwas and Cross Keys – based on factors such as stadium standards (there was a stated need to have a full, covered area accommodating 1,000 spectators), floodlighting and pitch quality.

At the time, the third issue of 'meritocracy' did not seem to automatically exclude the likes of Pontypool, provided that it could satisfy the first two criteria, the 'A' licence and the participation agreement.

As Sir Raymond Jack explained later in his judgment:

> The natural reading is that those clubs which can satisfy the first two conditions will be selected in order of meritocracy . . . The meritocracy standings were known to the clubs on 9 May . . . [but] . . . applications were sought and accepted from clubs outside the 10, including Pontypool. Ms [Julie] Paterson [the WRU compliance officer] was in close communication with Pontypool over its application for an A Licence. I am satisfied that she knew that it was wanted because Pontypool hoped that despite its position by meritocracy it could squeeze into the Premiership. She never told the club that it was misunderstanding the position.

Ultimately Sir Raymond Jack ruled that the WRU were fully within their rights to grant 'A' licences as they saw fit, without the need for the independent inspections Pontypool had asked for:

> As between a club and the WRU it is clear that the WRU could waive a requirement and grant a licence. Thus, on the assumption that Appendix A does provide for independent inspection of a club facility, *the WRU is entitled to waive the requirement and to grant a licence even if there has been no such inspection. That is straightforward as a matter of contract law*.
>
> The next question is whether it is a term of the agreement with a particular club that the WRU shall assess the other clubs

strictly in accordance with the rules. Once it is accepted that as between the WRU and a club the WRU may waive a provision, or the Criteria Appeals Panel may act as I have set out, the answer to this question must be no . . . I would add that there might well be valid reasons to treat two clubs in different ways. *It is important that the WRU's discretion to deal with a situation should not be usurped by the court.*

Sir Raymond Jack opined that the union had created the ground for a misunderstanding by leading Pontypool to believe it might have been eligible for selection despite its position in the meritocracy, and described the decision to add Bridgend and Carmarthen into the mix, 'as a result of pressure from two of the Regions in particular', as unfortunate. The judge concluded, however:

It is, of course, correct that the addition of the two clubs was not provided for by the Rules as they then stood. A change of the Rules was required. New Rules have been prepared but have not been given effect pending the resolution of Pontypool's case. *It must be accepted that the WRU has power to change the Rules.*

That spelled it out in black and white. (See www.monckton.com/docs/general/ParkPromotionPontypoolRugbyClubJuly2012.pdf for the full judgment.)

Pontypool had resolved to keep on fighting to the end. It was the Pontypool way, after all, although the more cold-blooded response might have been to accept the union's offer to 'drop hands' in May – which would have meant the union bearing its own legal costs. The WRU took its pound of flesh instead, deducting the 'parachute' payments due to Pontypool for its impending relegation from its legal costs during the trial (about £40,000). By the summer of 2012, Pontypool found itself within one week of being wound up. The club was on the point of extinction.

In July, the honorary Pontypool club president Graham Price doubted the club would be able to field a full 15-man team for the start of the coming season, and there were still legal costs of over £160,000 to be settled after the loss of the lawsuit. With no gate receipts to speak of bolstering the club, and with all the money raised by the 'fighting fund', plus individual contributions from the five directors, having been eaten up by the WRU lawsuit, there was nothing left for the daily running costs of the club. The ultimate saviour of Pontypool, however, was Peter Jeffreys, a self-made millionaire and owner of the online medical service provider Medinet. He pumped £100,000 into the club, which helped pay off the debt to the club's own solicitors, and undertook to cover the running costs out of his own pocket (see Appendix 1).

As Peter Jeffreys himself says: 'I contributed the money because I didn't want to see the club go. It's a great community up there and some people who might have wanted to save it didn't perhaps have the financial means to do so . . . I'm more involved now than I ever really wanted to be, to be honest, but I love the club. My dad brought me here, my sons come here, it means a lot to me.'

Peter Jeffreys recognises that the tale of the club over the recent past has been one of financial inefficiency and, ironically, of a failure of 'connection and extension' to the local community. He sees the need to build a corporate infrastructure behind the administration of the club and to get local businesses involved, beginning with the construction of a new hospitality area. At long last Pontypool RFC seems to have a guiding hand at the controls, one that can connect the past with the present, rugby with business. Jeffreys is someone who understands the tradition of the club and its importance to the community as a whole, on the one hand, and the need to implement a sensible commercial model that fits the requirements of the professional era on the other.

As Graham Price says, 'The difference between Peter and other benefactors, such as Bob Jude and Jeff Taylor, is that they were basically outsiders. Jeff might dispute that, but Peter has always been Pontypool, man and boy.'

When Bobby Windsor heard of the club's narrow escape from oblivion, he raised an imaginary toast to the absent Mr Jeffreys. 'I'll buy him a pint at Christmas, if I see him,' he said.

Behind Bobby Windsor, I see the ghosts of Eddie Mogford and Steve Jones winking at Jeffreys with that sense of mischief still in their eyes. Perhaps 'Jack' Jones will be nodding his approval from even further back in the club's past. Maybe even Pross will turn around from the long and lonely walk up to the Grotto tomorrow, take a look down to Pontypool Park and see something worth returning for. Who knows?

Pross belongs to a world where there was a closer tie between character and action, where how hard you worked for five or six days a week, or trained on a Monday or Thursday after work, or played on a wet Wednesday night or a Saturday afternoon, said everything about who you were. He would be a difficult man to convince.

When Ray glances back across his shoulder now, it is probably because he hears the footfall of memories behind him: the march of the 10,000 through Pontymoile to the Bank on a Wednesday night; the guttural chants of 'Poola! Poola!' as the human mountain came alive and red, white and black ran out onto the pitch; the suffering that followed. That all meant far more to him than any amount of talk about how the game should be run or played. Prosser was quoted in a newspaper article published 26 years ago, but the words he spoke then apply as much today: 'When I hear some of these critics propounding their theories, I think to myself, "Shut up, you stupid b*****d! You don't know what it's all about. You haven't got a buggered-up nose, burning ears and busted eyes, and your shoulder isn't so sore that you can't put your cap on." You get a lot of these men who have supposedly played the game. They've been on the field, but they don't know what the game is all about. They don't know what it's like to be that f***ed up when you get off the field that it's all you can do to lift up a pint of beer; when all you want to do is get into a corner, curl up and die.

'They make out they're big tough men and they rattle on about their theories, but they don't know any more about the game than the youngest girl on the Bank. They haven't suffered, see.' (*Western Mail*, 16 February 1987)

The world may be different now from the one Ray knew, but the fleeting sunny smile on the face of Welsh rugby near the M4 still needs to extend back to its heartland in the valleys and embrace its suffering before it is too late. Otherwise Welsh rugby will soon be just a peeling poster in a car park – or that unused season ticket blowing in the wind. And Thomas Raymond Prosser will keep on walking.

APPENDIX

The following statement appeared on the Pontypool RFC website:

Pontypool RFC are pleased to announce the Club has now amicably settled all its outstanding costs from the legal case with the Welsh Rugby Union and our solicitors Geldards.

The WRU have been paid £85,000 from the pledges to the fighting fund. The shortfall of £35,000 has been paid personally by the current and former directors. Every single pound that was pledged or donated was essential in securing survival for the Club.

The outstanding legal fees have been paid by Peter Jeffreys £60,000, and Dai Watt £15,000.

The money paid to settle the legal fees has no impact on the operating budget for the team.

There has been a huge drain on our resources over the past months and our main sponsor Medinet has pledged to support the Club financially until the end of the season to ensure stability.

While this has been a testing few months for everyone at the club we are delighted to now be able to draw a line under the issue and move forward.

THE GOOD, THE BAD AND THE UGLY

The club now have a number of exciting projects we are looking forward to putting in place ready for next season, including the renovation of the hospitality area which we hope to complete during Summer 2013.

Pontypool remain one of world rugby's most famous names and we look forward to working together with Sponsors, supporters, players, coaches and the community to help the club be successful both on and off the field.

Thank you to everyone who donated, pledged and supported Pontypool RFC throughout the Legal Challenge of 2012.